D1670250

COMMENTARIA ET LEXICA GRAECA
IN PAPYRIS REPERTA
(CLGP)

COMMENTARIA ET LEXICA GRAECA IN PAPYRIS REPERTA (CLGP)

ediderunt
Guido Bastianini · Daniela Colomo
† Herwig Maehler · Francesca Maltomini
Fausto Montana · Franco Montanari
Serena Perrone · Cornelia Römer

adiuvante Marco Stroppa

De Gruyter

COMMENTARIA ET LEXICA GRAECA IN PAPYRIS REPERTA (CLGP)

PARS I
COMMENTARIA ET LEXICA IN AUCTORES
VOL. 2
CALLIMACHUS – HIPPONAX

FASC. 5.1
EURIPIDES
Commentaria, marginalia, lexica

De Gruyter

ISBN 978-3-11-115557-9

e-ISBN (PDF) 978-3-11-116286-7

Library of Congress Control Number: 2006482798

Bibliografische Information der Deutschen Nationalbibliothek

Die Deutsche Nationalbibliothek verzeichnet diese Publikation in der Deutschen
Nationalbibliografie; detaillierte bibliografische Daten sind im Internet
über http://dnb.dnb.de abrufbar.

© 2023 Walter de Gruyter GmbH, Berlin/Boston

Druck: CPI books GmbH, Leck

www.degruyter.com

Prefazione

Dopo il completamento del volume I.1 Aeschines-Bacchylides (2004-2020), di cui sono in preparazione gli indici, la pubblicazione del volume I.2 dei *Commentaria et Lexica Graeca in Papyris reperta*, iniziata con il fascicolo I.2.6 Galenus-Hipponax (2019), prosegue con questa prima parte di Euripide, relativa ai papiri contenenti frammenti di *hypomnemata*, *marginalia* esegetici, attestazioni lessicografiche. Michael Haslam ha contribuito alla prima fase di elaborazione di questa parte con numerose indicazioni e preziosi suggerimenti.

A seguito dell'avanzamento delle ricerche sui materiali concernenti gli autori presi in considerazione, la struttura del volume I.2 è ora la seguente:

CLGP I.2: CALLIMACHUS-HIPPONAX

Fascicolo I.2.1 Callimachus
Fascicolo I.2.2 Cercidas-Cratinus
Fascicolo I.2.3 Demosthenes
Fascicolo I.2.4 Dionysius Thrax-Eupolis
Fascicolo I.2.5 Euripides
 I.2.5.1 Euripides. *Commentaria, marginalia, lexica* (2023)
 I.2.5.2 Euripides. *Hypotheseis*
Fascicolo I.2.6 Galenus-Hipponax (2019)

Il 29 ottobre 2021 Herwig Maehler ci ha lasciati. Desideriamo onorarne la memoria di studioso e di collega dedicandogli questo fascicolo.

GLI EDITORS

Criteri editoriali

I *Commentaria et Lexica Graeca in Papyris reperta* (CLGP) sono divisi in quattro parti:

I) *Commentaria et Lexica in auctores*. Testi papiracei che contengono testimonianze dell'esegesi ad autori identificati. Tali testi possono appartenere alle seguenti tipologie: *hypomnemata*; *hypotheseis*; *syngrammata*; glossari e lessici a singoli autori; voci di lessici riportabili a un autore; *marginalia* (annotazioni e semplici e glosse). Sono stati tralasciati i papiri che presentano segni marginali e varianti senza che si riscontri alcun commento e quelli di contenuto esclusivamente biografico, mentre sono inclusi i testi comprensivi di elementi sia esegetici che biografici. A discrezione del curatore, inoltre, potranno essere considerati altri materiali di carattere esegetico.

La parte I sarà costituita da quattro volumi, a loro volta suddivisi in fascicoli:
1. Aeschines-Bacchylides
2. Callimachus-Hipponax
3. Homerus
4. Hyperides-Xenophon

II) *Commentaria in adespota*. Testi esegetici riferiti a opere e autori non identificati, raggruppati secondo il genere letterario del testo commentato (epica, lirica etc.).

III) *Lexica*. Prodotti di carattere lessicografico generale (i glossari e i lessici a singoli autori rientrano nella parte I; non sono compresi i lessici bilingui). Si osservi che i termini 'glossario' e 'lessico' non sono usati come sinonimi: il glossario presenta i lemmi nell'ordine in cui compaiono in una determinata opera di un autore; nei lessici, invece, i lemmi seguono l'ordine alfabetico e possono essere tratti da autori e opere diversi.

IV) *Concordantiae et Indices*. Un articolato sistema di riferimenti incrociati permetterà il reperimento dei materiali secondo diverse "chiavi" di accesso (per es. le citazioni degli autori e dei grammatici).

In generale nel CLGP i papiri sono disposti per autori commentati, in ordine alfabetico secondo la forma latina del nome. Per ogni autore si prevede un'introduzione generale, quindi l'esame dei papiri che conservano materiali esegetici relativi alle opere, presentate in ordine alfabetico secondo la forma latina del titolo (quelle non identificate si trovano in fondo); quando questo criterio non risulta applicabile i testi seguono l'ordine alfabetico per collezione papirologica.

Un punto interrogativo dopo il numero assegnato a un determinato papiro contraddistingue, di norma, i reperti attribuiti a un autore in forma dubitativa. Se nessuna attribuzione risulta accettata dal curatore, il papiro sarà pubblicato fra i *Commentaria in adespota*. Se il carattere esegetico dell'opera non è sicuro, il punto interrogativo seguirà il titolo che identifica il genere dell'opera. Non sono numerati autonomamente, ma solo descritti in brevi schede, individuate da una lettera, i frammenti sulla cui natura permangono incertezze radicali.

Le sigle dei papiri sono tratte dalla *Checklist of Editions of Greek, Latin, Demotic and Coptic Papyri, Ostraca and Tablets*, disponibile *on line* all'indirizzo: http://papyri.info/docs/checklist.

Le riviste sono abbreviate secondo le sigle de *L'Année Philologique. Bibliographie critique et analytique de l'antiquité gréco-latine*, Paris 1928-.

Per i nomi e le opere degli autori greci si utilizzano le abbreviazioni del *Vocabolario della lingua greca* di Franco Montanari (= GI, 2013³), pp. 15-63: in caso di autori omonimi ivi diversificati con esponente o di opere indicate con un numero, si fa ricorso ad abbreviazioni perspicue, confrontando il LSJ ed eventualmente il *Thesaurus Linguae Graecae. Canon of Greek Authors and Works*, by L. Berkowitz-K.A. Squitier, New York-Oxford 1990³ (versione *on line* aggiornata al sito http://stephanus.tlg.uci.edu). Per le opere e gli scrittori latini si segue l'*Oxford Latin Dictionary*, Ed. by P.G.W. Glare, Oxford 2012² (versione *on line* aggiornata al sito https://www.oxfordscholarlyeditions.com/oseo/page/abbreviations).

All'inizio di ogni scheda si forniscono una serie di indicazioni così suddivise:

Prov.: *Provenit* (luogo di ritrovamento, secondo la denominazione latina).

Cons.: *Conservatur* (luogo di conservazione).

Ed./Edd.: *Edidit/Ediderunt* (edizioni del testo; le abbreviazioni bibliografiche che compaiono in questa sezione possono trovarsi anche sotto la voce *Comm.*).

Tab./Tabb.: *Tabula/Tabulae* (indicazioni delle immagini esistenti).

Comm.: *Commentationes* (numerazione in MP³ e in Pack², se differente; quindi il numero di LDAB e di TM. Le sigle MP³, LDAB e TM rimandano ai repertori disponibili *on line* agli indirizzi:

http://cipl-cloud09.segi.ulg.ac.be/cedopal/MP3/dbsearch.aspx

www.trismegistos.org/ldab

www.trismegistos.org/tm.

Segue la bibliografia in ordine cronologico e in forma abbreviata: le indicazioni bibliografiche complete si trovano nel *Conspectus librorum*.

Per ciò che concerne i commentari, dopo un'introduzione sul papiro, si offre la trascrizione interpretativa dell'intero testo con i lemmi in grassetto. Il grassetto è usato anche per contraddistinguere i lemmi nelle voci di lessico e nelle annotazioni marginali. Riguardo a queste ultime, si valuta caso per caso se fornire la trascrizione sia del testo letterario (a volte solo parziale), sia delle note, riproducendo fedelmente la posizione dei *marginalia,* oppure se indicare unicamente il lemma a cui le note marginali stesse si riferiscono.

Se nel papiro vi è *iota mutum,* nell'edizione del testo viene ascritto; in caso contrario, nel testo è sottoscritto. Le scritture anomale sul papiro sono riportate in apparato papirologico e normalizzate nel testo secondo gli usi correnti (ad es.: nel testo γίνομαι, in apparato γεινομαι pap.).

Sono usati i numeri romani per le colonne, i numeri arabi per i righi. Si adotta la numerazione dei righi per colonne, anche quando nell'edizione di riferimento compare la numerazione continua.

La traduzione, se presente (vi sono casi in cui il curatore non ritiene opportuno inserirla), è posta generalmente dopo gli apparati; a discrezione del curatore può trovarsi anche nelle note di commento.

A seconda della lingua moderna scelta dai singoli curatori, sono adottati opportuni adattamenti redazionali.

Per la citazione del CLGP si utilizzerà il seguente criterio: il nome dell'autore, accompagnato dal numero che contrassegna il papiro, quindi la sigla della raccolta (ad es. Aeschylus 1 CLGP). Per i rimandi interni si usa il simbolo di una freccia (⇒) in unione alle indicazioni della parte (in numero romano: ⇒ III, a significare CLGP III Lexica) o del nome dell'autore, cui si aggiunge il numero identificativo del papiro (ad es. ⇒ Aeschylus 1). All'interno della sezione su un autore, il richiamo a un papiro della stessa sezione è realizzato con il solo simbolo ⇒ seguito dal numero.

Marco Stroppa

Curatori

Euripides
      Kathleen McNamee
      Elena Esposito

Gli Editors sono citati in sigla:

GB	Guido Bastianini
DC	Daniela Colomo
HM	Herwig Maehler
FrM	Francesca Maltomini
FaM	Fausto Montana
FM	Franco Montanari
SP	Serena Perrone
CR	Cornelia Römer
Edd.	Editores omnes

Revisori dei papiri

or = originale
imm = immagine a stampa o digitale

Euripides 1	Kathleen McNamee	imm
Euripides 2	Kathleen McNamee	or
Euripides 3	Kathleen McNamee	or
Euripides 4	Kathleen McNamee	-
Euripides 5	Kathleen McNamee	imm
Euripides 6	Kathleen McNamee	or
Euripides 7	Kathleen McNamee	or
Euripides 8	Kathleen McNamee	or
Euripides 9	Kathleen McNamee	or
Euripides 10	Kathleen McNamee	or
Euripides 11	Kathleen McNamee	or
Euripides 12	Kathleen McNamee	or
Euripides 13	Kathleen McNamee	or
Euripides 14	Kathleen McNamee	or
Euripides 15	Kathleen McNamee	imm
Euripides 16	Kathleen McNamee	or
Euripides 17	Kathleen McNamee	or
Scheda (a)	Elena Esposito	or
Scheda (b)	Kathleen McNamee	imm

Siglorum et compendiorum explicatio

⟨ααα⟩	litterae coniectura additae
[ααα]	litterae coniectura restitutae
⟦ααα⟧	litterae a librario deletae
(ααα)	litterae per compendium a librario omissae
{ααα}	litterae delendae
α̣α̣α̣	litterae valde incertae
[. . .]	numerus litterarum quae perierunt
]. . .[	litterarum vestigia dubia
⌊ααα⌋	litterae ex testimonio alio antiquo allatae
|	versus finis

add.	addidit, addiderunt
ad l.	ad locum
ap.	apud
cet.	ceteri
cf.	confer
cfr.	confronta
col., coll.	colonna, colonne
comm.	commento
dub.	dubitanter
ed., edd.	editio, edidit, editor, editores
ed. pr.	editor, editio princeps
e.g.	exempli gratia
fin.	finis
fort.	fortasse
fr., frr.	frammento, frammenti
init.	initium
interl.	interlinea
inv.	inventory
l.	linea
leg.	legit
mg.	margo, in margine
n.	nota, note
no(s).	number(s)

p., pp.	page(s)
pap.	papyrus
sc.	scilicet
sch.	scholium, scholia
saec.	saeculum
sim.	simile
suppl.	supplevit, suppleverunt, etc.
susp.	suspicans, suspicatur, suspicantur etc.
s.v., s. vv.	sub voce, sub vocibus
v., vv.	verso, versi
vd.	vedi
vol.	volume

Conspectus librorum

ANDRIEU 1954   J. ANDRIEU, *Le dialogue antique: structure et présentation*, Paris, 1954.

ATHANASSIOU 1999   N. ATHANASSIOU, *Marginalia and Commentaries in the Papyri of Euripides, Sophocles and Aristophanes*, diss. University of London 1999, available at http://discovery.ucl.ac.uk/1348751/.

AUSTIN 1968   *Nova Fragmenta Euripidea in Papyris Reperta*, Ed. by C.A. AUSTIN, Berlin 1968.

AUSTIN 2005   C.A. AUSTIN, *Les papyrus des Bacchantes et le PSI 1192 de Sophocle*, in BASTIANINI-CASANOVA 2005, pp. 157-168.

BARBER 1938   E.A. BARBER, *Bibliography: Graeco-Roman Egypt, Papyrology (1937)*, JEA 24, 1938, pp. 92-117.

BARNS 1966   P.Oxy. XXXI 2543, in *The Oxyrhynchus Papyri* XXXI, Ed. with Trans. and Notes by J.W.B. BARNS et al., London 1966, pp. 53-54.

BASTIANINI-CASANOVA 2005   *Euripide e i papiri. Atti del convegno internazionale di studi, Firenze, 10-11 Giugno 2004*, Ed. by G. BASTIANINI-A. CASANOVA, Firenze 2005.

BATTEZZATO 2005   L. BATTEZZATO, *La parodo dell'Ipsipile*, in BASTIANINI-CASANOVA 2005, pp. 169-199.

BILLERBECK-ZUBLER 2010-   *Stephani Byzantii Ethnica*, Ed. by M. BILLERBECK-C. ZUBLER, Berlin 2010-.

BLASS-DEBRUNNER-FUNK 1961   F. BLASS-A. DEBRUNNER-R.W. FUNK, *A Greek Grammar of the New Testament and Other Early Christian Literature*, Cambridge-Chicago 1961.

BNJ   *Brill's New Jacoby*, Ed. by I. Worthington et al., Leiden 2009.

BNP   *Brill's New Pauly: Encyclopedia of the Ancient World*, Ed. by H. Cancik et al., Leiden 2006.

BOND 1963   *Euripides Hypsipyle*, Ed. by G.W. BOND, London 1963.

BOND 1981   *Euripides Heracles*, Ed. by G.W. BOND, Oxford 1981.

BOUQUIAUX-SIMON-MERTENS 1992   O. BOUQUIAUX-SIMON-P. MERTENS, *Les témoignages papyrologiques d'Euripide*, in *Papiri letterari greci e latini*, Ed. by M. Capasso, Galatina 1992 (Pap.Lup. 1), pp. 97-107.

BREMER 1983   J.M. BREMER, *Papyri Containing Fragments of Eur. Phoenissae. Some Corrections to the First Editions*, Mnemosyne 4th Ser. 36, 1983, pp. 293-305.

BREMER-WORP 1986   J.M. BREMER-K.A. WORP, *Papyri Containing Fragments of Eur. Phoenissae (2)*, Mnemosyne 4th Ser. 39, 1986, pp. 240-260.

BROGGIATO 2002   *Cratete di Mallo, I frammenti*, ed. by M. BROGGIATO, La Spezia 2002.

CALDERINI 1951   A. CALDERINI, Rev. of *The Antinoopolis Papyri, Part I*, Ed. by C.H. Roberts, London 1950, in *Aegyptus* 31, 1951, pp. 71-72.

CAMERON 2004   A. CAMERON, *Greek Mythography in the Roman World*, Oxford 2004.

CAPPELLETTO 2003   *I frammenti di Mnasea*, Ed. by P. CAPPELLETTO, Milano 2003.

CARRARA 2005   P.Schøyen I 8, Ed. by P. CARRARA, in *Papyri Graecae Schøyen (PSchøyen I)*, Ed. by R. Pintaudi, Firenze 2005, pp. 29-32.

CARRARA 2009   P. CARRARA, *Il testo di Euripide nell'antichità: ricerche sulla tradizione testuale euripidea antica, sec. IV a.C-sec. VIII d.C.*, Firenze 2009.

CASANOVA 2005   A. CASANOVA, *Quarant' anni di papiri euripidei*, in BASTIANINI-CASANOVA 2005, passim.

CAVALLO 2005   G. CAVALLO, *Γράμματα 'Αλεξανδρῖνα*, in *Il calamo e il papiro: la scrittura greca dall'età ellenistica ai primi secoli di Bisanzio*, Firenze 2005, pp. 174-202 = JÖBG 74, 1975, pp. 23-54.

CAVALLO-MAEHLER 1987 G. CAVALLO-H. MAEHLER, *Greek Bookhands of the Early Byzantine Period, A.D. 300-800*, London 1987.

CAVALLO-MAEHLER 2008 G. CAVALLO-H. MAEHLER, *Hellenistic Bookhands*, Berlin 2008.

CHRISTIANSEN 2017   T. CHRISTIANSEN, *Manufacture of Black Ink in the Ancient Mediterranean*, BASP 54, 2017, pp. 167-195.

CIAMPI 2009   A. CIAMPI, *I kimân di Ossirinco: Abu Teir e Ali el-Gammân*, in *Comunicazioni dell'Istituto Papirologico «G. Vitelli» 8*, Firenze 2009, pp. 123-154.

COCKLE 1987   *Hypsipyle: Text and Annotation Based on a Re-Examination of the Papyri*, Ed. by W.E.H. COCKLE, Roma 1987.

COLLARD ET AL. 2004   C. COLLARD-M.J. CROPP-K.H. LEE, *Euripides. Selected Fragmentary Plays* 2, Warminster 2004, pp. 218, 253-254.

COMUNETTI 2020   M. COMUNETTI, *s.v. Apollodorus [4]*, in LGGA, 2020.

COSTA 2007   *Filocoro di Atene. 1, Testimonianze e Frammenti dell'Atthis*, Ed. by V. COSTA, Tivoli 2007, pp. 247-254.

CPF   *Corpus dei papiri filosofici greci e latini*, I.1*, Firenze 1989; I.1**, Firenze 1992; I.1***, Firenze 1999; II.1*, Firenze 2019; II.1**, Firenze 2021; II.2, Firenze 2015; II.3, Firenze 2017; III, Firenze 1995; IV.1, Firenze 2002; IV.2, Firenze 2008.

CPP   *Catalogue of Paraliterary Papyri*, available at https://relicta.org/cpp/.

CRIBIORE 1996   R. CRIBIORE, *Writing, Teachers, and Students in Graeco-Roman Egypt*, Atlanta 1996.

CRIBIORE 1997   R. CRIBIORE, *Literary School Exercises*, ZPE 116, 1997, pp. 53-60.

CRIBIORE 2001a   R. CRIBIORE, *Gymnastics of the Mind*, Princeton 2001.

CRIBIORE 2001b   R. CRIBIORE, *The Grammarian's Choice: The Popularity of Euripides' Phoenissae in Hellenistic and Roman Education*, in *Education in Greek and Roman Antiquity*, Ed. by Yun Lee Too, Leiden-Boston 2001, pp. 241-259.

CRIBIORE 2007   R. CRIBIORE, *The School of Libanius in Late Antique Antioch*, Princeton 2007.

CRISCI 2000   E. CRISCI, *La produzione libraria nelle aree orientali di Bisanzio tra i secoli VII e VIII: i manoscritti superstiti*, in *I manoscritti greci tra riflessione e dibattito. Atti del V colloquio internazionale di paleografia greca, Cremona, 4-10 Ottobre 1998*, Ed. by G. Prato, Firenze 2000, vol. 1, pp. 3-28.

CRISCI 2003   E. CRISCI, *Papiro e pergamena nella produzione libraria in oriente fra IV e VIII secolo d.C.: materiali e riflessioni*, S&T 1, 2003, pp. 79-127.

CROPP 1982   M. CROPP, *The Text of Euripides' Herakles in P. Hibeh 179*, ZPE 48, 1982, pp. 67-73.

CULLHED-OLSON 2016-   *Eustathius of Thessalonica, Commentary on the Odyssey*, Ed. by E. CULLHED-S. DOUGLAS OLSON, Leiden 2016-.

DAVIES 1991   *Poetarum Melicorum Graecorum Fragmenta* 1, Ed. by M. DAVIES, Oxford 1991.

DEL CORSO 2006   L. DEL CORSO, *Lo 'stile severo' nei P.Oxy.: una lista*, Aegyptus 86, 2006, pp. 81-104.

DEL FABBRO 1979   M. DEL FABBRO, *Il commentario nella tradizione papiracea*, StudPap 18, 1979, pp. 69-132.

DEUBNER 1942   L. DEUBNER, *Oedipusprobleme*, Abhandlungen der Preussischen Akademie der Wissenschaften 4, Berlin 1942.

DI BENEDETTO 1965   V. DI BENEDETTO, *La tradizione manoscritta euripidea*, Padova 1965.

DIGGLE 1971   J. DIGGLE, Rev. of A. Tuilier, *Recherches critiques sur la tradition du texte d'Euripide*, Paris 1968, in CR 21, 1971, pp. 19-21.

DIGGLE 1981-1994   *Euripidis fabulae*, Ed. by J. DIGGLE, 3 vol., Oxford 1981-1994.

DIGGLE 1983   J. DIGGLE, *On the Manuscripts and Text of Euripides Medea*, CQ 33 1983, pp. 339-357.

DIGGLE 1984   J. DIGGLE, *On the Manuscripts and Text of Euripides, Medea: II. The Text*, CQ 34, 1984, pp. 50-65.

DIGGLE 1991   J. DIGGLE, *The Textual Tradition of Euripides' Orestes*, Oxford 1991.

DIGGLE 1998   J. DIGGLE, *Tragicorum Graecorum Fragmenta Selecta*, Oxford 1998.

DINDORF 1863   *Scholia Graeca in Euripidis tragoedias: ex codicibus aucta et emendata*, Ed. by W. DINDORF, Oxford 1863.

DONOVAN 1969   B.E. DONOVAN, *Euripides Papyri*, New Haven, Conn. 1969.

EITREM-AMUNDSEN 1956   S. EITREM-L. AMUNDSEN, *From a Commentary on the 'Troades' of Euripides, P.Osl. Inv. No. 1662*, in *Studi in onore di Aristide Calderini e Roberto Paribeni*, Milano 1956, II, pp. 147-150.

ERBSE 1977   *Scholia Graeca in Homeri Iliadem (Scholia Vetera)* 5, Ed. by H. ERBSE, Berlin 1977.

ESSLER 2009   H. ESSLER, *Zur Geschichte der Würzburger Papyrussammlung*, Würzburger Jahrbücher für die Altertumswissenschaft, Neue Folge 33, Würzburg 2009, pp. 165-192.

ESSLER-MASTRONARDE-MCNAMEE 2013   H. ESSLER-D. MASTRONARDE-K. MCNAMEE, *The Würzburg Scholia on Euripides' Phoenissae. A New Edition of P.Würzb. 1 with Translation and Commentary*, WJA 48, 2013, pp. 31-97.

FGrHist   F. Jacoby, *Die Fragmente der griechischen Historiker*, Berlin 1923-1958.

FINGLASS 2015   P.J. FINGLASS, *Reperformances and the Transmission of Texts*, Trends in Classics 7, 2015, pp. 259-276.

FINGLASS 2020   P. J. FINGLASS, *The Textual Tradition of Euripides' Dramas*, in *Brill's Companion to Euripides* vol. 1, Ed. by A. Markantonatos, Leiden-Boston 2020, pp. 29-48.

FOURNET 2007   J.-L. FOURNET, *Disposition et réalisation graphique des lettres et des pétitions protobyzantines: pour une paléographie 'signifiante' des papyrus documentaires*, in *Proceedings of the 24th International Congress of Papyrology, Helsinki, 1-7 August, 2004*, Ed. by J. Frösén-T. Purola-E. Salmenkivi, Helsinki 2007, pp. 353-367.

FOURNET 2009   J.-L. FOURNET, *Esquisse d'une anatomie de la lettre antique tardive d'après les papyrus*, in *Correspondances: document pour l'histoire de*

	l'antiquité tardive, Ed. by R. Delmaire-J. Desmuliez-P.-L. Gatier, Lyon 2009, pp. 23-66.
FOURNET 2020	J.-L. FOURNET, *Les signes diacritiques dans les papyrus documentaires grecs,* in *Signes dans les textes,* Ed. by N. Carlig et al., Liège 2020, pp. 145-166.
FOWLER 2001	R.L. FOWLER, *Early Greek Mythography,* Oxford 2001-2013.
FUNGHI 2003	M.S. FUNGHI, *Aspetti di letteratura gnomica nel mondo antico,* I, Firenze 2003.
FUNGHI-ROSELLI 1997	M.S. FUNGHI-A. ROSELLI, *Papiri filosofici. Miscellanea di Studi,* I, Firenze 1997.
GAMMACURTA 2006	T. GAMMACURTA, *Papyrologica scaenica: i copioni teatrali nella tradizione papiracea,* Alessandria 2006.
GÖRSCHEN 1969	F.C. GÖRSCHEN, *Der Aufbau der Euripideischen Hypsipyle,* APF 19, 1969, pp. 5-61.
GRENFELL-HUNT 1898	B.P. GRENFELL-A.S. HUNT, *The Oxyrhynchus Papyri, Part I,* London 1898.
GRENFELL-HUNT 1899	B.P. GRENFELL-A.S. HUNT, *The Oxyrhynchus Papyri, Part II,* London 1899.
GRENFELL-HUNT 1908	B.P. GRENFELL-A.S. HUNT, *The Oxyrhynchus Papyri Part VI,* London 1908.
GRENFELL-HUNT 1915	B.P. GRENFELL-A.S. HUNT, *The Oxyrhynchus Papyri, Part XI,* London 1915.
GRENFELL-HUNT 1919	B.P. GRENFELL-A.S. HUNT, *The Oxyrhynchus Papyri, Part XIII,* London 1919.
GUÉRAUD-JOUGUET 1938	O. GUÉRAUD-P. JOUGUET, *Un livre d'écolier du IIIe siècle avant J.-C.,* Cairo 1938.
HAMILTON 1974	R. HAMILTON, *Objective Evidence for Actors' Interpolations in Greek Tragedy,* GRBS 15, 1974, pp. 387-402.
HARDER 1985	A. HARDER, *Euripides' Kresphontes and Archelaos: Introduction, Text, and Commentary,* Leiden 1985.
HASLAM 1974	M.W. HASLAM, *Stesichorean Metre,* QUCC 17, 1974, pp. 7-57.
HASLAM 1986a	P.Oxy. LIII 3719, in *The Oxyrhynchus Papyri* LIII, Ed. by M.W. HASLAM, London 1986, pp. 148-149.
HASLAM 1986b	P.Oxy. LIII 3716, in *The Oxyrhynchus Papyri* LIII, Ed. by M.W. HASLAM, London 1986, pp. 130-133
HASLAM 1986c	P.Oxy. LIII 3718, in *The Oxyrhynchus Papyri* LIII, Ed. by M.W. HASLAM, London 1986, pp. 135-148.
HASLAM 1986d	P.Oxy. LIII 3712, in *The Oxyrhynchus Papyri* LIII, Ed. by M.W. HASLAM, London 1986, pp. 127-128.
HEICHELHEIM 1940	F.M. HEICHELHEIM, *Another Literary Papyrus in the Fitzwilliam Museum, Cambridge,* AJP 61, 1940, pp. 209-210.
HERWERDEN 1909	*Euripidis Hypsipylae fragmenta,* Ed. by H. VAN HERWERDEN, Utrecht 1909.
HOMBERT 1965	M. HOMBERT , *P. Oslo inv. 1662,* REG 78, 1965, p. 244.
HOUSTON 2007	G. HOUSTON, *Grenfell, Hunt, Breccia, and the Book Collections of Oxyrhynchus,* GRBS 47, 2007, pp. 327-359.
HUGHES-NODAR 2001	P.Oxy. LXVII 4550, in *The Oxyrhynchus Papyri* LXVII, Ed. with Trans. and Notes by R. Coles, London 2001, pp. 26-28.

HUNT 1912   A.S. HUNT, *Tragicorum Graecorum Fragmenta Papyracea Nuper Reperta*, Oxford 1912.

IPPOLITO 2020   A. IPPOLITO, *s.v. Parmeniscus*, in LGGA, 2020.

IRIGOIN 1984   J. IRIGOIN, *Livre et texte dans les manuscrits byzantins de poètes*, in *Il libro e il testo. Atti del convegno internazionale: Urbino, 20-23 Settembre 1982*, Ed. by C. Questa-R. Raffaelli, Urbino 1984, pp. 85-102.

ITALIE 1923   *Euripidis Hypsipyla*, Ed. by G. ITALIE, Berlin 1923.

JANKO 2001   R. JANKO, *More of Euripides' Hercules bis in P. Hibeh 179*, ZPE 136, 2001, pp. 1-6.

JANKO 2002   R. JANKO, *The Derveni Papyrus: An Interim Text*, ZPE 141, 2002, pp. 1-62.

JOHNSON 2004   W.A. JOHNSON, *Bookrolls and Scribes in Oxyrhynchus*, Toronto 2004.

JOHNSON 2009   W.A. JOHNSON, *The Ancient Book*, in *The Oxford Handbook of Papyrology*, Ed. by R.S. Bagnall, Oxford 2009, pp. 256-281.

JONES 2016   N.F. JONES, *Philochoros of Athens (328)*, BNJ 328 F 34c.

JOUAN-LOOY 1998   *Euripide tragédies 8 1ère partie*, Ed. by F. JOUAN-H. VAN LOOY, Paris 1998.

KANNICHT 1976   R. KANNICHT, *Euripidea in P. Hibeh 2.179*, ZPE 21, 1976, pp. 117-133.

KANNICHT 2004   *Tragicorum graecorum fragmenta* (TrGF), 5, *Euripides*, Ed. by R. KANNICHT, Göttingen 2004.

KANNICHT 2007   *Tragicorum graecorum fragmenta* (TrGF) 2, *fragmenta adespota*, Ed. by R. KANNICHT, Göttingen 2007.

KASSEL-AUSTIN 1984   *Poetae comici graeci* (PCG), 3.2, Ed. by R. KASSEL-C.A. AUSTIN, Berlin 1984.

KOENEN-SIJPESTEIJN 1989   L. KOENEN-P.J. SIJPESTEIJN, *Euripides, Orestes 835-846 (P. Mich. Inv. 3735)*, ZPE 77, 1989, pp. 261-266.

KOVACS 1994   D. KOVACS, *Euripidea*, Leiden 1994.

KOVACS 2003   D. KOVACS, *Toward a Reconstruction of Iphigenia Aulidensis*, JHS 123, 2003, pp. 77-103.

LAMA 1991   M. LAMA, *Aspetti di tecnica libraria ad Ossirinco*, Aegyptus 71, 1991, pp. 55-120.

LEONE 1984   G. LEONE, *Epicuro, Della natura, libro XIV*, CErc 14, 1984, pp. 17-107.

LEWIS 1936   N. LEWIS, *Greek Literary Papyri from the Strasbourg Collection*, ÉdP 3, 1936, pp. 52-79.

LGGA   *Lexicon of Greek Grammarians of Antiquity*, Ed. by F. Montanari-F. Montana-L. Pagani, Leiden 2015-.

LOOY 1964   H. VAN LOOY, *Zes verloren Tragedies van Euripides*, Bruxelles 1964.

LUISELLI 2011   *Aratus 2*, Ed. by R. LUISELLI, CLGP I.1.3, Berlin-Boston 2011, pp. 60-96.

LUPPE 1977   W. LUPPE, *Ein weiteres Indiz für eine 'Zweitfassung' des euripideischen Herakles?*, ZPE 26, 1977, pp. 59-63.

LUPPE 1980   W. LUPPE, *Literarische Texte: Drama*, APF 27, 1980, pp. 233-250.

LUPPE 1991   W. LUPPE, *Literarische Texte: Drama*, APF 37, 1991, pp. 77-91.

LUPPE 1993   W. LUPPE, *Zum Herakles-Papyrus P. Hibeh 179*, ZPE 95, 1993, pp. 59-64.

LUPPE 2001   W. LUPPE, *Griechische literarische Texte: Drama*, APF 47, 2001, pp. 187-195.

LUPPE 2008   W. LUPPE, *Griechische literarische Texte: Drama*, APF 54, 2008, pp. 259-65.

MAEHLER 1993   H. MAEHLER, *Die Scholien der Papyri in ihrem Verhältnis zu den Scholiencorpora der Handschriften*, in *La philologie grecque à l'époque hellénistique et romaine*, Vandoeuvres-Genève 1993, pp. 94-141 = *Schrift, Text und Bild: kleine Schriften von Herwig Maehler*, Ed. by C. Láda-C. Römer, Munich 2006, pp. 79-99.

MAEHLER 2000   H. MAEHLER, *L'évolution matérielle de l'hypomnèma jusqu'à la basse époque*, in *Le commentaire entre tradition et innovation: actes du colloque international de l'Institut des Traditions Textuelles, Paris et Villejuif, 22-25 Septembre 1999*, Ed. by T. Dorandi-M.-O. Goulet-Cazé et al., Paris 2000, pp. 29-36, = *Schrift, Text, und Bild: kleine Schriften von Herwig Maehler*, Ed. by C. Láda-C. Römer, Munich 2006.

MAEHLER 2021   H. MAEHLER, *Die Papyrus-Scholien zu Euripides*, in *Der Wandel des Euripidesbildes von der Antike bis heute*, Ed. by S. Büttner-A. Dunshirn, Heidelberg 2021, pp. 135-148.

MARTIN 2018   *Euripides. Ion*, Ed. and Comm., by G. MARTIN, Berlin-Boston 2018.

MASTRONARDE 1988   *Euripides Phoenissae*, Ed. by D.J. MASTRONARDE, Leipzig 1988.

MASTRONARDE 2010   D.J. MASTRONARDE, *Euripides Scholia (an Open-Access Digital Edition)*, available at http://euripidesscholia.org/.

MASTRONARDE 2011   D.J. MASTRONARDE, Rev. of *Il testo di Euripide nell'antichità* by P. Carrara, Firenze 2009, in Gnomon 83, 2011, pp. 193-197.

MASTRONARDE 2017   D. MASTRONARDE, *Preliminary Studies on the Scholia to Euripides*, available at https://escholarship.org/uc/item/5p2939zc.

MASTRONARDE-   D.J. MASTRONARDE-J.M. BREMER, *The Textual Tradition of Euripides'*
BREMER 1982   *Phoinissai*, Berkeley 1982.

MATIJAŠIĆ 2020   *Timachidas Rhodius*, Ed. by I. MATIJAŠIĆ, *Supplementum Grammaticum Graecum* 4, Leiden-Boston 2020.

MATTHAIOS 2020   S. MATTHAIOS, *Greek Scholarship in the Imperial Era and Late Antiquity*, in *Ancient Greek Scholarship from the Beginnings to the End of the Byzantine Age*, Ed. by F. Montanari, Leiden-Boston 2020, pp. 260-372.

MATTHIESSEN 2010   *Euripides Hekabe*, Ed. und Komm. von K. MATTHIESSEN, Berlin-New York 2010.

MAYSER 1906   E. MAYSER, *Grammatik der griechischen Papyri aus der Ptolemäerzeit, mit Einschluss der gleichzeitigen Ostraka und der in Ägypten verfassten Inschriften*, Leipzig 1906.

MCNAMEE 1981   K. MCNAMEE, *Abbreviations in Greek Literary Papyri and Ostraca*, Chico, Calif. 1981.

MCNAMEE 1992   K. MCNAMEE, *Sigla and Select Marginalia in Greek Literary Papyri*, Bruxelles 1992.

MCNAMEE 1994   K. MCNAMEE, *School Notes*, in *Proceedings of the 20th International Congress of Papyrologists, Copenhagen 23-29 August 1992*, Ed. by A. Bülow-Jacobsen, Copenhagen 1994, pp. 177-184.

MCNAMEE 2007a   K. MCNAMEE, *Finding Libraries*, in *Proceedings of the 24th Inter-*

national Congress of Papyrology, Helsinki, 1-7 August, 2004, Ed. by J. Frösén-T. Purola-E. Salmenkivi, Helsinki 2007, II, pp. 692-707.

McNamee 2007b K. McNamee, *Annotations in Greek and Latin Texts from Egypt*, New Haven, Conn. 2007.

McNamee 2012 K. McNamee, *Ancient Exegesis on Euripides for Commentaria et Lexica Graeca in Papyris Reperta*, in *Actes du 26e congrès international de papyrologie (Genève 2010)*, Ed. by P. Schubert, Geneva 2012, pp. 499-506.

Meccariello 2019 C. Meccariello, *The First Medea and the Other Heracles*, Philologus 163, 2019, pp. 198-213.

Medda 2008 E. Medda, *Il frammento tragico adespoto F 665 K.-Sn. (= PSI XIII 1303). Una tragedia tebana?*, Lexis 26, 2008, pp. 119-143.

Merkelbach 1956 R. Merkelbach, *Literarische Texte unter Ausschluss der christlichen*, APF 16, 1956, pp. 82-129.

Milne 1908 J.G. Milne, *Relics of Graeco-Egyptian Schools*, JHS 28, 1908, pp. 121-132, nos. VIII and XV.

Milne 1923 J.G. Milne, *More Relics of Graeco-Egyptian Schools*, JHS 43, 1923, pp. 40-43.

Montana 2006 F. Montana, *s.v. Timachidas*, in LGGA, 2006.

Montana 2007-2008 F. Montana, *s.v. Callistratus*, in LGGA, 2007-2008.

Montana 2011 F. Montana, *The Making of Greek Scholiastic Corpora*, in *From Scholars to Scholia: Chapters in the History of Ancient Greek Scholarship*, Ed. by F. Montanari-L. Pagani, Berlin-New York 2011, pp. 105-161.

Montana 2012² a *Aristophanes 1*, Ed. by F. Montana, CLGP I.1.4, Berlin-Boston 2012², pp. 13-36.

Montana 2012² b *Aristophanes 16*, Ed. by F. Montana, CLGP I.1.4, Berlin-Boston 2012², pp. 102-106.

Montana 2012² c *Scheda: P.Oxy. XIII 1611* in CLGP I.1.4, Berlin-Boston 2012², pp. 238-239.

Montana 2018 F. Montana, *s.v. Alexander [5] Aetolus*, in LGGA, 2018.

Montana 2020 F. Montana, *Hellenistic Scholarship*, in *Ancient Greek Scholarship from the Beginnings to the End of the Byzantine Age*, Ed. by F. Montanari, Leiden-Boston 2020, pp. 132-259.

Montanari, E. 1999 *Theophrastus 8T (De regno 2)*, Ed. by E. Montanari, in CPF 1.1***, pp. 860-867.

Montanari, F. 1987 F. Montanari, *Un 'nuovo' papiro dell'Ecuba di Euripide (P.Tebt. 683 recto)*, RFIC 115, 1987, pp. 24-32 and 441-443.

Montanari, F. 2009 F. Montanari, *L'esegesi antica di Eschilo da Aristotele a Didimo*, in *Eschyle à l'aube du théatre occidental, Neuf exposés suivis de discussions*, Ed. by J. Jouanna-F. Montanari, Vandoeuvres-Genève 2009, pp. 379-433.

Mossay 1972 J. Mossay, *Les fragments d'Euripide du parchemin De Langhe*, AC 41, 1972, pp. 500-518.

Murray 2001 K.M.E. Murray, *Caught in the Web of Words: James A.H. Murray and the Oxford English Dictionary*, New Haven 2001.

Musso 1966 O. Musso, *De Eurip. Hypsip. POx 852 fr. 18 v. 6*, Aegyptus 46, 1966, p. 185.

Musso 1983   O. Musso, *Un nuovo papiro di Euripide e conseguenze critico-testu-ali*, Prometheus 9, 1983, pp. 49-56.

Norsa 1921   M. Norsa, *Elenco di opere letterarie*, Aegyptus 2, 1921, pp. 17-22.

Norsa 1949   *Papiri greci e latini XIII*, Ed. by †G. Vitelli-M. Norsa-V. Bartoletti, Firenze 1949-1953.

Obbink 2001   D. Obbink, *Papyri of Euripides*, in *The Oxyrhynchus Papyri, Part LXVII*, London 2001, pp. 2-16.

Oellacher 1939   H. Oellacher, *Griechische literarische Papyri II*. Mitteilungen aus der Papyrussammlung der Österreichischen Nationalbibliothek, neue Serie, III. Folge (M.P.E.R., N.S. III), Vienna 1939, p. 21.

Otranto 2000   R. Otranto, *Antiche liste di libri su papiro*, Roma 2000.

Page 1934   D.L. Page, *Actors' Interpolations in Greek Tragedy, Studied with Special Reference to Euripides' Iphigeneia in Aulis*, Oxford 1934.

Page 1938   D.L. Page, *A New Papyrus Fragment of Euripides' Medea*, CQ 32, 1938, pp. 45-46.

Page 1942   D.L. Page, *Greek Literary Papyri in Two Volumes*, Cambridge, Mass. 1942

Page 1952   D.L. Page, *Euripides Medea*, Oxford 1952.

Page 1962   *Poetae Melici Graeci (PMG)*, Ed. by D.L. Page, Oxford 1962.

Page 1963   *The Oxyrhynchus Papyri, Part XXIX, [no. 2506]*, Ed. by D.L. Page, London 1963.

Papathomopoulos 1964 M. Papathomopoulos, *Un argument sur papyrus de la Médée d'Euripide*, Recherches de papyrologie 3, 1964, pp. 37-39.

Pasquali 1952   G. Pasquali, *Storia della tradizione e critica del testo*, Firenze 1952².

Perrone 2009a   *Comoedia 8[?]*, Ed. by S. Perrone, CLGP II.4, Berlin 2009, pp. 63-81.

Perrone 2009b   S. Perrone, *Lost in Tradition. Papyrus Commentaries on Comedies and Tragedies of Unknown Authorship*, Trends in Classics 1, 2009, pp. 203-240.

Pfeiffer 1968   R. Pfeiffer, *History of Classical Scholarship from the Beginnings to the End of the Hellenistic Age*, Oxford 1968.

Piano 2020   V. Piano, *Euripide autore di TrGF II, 455 K.-Sn.: una nuova (e antica) testimonianza*, MD 84, 2020, pp. 147-156.

Pöhlmann-West 2001   E. Pöhlmann-M.L. West, *Documents of Ancient Greek Music*, Oxford 2001.

Ponzio 1996   A. Ponzio, *La tradizione papiracea della Medea di Euripide*, APapyrol 8-9, 1996, pp. 95-142.

Porro 1985   A. Porro, *Manoscritti in maiuscola alessandrina*, S&C 9, 1985, pp. 169-215.

Powell 1936   P.Harr. I 38, in J.E. Powell, *The Rendel Harris Papyri of Woodbrooke College, Birmingham*, Cambridge 1936, pp. 23-26.

Prato 1964   C.P. Prato, *Il contributo dei papiri al testo dei tragici greci*, SIFC n.s. 36, 1964, pp. 1-79.

Puglia 1996   E. Puglia, *Il catalogo di un fondo librario di Ossirinco del III d.C. (PSILaur. inv. 19662)*, ZPE 113, 1996, pp. 51-65.

Puglia 1997   E. Puglia, *La cura del libro nel mondo antico: guasti e restauri del rotolo di papiro*, Napoli 1997.

Renner 1990   P.Col. VIII 202, in *Columbia Papyri VIII*, Ed. by. R.S. Bagnall-T.T. Renner-K.A. Worp, Atlanta 1990, pp. 48-54.

RISPOLI 2005   G.M. RISPOLI, *Tragedia e tragici nei papiri ercolanesi*, Vichiana 4.7, 2005, pp. 195-230.

ROBERTS 1950   P.Ant. I 23, in *The Antinoopolis Papyri*, Part I, Ed. with Trans. and Notes by C.H. ROBERTS, London 1950, pp. 61-63.

ROBERTS 1955   C.H. ROBERTS, *Greek Literary Hands, 350 B. C.-A. D. 400*. Oxford 1955.

ROSSINI 2019   C. ROSSINI, *Eur. Hec. 23 e P. Hib. II 172 c. IV 90*, Eikasmós 30, 2019, pp. 75-79.

RUTHERFORD 2001   I. RUTHERFORD, *Pindar's Paeans: A Reading of the Fragments with a Survey of the Genre*, Oxford 2001.

SALOMONS 1996   *Papyri Bodeleianae* (P.Bodl. I), Ed. by R.P. SALOMONS, Amsterdam 1996, pp. 316-317.

SAVIGNAGO 2008   L. SAVIGNAGO, *Eisthesis. Il sistema dei margini nei papiri dei poeti tragici*, Alessandria 2008.

SCATENA 1934   U. SCATENA, *Studio sulla Ipsipile euripidea*, Roma 1934.

SCHADEWALDT 1952   W. SCHADEWALDT, *Zu einem Florentiner Papyrusbruchstück aus dem 'Alkmeon in Psophis' des Euripides*, Hermes 80, 1952, pp. 46-66 = *Hellas und Hesperien. Gesammelte Schriften zur Antike und zur neueren Literatur*, Zürich 1960, pp. 316-334.

SCHMIDT 1918   K.F.W. SCHMIDT, Rev. of *The Oxyrhynchus Papyri, Part XI*, Ed. by B.P. Grenfell-A.S. Hunt, in GGA 180, 1918, pp. 81-126.

SCHUBART 1925   W. SCHUBART, *Griechische Palaeographie*, München 1925.

SCHWARTZ 1887   *Scholia in Euripidem*, Ed. by E. SCHWARTZ, Berlin 1887.

SNELL 1937   B. SNELL, *Euripides Alexandros und andere Strassburger Papyri mit Fragmenten griechischer Dichter*, Berlin 1937.

STROPPA 2008   M. STROPPA, *Lista di codici tardoantichi contenenti hypomnemata*, Aegyptus 88, 2008, pp. 49-69.

STROPPA 2009   M. STROPPA, *Some Remarks Regarding Commentaries on Codex from Late Antiquity*, Trends in Classics 1, 2009, pp. 298-372.

SUDHAUS 1892   *Philodemi volumina rhetorica* 1, Ed. by S. SUDHAUS, Leipzig 1892.

SUDHAUS 1896   *Philodemi volumina rhetorica* 2, Ed. by S. SUDHAUS, Leipzig 1896.

TOBIAS 1928   Y. TOBIAS, *L'Hypsipyle d'Euripide*, diss. Bruxelles 1928.

TrGF   *Tragicorum Graecorum Fragmenta*

TUILIER 1968   A. TUILIER, *Recherches critiques sur la tradition du texte d'Euripide*, Paris 1968.

TURNER 1955   *The Hibeh Papyri*, II, Ed. with Transl. and Notes by E.G. TURNER, London 1955.

TURNER 1977   E.G. TURNER, *The Typology of the Early Codex*, Philadelphia 1977.

TURNER-PARSONS 1987 E.G. TURNER-P.J. PARSONS, *Greek Manuscripts of the Ancient World*, London 1987[2].

TURYN 1957   A. TURYN, *The Byzantine Manuscript Tradition of the Tragedies of Euripides*, Urbana, Ill. 1957.

WEBSTER 1966   T.B.L. WEBSTER, *Three Plays by Euripides*, in *The Classical Tradition: Literary and Historical Studies in Honor of Harry Caplan*, Ed. by L. Wallach, Ithaca, N.Y. 1966, pp. 83-97.

WEBSTER 1967   T.B.L. WEBSTER, *The Tragedies of Euripides*, London 1967.

WEIL 1907   *Euripide. Iphigénie en Tauride*, téxte grec, rec. nouv. avec un comm crit. et explic. et une notice par H. WEIL, Paris 1907.

WEST, M.L. 1967   M.L. WEST, *Prose in Simonides*, CR 17, 1967, p. 133.

WEST, S. 1967   S. WEST, *The Ptolemaic Papyri of Homer*, Köln-Opladen 1967.

WILAMOWITZ 1900   U. WILAMOWITZ-Moellendorf, Rev. of *The Oxyrhynchus Papyri,
                       Part II*, Ed. by B.P. Grenfell-A.S. Hunt, London 1899, in GGA
                       162, 1900, pp. 29-58.

WILCKEN 1934   *Mitteilungen aus der Würzburger Papyrussammlung*. Abhandlun-
                       gen der preussischen Akademie der Wissenschaften 1933,
                       Philosophisch-Historische Klasse 6, Ed. by U. WILCKEN, Berlin
                       1934 = U. WILCKEN, *Berliner Akademieschriften zur alten Geschichte
                       und Papyruskunde (1883-1941)*, Leipzig 1970, pp. 7-22.

WILLIS 1968   W.H. WILLIS, *A Census of Literary Papyri from Egypt*, GRBS 9,
                       1968, pp. 205-241.

WOUTERS 1973   A. WOUTERS, *The Hand and the Date of the R. De Langhe Parchment*,
                       AC 42, 1973, pp. 516-518.

ZUNTZ 1963   G. ZUNTZ, *The Political Plays of Euripides*, Manchester 1963.

ZUNTZ 1965   G. ZUNTZ, *An Inquiry into the Transmission of the Plays of Euripides*,
                       Cambridge 1965.

PARS I
COMMENTARIA ET LEXICA IN AUCTORES

VOL. 2
CALLIMACHUS – HIPPONAX

FASC. 5.1
EURIPIDES
Commentaria, marginalia, lexica

EURIPIDES: COMMENTARIA, MARGINALIA, LEXICA

Fragments of ancient manuscripts containing or connected with Euripidean tragedy survive from every century of the millennium from the third B.C.E.
to the seventh C.E.[1] To judge from their numbers, his stature among poets was
second in antiquity only to Homer's.[2] In addition to fragments of known and
unknown plays and scripts evidently connected with performance,[3] we also
have parts of hypotheses (to appear in a separate volume of CLGP edited by
M. Magnani), lexicon entries (in Scheda (a) of this volume E. Esposito identifies some dozen Euripidean lemmata in a list of poetic epithets), anthologized
excerpts, critiques and illustrative quotations in treatises of various kinds, references in book lists,[4] and copying exercises from ancient schools. The span of
time in which these latter were written—from the first appearance of Greek
papyri in Egypt until the end of antiquity—marks him also as the second most
important poet in the educational curriculum.

The earliest effort to secure, in any form, the text of Euripides and the other great tragedians comes with Lycurgus' order about 330 B.C.E. that official

---

[1] For the most up-to-date bibliographic information on Euripidean papyri see TM (https://www.
trismegistos.org/authors), LDAB (http://www.trismegistos.org/ldab), and MP³ (http://cipl93.
philo.ulg.ac.be/Cedopal/MP3/dbsearch.aspx).

[2] A search in TM for Euripides as author yields precisely 300 results as of October 2020. Some of
the entries are anthologies or school exercises, while others are texts containing citations, or else
are assigned to Euripides only speculatively. Casanova 2005 offers a review of Euripidean
papyrology. Maehler 2021 discusses the history of Euripidean scholarship with particular attention to annotated texts. An older but still instructive survey of the numbers of Euripidean papyri
relative to those of other authors is Willis 1968.

[3] Texts probably connected with performance: P.Oxy. LXVII 4546, *Alc.* 344-382, Admetus' lines
only (TM 68623, MP³ 378.01, LDAB 9895; Marshall 2004); P.Oxy. XXVII 2458, *Cresphontes* (TM
59862, MP³ 436, LDAB 967; Harder 1985; Gammacurta 2006, pp. 95-110); Pöhlmann and West
2001, pp. 12-17 no. 3, Gammacurta 2006, pp. 131-142, *Or.* with musical notation (TM 59935, MP³
411, LDAB 1047).

[4] A list of Euripidean tragedies: P.Oxy. XXVII 2456, alphabetical list of Euripidean plays, IIᵖ (TM
59821, MP³ 452, LDAB 926, Otranto 2000, pp. 51-54, no. 10); a list of tragedians: PSI inv. 19662v, a
catalogue of mainly of prose titles but also including Homer, Menander, and Euripides, to each of
whose names is attached the label ὅσα εὑρίσκ(εται), "as much as can be found," IIIᵖ (TM 64042, MP³
2087, LDAB 5258; see Puglia 1996, pp. 59-60; Otranto 2000, pp. 79-95 no. 16; interpreting the
phrase differently; Norsa 1921).

copies be made of their plays.[5] Aristotle's contemporaneous Διδασκαλίαι,[6] culled from official records, fixed the performance details of the tragedies. His *Poetics* provides the earliest analytical critique of tragic poetry and naturally considers Euripides. Dicaearchus, slightly younger than Aristotle, composed hypotheses, which recorded the versions of the myths staged by Sophocles and Euripides.[7] The title and presumably the contents (ὑποθέσεις τῶν Εὐριπίδου καὶ Σοφοκλέους μύθων) reflect Aristotle's insistence on the primacy of plot in effective tragedies (ἀρχὴ μὲν οὖν καὶ οἷον ψυχὴ ὁ μῦθος τῆς τραγῳδίας, *Poetics* 1450a 38). In the hypotheses, in fact, Dicaearchus seems to have braided together two strands of Peripatetic work: the fact-based antiquarian research represented by Aristotle's *Didascaliae*, which he must have consulted in order to identify the plays produced, and the philosophical analysis of tragedy that is a main focus of *Poetics*.[8] A little later, at Alexandria, Alexander Aetolus (early third century B.C.E.) first undertook to revise and emend the texts of Attic tragedy. The technical term describing this work (and that simultaneously of Lycophron on comedy), is διορθοῦνται. The word seems to indicate that Alexander's work involved textual revision and emendation of the plays, perhaps in preparation for a critical edition.[9] In the later third and early second centuries B.C.E., also at Alexandria, the expansive work of Aristophanes of Byzantium did include actual editions of Attic drama, as well as an established colometry for its lyric passages and hypotheses to the plays of tragedy. Portions of the latter survive in the preserved hypotheses of mediaeval manuscripts and must derive, ultimately, from Aristotle's Διδασκαλίαι, mediated by Dicaearchan hypotheses and by the bibliographical *Pinakes* that Callimachus created for the Alexandrian library in the early third century B.C.E.[10]

Scholarly attention in the form of hypomnemata on Euripidean tragedy came later, although at whose hand first is not clear. Callistratus (first half of the 2nd century B.C.E.), probably a student of Aristophanes, figures in three Euripidean scholia that could derive from a commentary by his hand:[11] one explains a conundrum, one credits Aristophanes with a reading, and the third supplies a variant. Callistratus' coeval Aristarchus is cited in scholia to three Euripidean plays. The source of the notices is unidentified, but Pfeiffer

---

[5] Plut. *Moralia* 841f. For the following overview of Euripidean exegesis, I draw especially on Pfeiffer 1967, Mastronarde 2017, Montana 2020, *LGGA*, and *BNP*. For a parallel review of the text tradition of Euripides, see Finglass 2020.
[6] Arist. frr. 619, 624, 628, 629 Rose; Pfeiffer 1968, p. 81.
[7] Dicaearch. fr. 112 Mirhady = Sext. Emp. *Math.* 3.3. On the reliability of the ancient testimony see Montanari 2009, pp. 384-388.
[8] On the latter point, see Montana 2020, pp. 196-197.
[9] Tz. *Proll.Com.* 1; Montana 2018; Montana 2020, p. 175 with n. 175.
[10] Montana 2020, pp. 191-200.
[11] *Sch. in Or.* 314, 434, and 1038.

feels confident that it was hypomnemata on Euripides by Aristarchus, who is known to have written them for Aeschylus and Sophocles. A tantalizing fact that may support this case is a similarity in wording between certain Euripidean scholia and the Aristarchan scholia on Homer. Against this is the fact that such parallels might simply be the result of cross-fertilization between the Homeric and the Euripidean traditions, and could have been introduced by Didymus in the course of compiling commentaries on those authors late in the next century.[12] Contemporary with Aristarchus but working at Pergamum is Crates of Mallos, from whom we have four fragments of exegesis pertaining to *Or.*, *Ph.*, and *Rh.* Here too the original context of the comments is unclear; at least three of the four fragments could equally well derive from works on astronomy or geography; the fourth is genealogical.[13] The Alexandrian Parmeniscus, probably active in the time just after Aristarchus, is cited in several scholia on *Med.*, *Tr.*, and *Rh.*, but the source of the excerpts remains, again, uncertain. Because the topics treated include astronomy, geography, and lexicography, some regard Parmeniscus' treatise *Against Crates* as a possible source, since each of these is a subject that engaged Crates. Others see some form of specifically exegetic work on Euripides as likelier.[14] Scarcely anything is known of Apollodorus of Tarsus, who perhaps worked in the period between Aristarchus and Didymus and is cited twice in scholia to *Med.* for problems in line assignment.[15] An actual commentary on Euripides' *Med.* is explicitly credited, at last, to the Rhodian grammarian Timachidas, who probably was active in the last half of the first century B.C.E. Whether he also wrote commentaries on other Euripidean plays is unknown, however.[16] Perhaps contemporary with Timachidas, but certainly earlier than the first century C.E., is Apollodorus of Cyrene, credited in a scholion on *Or.* for the suggestion that a certain part of the text might be a stage direction.[17] In the late first century B.C.E. Didymus Chalcenterus, the great consolidator of learned commentaries on several authors, produced a hypomnema on *Medea*, and this is identified as a source for the scholia in an eleventh-century Paris manuscript, as we learn from a subscription.[18] Given his legendary productivity in compiling the exegetical

---

[12] *Sch. in Alc.* 1154, *sch. in Ph.* 126, *sch. in Rh.* 540. Pfeiffer 1968, p. 223.

[13] Broggiato 2001, pp. xxiv-xxv and frr. 86-89.

[14] Ippolito 2020; Mastronarde 2017, p. 20.

[15] Comunetti 2020; Mastronarde 2017, pp. 20-21.

[16] Matijašić 2020, Timachidas frr. 31a-b, 32 = frr. 15-16 Blinkenberg.

[17] Mastronarde 2017, p. 21; "Apollodorus [13] of Cyrene," BNP.

[18] Paris, Bibliothèque Nationale, gr. 2713, XIth cent., fol. 129r: πρὸς διάφορα ἀντίγραφα Διονυσίου ὁλοσχερὲς καί τινα τῶν Διδύμου; see Montana 2011, p. 151 with n. 147; "Didymus" [1], *BNP*; Mastronarde 2017, pp. 22-23.

work of his predecessors, it is entirely likely he also gave attention to creating hypomnemata for the other plays of Euripides.

After Didymus, hardly any information survives about further exegetic and philological work on Euripides. Various related reasons for this poverty of fact suggest themselves. One is the inclination, even in antiquity, to see precisely that period of Hellenistic scholarship as the pinnacle of ancient learning to regard what came after as of less consequence. Another is the (therefore inevitable) paucity of references to post-Alexandrian scholarship. Lastly, and probably most important, there is the generally messy nature of the transmission of exegetic material from antiquity, subject as it perpetually was to excerpting, modifying, condensing, and recombination; much was simply lost. As Mastronarde observes, "It is indeed sobering to see how rarely the names of the philological experts earlier than Didymus appear in the extant scholia."[19] Still, a demand for commentaries, whether amalgamated, excerpted, or written anew, must have persisted as long as teachers, whatever the level of their students, continued to teach the classics. Even though post-Alexandrian work is barely discernible in the scholia, there is still some evidence of it.

We can tease out a sense of its quality from references to post-Hellenistic authorities in, e.g., scholia and the Suda. Evidence for work on Euripides is meager. Seleucus, working in the first half of the first century C.E., that is, a bit later than Didymus, is called Ὁμηρικός and said to have produced exegetical works on Euripides and also on more or less "every poet." The similarly prolific Soteridas of Epidaurus (mid-first century C.E.), wrote on Homeric questions, comedy, orthography, and meter, and also produced commentaries on Menander and Euripides.[20] Exegesis by Irenaeus (2nd half of the second century C.E.?) survives in scholia to *Med.* 214 and 219. Less philological and more explanatory in nature than that of Seleucus or Soteridas, but not without human insight, his work on Euripides seems aimed more at students than scholars.[21] Scholia dealing with a matter of custom and with language derive from work by Aeschines. Aeschrion is credited in another scholion with information about a river with fantastic properties.[22] The exiguous fragments of both these writers—neither of whom is datable or otherwise known—suggest they took a more traditionally philological approach than Irenaeus, but obscurity

---

[19] Mastronarde 2017, pp. 14-23.

[20] *Sud.* ϲ 200 Adler Ϲέλευκος; *Sud.* ϲ 875 Adler Ϲωτηρίδαϲ; Mastronarde 2017, pp. 23-26.

[21] See, e.g. *sch. in Med.* 214. On the distinction between the Irenaeus named in scholia to Euripides and Herodotus and the student of Heliodorus (Eirenaeus. Irenaeus [1] *BNP*), see Mastronarde 2017, pp. 24-25.

[22] Aeschines: *sch. in Or.* 12, *sch. in Or.* 1371. Aeschrion: *sch. in Tr.* 228. See Mastronarde 2017, pp. 24-25.

shrouds all three. Similarly Dionysius, identified in the subscription to the *Medea* scholia in ms. Paris gr. 2713 (cited above, n. 18) as the principal source of the scholia there, is also cited in the subscription to the *Orestes* scholia in a twelfth-century Venetian manuscript but is otherwise unknown.[23] That even scholars as prolific and significant as Didymus and, apparently, Dionysius figure so sparingly in Euripidean scholia underscores how much Euripidean exegetic work is lost not only from the Hellenistic centuries but also from the centuries that followed.

Given the wide readership that several centuries of learned activity reflects, one might expect to find a fair amount of exegetic material in papyri directed especially at learners and occasionally also at scholarly readers of the poet. In fact, there is very little indeed. Only two fragmentary commentaries on individual plays survive (⇒ 16, 17), and only fifteen texts with annotations. All the annotated texts except three or four[24] are from Oxyrhynchus, and all but two are copies of the 'select' plays. Six manuscripts (three rolls and three codices) contain plays of the Byzantine triad. Texts outside the select group are represented by one copy each of an *Hypsipyle* and an *Alcmaeon*. Nine annotated fragments are from rolls and six from codices, with dates ranging over seven hundred years: the earliest two date from the II^a-I^a and I^a. Five were copied in the II^p century, two in the III^p, three in the V^p and three in the VI^p.

Notes that survive are meager and in sorry condition. The largest number of reasonably legible marginalia in a single text is twelve, but thirteen papyri have only one or two notes apiece. Many of those additions are only doubtfully read. With one exception (a query, ζή(τει), in ⇒ 11) they offer elementary lectional help: glosses, metaphrases, and simple explanations of what is going on in the text. *Notae personarum*, the names of speaking characters in drama, written (usually in abbreviated form) at the beginning of speeches assigned to particular characters, are not included.[25] Commonly they are the work of the principal scribe, a fact that suggests they belonged to the text tradition and were copied along with the play.[26]

The two surviving hypomnemata on Euripides are both papyrus codices of very late date. One (⇒ 17), copied in the VI^p, is actually a single, long note

---

[23] Venezia, Biblioteca Nazionale Marciana, gr. 765, olim 471, XIIth cent., fol. 75r: πρὸς διάφορα ἀντίγραφα παραγέγραπται ἐκ τοῦ Διονυσίου ὑπομνήματος ὁλοσχερῶς καὶ τῶν μικτῶν; *BNP Dionysius* [22].

[24] The provenance of three texts (⇒ 4, ⇒ 5, ⇒ 15) is unknown, while P.Mich. inv. 3735 ⇒ 10 was described as coming from Oxyrhynchus.

[25] A notable exception to the use of speaker names in *notae personarum* appears in P.Oxy. XXVII 2458, *Cresphontes*, III^p (TM 59861, MP³ 436, LDAB 967; Harder 1985, Gammacurta 2006, pp. 95-110; not included in this corpus), where the scribe indicated speaker changes by numerals; see above, n. 3.

[26] A speaker note in TM 59843 (MP³ 421, LDAB 948) written by a second hand is an exception.

on a line from *Tr.* and may in fact be an excerpt on a loose slip of paper and not a page from a full commentary. It is exceptionally learned, dealing with historical matters and including ample quotations from Thucydides and Philochorus (Th. 1.112.5; Philoch. *BNJ* 328 F 34c). The other commentary, treating *Phoenissae* (⇒ 16), is an odd concoction, also from the VI^p, containing extracts from hypomnemata. It is curious because of the disorder of its entries and their superficial coverage of the play: just 85 lines account for about three-quarters of the tragedy. Most of the discussion is exegesis developed for the classroom. Date of composition, as usual, is uncertain for both commentaries.

Both the papyrus commentaries show clear correspondence to scholia, although in very different ways. In the *Phoenissae* commentary (⇒ 16), verbal anticipations of the corresponding scholia are numerous but generally inexact. The *Troades* commentary (⇒ 17), with its close attention to historical matters, is far more learned than the relevant scholia, which largely bypass history and offer general information about genealogy and the stewardship of the Delphic shrine. Curiously a much closer connection is evident between the papyrus and a passage in the scholia vetera to Aristoph. *Av.* 558. The rare marginalia in annotated texts of Euripides only occasionally connect with tradition and never, in fact, to the relevant Euripidean scholia. Most are short glosses or geographical identifications, some of which show affinity to lexica or to scholia on other authors' texts. In ⇒ 6 there are correspondences with scholia, for example, of Lycophron, Theocritus, and Eur. *Hec.*, and to Stephanus of Byzantium. Papyrus ⇒ 13 has a connection with the *scholia recentiora* on the play in question. Because hypomnemata typically blend explanatory material with the lexical, it is impossible to know whether one or the other was the source of these notes. That said, it is clear from this group of texts that it was lexical material the annotators found most consistently useful.

Undoubtedly the number of surviving marginal and interlinear additions would be higher if longer fragments of Euripidean plays had survived. Certain factors suggest, however, that annotation was possibly never really extensive in manuscripts of Euripides. One is the playwright's prominence as a school author, especially at the elementary level; a list of Euripidean school texts is given in Appendix 1.[27] When children are just learning to write and read, exegesis is relatively unimportant and marginalia fairly pointless. The second consideration is the strong emphasis on oral recitation in ancient education from the earliest level. Its importance continued at the grammatical

---

[27] On ancient education, see the work of Raffaella Cribiore, in particular, Cribiore 1996 on the work of beginners and advanced beginners, Cribiore 1997 and Cribiore 2001b on Euripidean and other literary texts used as school exercises, Cribiore 2001a on post-elementary education, and Cribiore 2007 on rhetorical education as revealed through the letters of Libanius.

stage, when students composed exercises for oral delivery and read classical texts aloud with attention to proper expression as well as proper word division. Each preliminary stage was preparation for the highest level of instruction, when students worked with a rhetor to perfect composition and delivery skills so that their public speaking might be well informed and persuasive. Except at the grammatical level, when full comprehension of the texts being read was a priority, exegesis was generally beside the point. Annotations are in fact absent from elementary school exercises; papyrus ⇒ 14 is a more advanced school copy of *Phoenissae* with interlinear notes.[28]

Unsurprisingly for a poet whose works were ingrained since childhood in the consciousness of readers, Euripides is widely quoted and cited in works of diverse sorts, gathered together in three appendices. Appendix 1 lists school texts, most of them copying excercises based on quotations from his plays. Appendix 2 contains a diverse group of texts in which authors evaluate Euripidean poetry. Philodemus, for example, naturally incorporates quotations to illustrate his points in *On Poetry*, and several citations are from Euripides. Demetrius Laco, in a work on literary criticism, sometimes draws on the poet to support a thesis. Satyrus' biography of Euripides is unsurprisingly replete with quotations justifying the author's anecdotes about the poet's life. A certain amount of judicious criticism underlies these citations and those in a few other texts, but because these remarks were not intended as exegesis, they are excluded here. Appendix 3 is a short list of texts formerly thought to have contained exegetic comment on Euripides.

Appendices

Appendix 1: Euripidean school texts (see Cribiore 1996, Cribiore 1997)
A. School exercises
> BKT V 2, pp. 96-97, *Hip.*, II^a, Dios Polis (Thebes East) (TM 59908, MP³ 396, LDAB 1018, Cribiore 1996, no. 242)
> BKT V 2, p. 98 no. XVII 6, *Tr.*, I^p (TM 59789, MP³ 430, LDAB 893, Cribiore 1996, no. 182)
> MPER N.S. III 32, hypothesis to *Autolycus* I, II^p (TM 59684, MP³ 1989,

---

[28] Papyri of Homer, Menander, and Demosthenes, the other principal school authors, follow generally the same pattern as those of Euripides: elementary copying exercises are free of annotation, but longer passages that may plausibly be thought useful for students of the grammarian sometimes contain glosses and short explanatory notes. The learned marginalia in some texts of the authors traditionally read in school are probably unrelated to pedagogy even at the grammatical level: see, e.g., TM 60674 (MP³ 778, LDAB 1799), Hom. *Il.* 6; TM 61144 (MP³ 998, LDAB 2283), Hom. *Il.* 23; TM 60262 (MP³ 1039, LDAB 1382), Hom. *Od.* 3; TM 60548 (MP³ 1149.3, LDAB 1672), Hom. *Od.* 23; TM 61505 (MP³ 1297.6, LDAB 2652), Men. *Col.* (McNamee 2007b, pp. 272-273, 275-276, 276-281, 284, 298).

LDAB 788, Cribiore 1996, no. 192)

MPER V pp. 74-77, *SH* 288.1-43A, *Ph.*, IV-V[p], Oxyrhynchus (TM 59430, MP[3] 425, LDAB 529, Cribiore 1996, no. 303)

O.Bodl. Gk. Inscr. 2941+2942, Milne 1908; school exercise containing a text perhaps by Philemon in which Euripides is commended for misogynistic statements about women (O.Bodl. 2943, next, is another copy of the same text), II[p], Dios Polis (Thebes East) (TM 62367, MP[3] 2721, LDAB 3532, Cribiore 1996, no. 267, Kassel-Austin 1984 no. 1047, Funghi 2003, pp. 6-10)

O.Bodl. Gk. Inscr. 2943, Milne 1923, copy of the preceding, II[p], Dios Polis (Thebes East) (TM 62368, MP[3] 2721.1, LDAB 3533, Cribiore 1996, no. 268, Kassel-Austin 1984, no. 1048, Funghi 2003, pp. 6-10)

O.Claud. I 183, *Hypsipyle* fr. 60 = Aeschl. *Pers.* 483, II[p], Mons Claudianus (Eastern Desert) (TM 63415, MP[3] 1982.01, LDAB 4623, Cribiore 1996, no. 277)

P.Berol. inv. 12311, anthology including a quotation of TrGF Eur. F11 (*Aegeus*), III-II[a], Philadelphia (TM 59946, MP[3] 1575, LDAB 1058, Cribiore 1996, no. 236)

P.Berol. inv. 12319, *El.*, *Hec.*, III-II[a], Philadelphia (TM 62676, MP[3] 1567, LDAB 3864, Cribiore 1996, no. 234)

P.Cairo 65445, schoolteacher's manual, including poetic anthology with passages of *Ph.* and *Ino*, the version slightly different from that of Stobaeus; III[a], Arsinoite nome (TM 59942, MP[3] 2642, LDAB 1054, Cribiore 1996, no. 379; Guéraud-Jouguet 1938, TrGF Eur. F421)

P.Didot pp. 16-18 (Paris Louvre 7171+7172), *Med.*, II[a], Oxyrhynchus (TM 59936, MP[3] 401, LDAB 1048, Cribiore 1996, no. 244)

P.IFAO inv. 172, gnomic anthology including part of *Med.*, IV[p], Egypt (TM 61301, MP[3] 1612.1, LDAB 2443, Cribiore 1996, no. 304)

P.Heid. inv. G 1744 ll. 12-22, *Ph.*, II[p] (TM 59818, MP[3] 420.01, LDAB 923)

P.Hib. I 25 = P.Yale I 20, Euripidean anthology, III[a], Hibeh (TM 59931, MP[3] 378, LDAB 1041, Cribiore 1996, no. 240)

P.Lond.Lit. 75, *Ph.*, II[a] (TM, 59912, MP[3] 416, LDAB 1022, Cribiore 1996, no. 241)

P.Med. 1 recto [a], *Telephus*, II[a], Memphis (Saqqara, Serapeum) (TM 59914, MP[3] 447, LDAB 1024, Cribiore 1996, no. 246)

P.Mert. II 54 verso, *Ph.*, II[p], Arsinoite nome (TM 59815, MP[3] 422, LDAB 919, Cribiore 1996, no. 282)

P.Mil.Vogl. II 44, *Hip.*, I[p] (TM 59791, MP[3] 398, LDAB 895)

P.Oxy. XXIV 2400, list of subjects for declamation, including that of Euripides being tried for impiety for displaying Heracles mad, III[p] (TM 64082, MP[3] 2529, LDAB 5300)

P.Tebt. III 901, *Bac.*, II^a, Tebtunis (TM 59909, MP³ 384, LDAB 1019, Cribiore 1996, no. 129)

Pap.Lugd.Bat. XVII 18, Hypothesis to *Temenos* or *Temenidae*, III-IV^P (TM 59869, MP³ 2649.1, LDAB 976, Cribiore 1996, no. 301)

B. Imitations of Euripidean plays (advanced school exercises?):

O.Clermont-Ganneau pp. 435-438, no. X 32, quotation from Chaeremon, but presented by the writer as if by Euripides, II^P, Elephantine (TM 59440, MP³ 2656, LDAB 539, Cribiore 1996, no. 190)

P.Schub. 8, *SH* 952, hexameters containing an imitation of *Hel.* 678, I^a/I^P (TM 65558, MP³ 1838, LDAB 6809)

PSI XIII 1303, the events of *Ph.* 446-637 recast in different language, II-III^P (TM 59841, MP³ 420, LDAB 946, Oxyrhynchus (TrGF Eur. F665, Medda 2008)

Appendix 2: Miscellaneous texts containing references to Euripides

A. Euripidean citations and quotations appearing in commentary or annota-tion on other authors:

MPER N.S. I 23, marginal commentary on Pind. *P.* 1, VI^P (TM 62559, MP³ 1356, LDAB 3741)

P.Berol. inv. 9571v, commentary on Pind. *Dith.* or treatise on the dithyramb, quoting opening lines of *Hyps.* (TrGF Eur. F752) with attribution, in a discussion of the epithets of Dionysus, III^P (TM 59145, MP³ 1381, LDAB 240)

P.Oxy. VI 853, commentary on Thuc. 2.15.1 ὥσπερ καὶ Ἐλευσίνιοι μετ' Εὐμόλπου πρὸς Ἐρεχθέα that draws attention to Eur. *Erechtheus* (TrGF Eur. F369c), II^P (TM 62878, MP³ 1536, LDAB 4069)

P.Oxy. VI 856 ⇒ Aristophanes 1 (Montana 2012²a, pp. 13-36), commentary on Aristoph. *Ach.*, treating Dicaeopolis' conversation with Euripides, IV^P (TM 59257, MP³ 138, LDAB 354)

P.Oxy. VIII 1087, commentary on Hom. *Il.* 7.75-83. Grammatical notes on παρώνυμα offering illustrations from Euripides and others (TrGF Eur. F11c and F751a), I^P (TM 61125, MP³ 1186, LDAB 2264)

P.Oxy. XVII 2086r ⇒ Comoedia 8 (?), commentary on unidentified comedy with a possible quotation of *Stheneboea* 1 (TrGF Eur. F61) and perhaps a reference to *Alcmaeon in Psophis* (TrGF Eur. F5); Perrone 2009b, II^P (TM 63601, MP³ 2860, LDAB 4810)

P.Oxy. XX 2258 C fr. 2 recto marg. lines 13-19, marginal note on Callim. *Sosibiou Nike* linking Μυριναῖον γάλα (fr. 384 Pf. lines 25-26) with Euripides' Hypsipyle of Myrina, the nurse of Archemorus; VI-VII[P] (TM 59424, MP[3] 186, LDAB 523)

P.Oxy. XXXI 2536, commentary by Theon on Pind. *P.* 12 with a quotation from Eur. *Oedipus* (TrGF Eur. F556), II[P] (TM 62825, MP[3] 1498.2, LDAB 4015)

P.Oxy. XXXV 2742 ⇒ Comoedia 4, commentary on old comedy with a quotation from *Hyps.* (TrGF Eur. F71), II[P] (TM 63613, MP[3] 1631.1, LDAB 4822)

P.Stras. G. 621 ⇒ Aristophanes 16 (Montana 2012[2]b, pp. 102-106), marginal note on *Nub.* 1371-1372 identifying the source of a paraphrase from Euripides as coming from *Aeolus* (TrGF Eur. F2), VI[P] (TM 59287, MP[3] 149, LDAB 384).

B. Treatises drawing on Euripides to strengthen or illustrate arguments:[29]

P.Berol. inv. 13407, P.Schub. 38, treatise on old age citing Eur. *HF* 673-75, I-II[P], Hermopolis (TM 63217, MP[3] 2596, LDAB 4422)

P.Fay. 337 (descr.), see CPF II.1** (2021), pp. 123-140: 137, treatise on gods, sacrifices, and fate citing TrGF II 455 Kn.-Sn. (Euripides: V. Piano, MD 84 [2020], pp. 147-156), I/II[P], Theadelphia (Arsinoite nome) (TM 63322, LDAB 4529)

P.Herc. 207, Philodemus *On Poems* 4, discussion of the nature of tragic poetry, mentioning Euripides, I[a] (TM 62391, LDAB 3556)

P.Herc. 220, Philodemus *De Rhetorica*, quoting TrGF Eur. F850, adapted (*incert. fab.*), I[a], (TM 62448, LDAB 3621)

P.Herc. 221, Philodemus *De rhetorica* 4, quoting Pl. *Gorg.* 486, in which TrGF Eur. F186 (*Antiope*) is embedded, I[a] (TM 62393, LDAB 3558)

P.Herc. 460+1073+1081a, Philodemus, *On Poems* 1, features of Euripides' poetry cited to support the argument, with quotations from *El.*, *Ion*, and TrGF 954[a], I[a] (TM 62419, LDAB 3592)

P.Herc. 463 fr. 13, Philodemus *De rhetorica* Book 4, quoting Eur. *Ph.* 1175-76 to add force to a point, I[a] (TM 62393, LDAB 3558)

P.Herc. 1004, Philodemus *De rhetorica* 9, quoting *Med.* 582-83 (adapted, with an unattested possible variant), I[a] (TM 62436, LDAB 3609)

P.Herc. 1007/1673, Philodemus *De rhetorica* 4, quoting TrGF Eur. F1103a (*incert. fab.*), I[a] (TM 62460, LDAB 3635)

P.Herc. 1014, Demetrius Laco *On Poems* 2, with quotations from *Licymnios* and another unidentified play by Euripides to support the arguments, II-I[a] (TM 59502, LDAB 602)

---

[29] On references to tragedy and tragedians in Herculaneum papyri, see Romeo 1982 and Rispoli 2005 (esp. pp. 224-225 on Euripides); on Philodemus' use of Euripides see Nardelli 1982.

P.Herc. 1014, Demetrius Laco *op. incert.*, with quotation from *Or.* to support an argument, II-I^a (TM 59506, LDAB 606)

P.Herc. 1015+832, Philodemus *De rhetorica* 5 or 8, quoting Aristotle's use of TrGF Eur. F796, modified (*Philoctetes*), I^a (TM 62429, LDAB 3602)

P.Herc. 1081b+1074b+1676+994, Philodemus, *On Poems* 2, features of Euripides' poetry cited to support the argument, with quotation from TrGF 330b, I^a (TM 62433, LDAB 3606)

P.Herc. 1087+1403, Philodemus *On Poems* 3, quotation from an unknown tragedy by Euripides used to support the arguments, I^a (TM 62450, LDAB 3625)

P.Herc. 1384, Chrysippus(?): TrGF Eur. F1052 (*incert. fab.*, slightly altered) and TrGF Eur. F789+788, adapted (*Philoctetes*), in the context of a discussion of modes of living, I^a (TM 62466, LDAB 3642)

P.Herc. 1425 col. xxxiv / P.Herc. 1538 col.vi (two copies of the same work), Philodemus *On Poems* 5, containing general allusions to Euripides in the context of a refutation of a Stoic critic's definition of the Good Poet, I^a (TM 62411 and 62481. LDAB 3562 and 3657)

P.Herc. 1471, Philodemus *De libertate loquendi*, quoting TrGF Eur. F978, adapted (*incert. fab.*), I^a (TM 62476, LDAB 3652)

P.Herc. 1573, Philodemus *De rhetorica* 2, quoting TrGF Eur. F978, adapted (*incert. fab.*), I^a, (TM 62499, LDAB 3679)

P.Herc. 1609, Philodemus *On Piety*, with supportive quotation from *Ph.* (col. i.), I^a (TM 62400, LDAB 3563)

P.Herc. 1669, Philodemus *De rhetorica*, quoting TrGF Eur. F542, adapted (*Oedipus*), I^a (TM 62448, LDAB 3621)

P.Herc. 1674 col. XLV.2-3, Philodemus *De rhetorica*, naming Homer and Euripides as objects of pointless research by sophists, I^a (TM 62500, LDAB 3680)

P.Herc. 1736, ?Philodemus ?*On Poems*, a reference to the recognition scene in *El.*, II^a-I^p (TM 63156, LDAB 4361)

P.Lond.Lit. 159a+591 b, philosophical dialogue with a possible paraphrase of Euripides, III^a, Gurob (TM 62834, MP³ 2593, LDAB 4024)

P.Lond.Lit. 183, treatise on literary criticism or on Attic usage, quoting Eur. *Bac.* 642, II^p, Egypt (TM 62518, MP³ 2291, LDAB 3699)

P.Louvre N 2326, Chrysippus περὶ ἀποφατικῶν, citing Euripidean passages beginning with οὐκ: *Andr.* 205, *Hel.* 1245, *IA* 28, *Suppl.* 270, TrGF Eur. F333.2 (*Dictys*), TrGF Eur. F661.1 (*Stheneboia*); TrGF Eur. F817.3 (*Phoenix*), and TrGF Eur. F880.1 (*incert. fab.*), II^a, Memphis (Saqqara, Serapeum) (TM 59451, MP³ 246, LDAB 550)

P.Oxy. III 410, treatise on oratory, in Doric dialect, quoting *Phoenix* (TrGF Eur. F809) to illustrate a point, II^p (TM 60577, MP³ 2295, LDAB 1701)

P.Oxy. IV 684, ?philosophy (advice for dealing with kings) containing a paraphrase of TrGF Eur. F1001-1002, III^P (TM 64070, MP^3 2591, LDAB 5287)

P.Oxy. IX 1176, Satyrus, biography of Euripides illustrated by quotations from the plays, II^P (TM 62717, MP^3 1456, LDAB 3905)

P.Oxy. XIII 1611, work on literary criticism or portions of a hypomnema?, quoting Eur. *Alcmaeon in Corinth* (TrGF Eur. F73a), III^P (TM 62411, MP^3 2290, LDAB 5430)

P.Oxy. XX 2260 Apollodorus ? quoting Euripides (TrGF Eur. F1009a) in reference to Athena's spear, I-II^P (TM 59148, MP^3 96.11, LDAB 243)

P.Oxy. LIII 3699, philosophical dialogue: remains of five lines quoting from *Autolycus* (TrGF Eur. F282), II^P (TM 63650, MP^3 2592.61, LDAB 4859)

P.Oxy. LXXVI 5093, rhetorical epideixis discussing Euripides' dramaturgy and quoting from an alleged revision of *Med.*, I^P (2nd half) (TM 129891, LDAB 129891)

PSI IX 1093, gnomic treatise containing a reference to Euripides' style, II^P, Oxyrhynchus (TM 59666, MP^3 2292, LDAB 768)

P.Yale II 106, rhetorical treatise discussing the proper use of poetic language and quoting *Ph.* 543 as negative example, IV-V^P, Egypt (TM 64258, MP^3 311, LDAB 5478)

Pap.Vat.Gr. 11 verso (formerly *P.Marm.*), Favorinus *De exilio*, quoting (in some places with attribution to the poet) *HF*, *Ph.*, *Antigone* (TrGF Eur. F157-58) and perhaps *Andromeda* (TrGF Eur. 10), and paraphrasing the first line of *Auge* (TrGF Eur. F264a), III^P, Libya (Marmarica) (TM 59953, MP^3 455, LDAB 1065)

Appendix 3: Texts formerly thought to contain Euripidean exegesis:

P.Ashm. s.n., gnomologium possibly containing a very fragmentary copy of TrGF Eur. F1017, II-I^a, Crocodilopolis (TM 59943, MP^3 1574, LDAB 1055)

P.Col. VIII 202, Eur. *Or.* 205-247 written on a recycled papyrus in which illegible traces in the upper margin appear to be insufficiently expunged writing, not annotations. For plates see Renner 1990, pl. 11 and Cavallo-Maehler 2008, pl. 40; II^a, Egypt (TM 59903, MP^3 410, LDAB 1012)

P.Oxy. II 221, hypomnema on Hom. *Il.* 21, in which the commentator credits one Euripides (name restored by Blass at vi.17-18; see P.Oxy. II p. 57) with a plus-verse, *Il.* 2.866a, which Eustathius also reports (4.475.17). This Euripides, however, is not the playwright but an evidently pre-Alexandrian editor of Homer, perhaps the person mentioned at *Sud.* ε 3694 Adler; II^p, Oxyrhynchus (TM 60508, MP^3 1205, LDAB 1631)

P.Oxy. LXVII 4551, Eur. *Andr.* 46-62, with an interlinear correction previously thought possibly to be an explanatory note; IV^p, Oxyrhynchus (TM 59873, MP^3 379.1, LDAB 980)

P.Tebt. II 683 recto descr., Berkeley, Bancroft Library UC 2341, *Hec.* 216-231, seemingly with part of the text misread as a marginal note; Montanari 1987; I-II^p, Tebtunis (TM 59795, MP^3 388.1 = Pack 2456, LDAB 899)

PSI XIII 1302

saec. II^P

Marginal notes or variant readings on Alcmaeon (in Psophis *or* in Corinth?)

Prov.: Oxyrhynchus.

Cons.: Cairo, Egyptian Museum PSI 1302.

Edd.: Norsa 1949, pp. 54-56; Schadewaldt 1952; Austin 1968, p. 83 (fr. 150); Jouan-Van Looy 1998, p. 111; Kannicht 2004, 5.1 pp. 216-217 (TrGF Eur. F86).

Tab: Norsa 1949, pl. 3; Donovan 1969, pl. 14; http://www.psi-online.it/documents/psi;13;1302.

Comm.: MP³ 431; LDAB 916; TM 59812   Merkelbach 1956, p. 103; Looy 1964; Webster 1967, p. 41; Donovan 1969, pp. 64-66, no. 12; Athanassiou 1999, pp. 19-20; Johnson 2004, p. 63 (scribe A24); Houston 2007, p. 342; McNamee 2007a; McNamee 2007b, p. 257; Savignago 2008, pp. 266-268 (no. 51); Carrara 2009, pp. 321-323; Ciampi 2009, p. 146.

PSI XIII 1302 was the last fragment studied by Vitelli. Norsa published his transcription and notes without change, but also without incorporating suggestions of Schadewaldt, since the letter containing them was destroyed in an air raid of March 23, 1944. Schadewaldt made good the loss with an edition of his own in 1952. The papyrus has been returned to Cairo, but a digitalized version of a black and white photograph was available.

Overall dimensions are reported in the ed.pr. as 23 by 15 cm (measured at the bottom, which is about twice as wide as the top). The full width of the top and bottom margins appears to be preserved. Calculations based on measurements from the photograph indicate they are 4.6 and 7 cm wide, respectively. At the left of the surviving text is a generous but incomplete intercolumn measuring 3 cm and, where indented, 3.8 cm. The left edge of a column of twenty lines is preserved. At the bottom of the column, a 3-cm-wide portion of the right intercolumn also survives, but only the final line of text survives complete. The first seven verses of the papyrus are trimeters. A coronis plus forked paragraphus below line 7 separate that section from the choral lyric that follows, which is indented by 1.8 cm. Writing is on the side with horizontal fibers; the verso is blank. Two marginalia that survive in the left intercolumn refer to text in the lost preceding column (modify McNamee 2007b, p. 257).

The script is a beautiful and carefully executed example of the so-called mixed type, with marked contrast between narrow letters (ε, ο, ρ, c) and wide ones (δ, η, μ, ν, π). Bilinear except for the descenders of ρ, τ, and υ, with that of τ being generally shorter than the others. The saddle of μ is curved. Handwriting is very like that of Turner 1987, no. 27, which is assigned to the second century; there, however, the contrast is less exaggerated between letters that break the bilinear continuity and those that do not. Johnson 2004 assigns the manuscript to the group produced by Scribe A24, whose other output included four lost tragedies and three prose texts. The extravagance of the margins and the elegance of the script mark this as an edition deluxe. At the level of lines 1 and 3, at the left of the column, are two fragmentary marginalia.

The text was part of a collection of at least 52 books analyzed in Houston 2007 (see also McNamee 2007a) that Breccia excavated in 1932 at the Kom Ali el-Gamman. Although the writer of the papyrus is not otherwise represented in that group, five other papyri from the same excavation contain exegetic or possibly exegetic marginalia: PSI XI 1211 (MP³ 34, Aeschylus), PSI XI 1216+ P.Oxy. XVIII 2171-2172 and pp. 183-184 + P.Oxy. XIX p. 149 (MP³ 222, Callimachus), PSI XIV 1390 (MP³ 371, Euphorion), PSI XI 1192 (MP³ 1466, Sophocles), and PSI XI 1214 (MP³ 1482, Sophron). The first two of these, MP³ 34 and MP³ 222, may have shared an annotator with PSI XIII 1302, for in quickly written, sloping angled capitals of the additions are alike; the top of τ in a note in MP³ 222 has the same rake as in the Euripides papyrus, and the ductus of the writing in the two texts is similar. Given the conventional nature of the script and the scanty remains of notes in each papyrus, however, this is not compelling evidence for identification.

The trimeters at the top of the column evidently belong to a single speech, as there are no paragraphi to mark a change of speaker. Although only the first half of each line survives, the speaker is clearly ordering the listener inside and warning that person, threateningly, to keep something secret. Lines 6 and 7 conclude the speech with a comment on the stupidity of trusting a slave, a remark that no doubt discloses the status of the silent interlocutor. This gnomic observation is preserved by Stobaeus, who attributes it simply to Euripides *Alcmaeon*: Εὐριπίδου Ἀλκμέωνος· ὅστις δὲ δούλῳ φωτὶ πιστεύει βροτῶν/πολλὴν παρ' ἡμῖν μωρίαν ὀφλισκάνει (Stob. 4.19.25; TrGR F86). Whether the source is *Alcmaeon in Psophis*, produced in 438, or the posthumous *Alcmaeon in Corinth* is not finally resolved. Vitelli cautiously favored attributing the text to the earlier play. Schadewaldt finds confirmatory links to Apollodorus' account of Alcmaeon's return to Psophis to retrieve the necklace and robe of Eriphyle (Apollod. 3.7.5; Schadewaldt 1952, pp. 51-53).

Right of col. i 1 (lost)

?

] . ιαυτηι

]. elongated vertical bending slightly to the right at the top (part of a ligature to the preceding stroke?); to the left of this, a short horizontal at the top of the writing space that may connect with the vertical at the right. Attached to the left end of the horizontal is a vertical descender of 0.5 mm. which breaks off at a break in the papyrus: possibly γ; less likely ν; if η, the form is different from that of η at the end of the note

───

].ι αὐτῆ? τ]οιαύτηι does not fit the traces   GB suggests]ε̣παυτηι, i.e.,] ε̣π' αὐτῆι, with π made in a single stroke but with abrasion at the top of the arch.

Right of col. i 3 (lost)

?

]ην αυ( ) δαί

There is a space between ν and α

───

]ην α°δ̓ἀί pap.:].. ν̣α°δᾱ̓' Kannicht, utilizing notes of Snell, who also examined the papyrus (]το̣ν Snell ap. Looy 1964):].ν̣α°δαι (with two dots of uncertain letters above α and ι) Vitelli, Schadewaldt

Bastianini *per litt.* suggests that [οὕ(τως)] ἦν (i.e., *sic*) may have begun the note. If the revisor also included the relevant text from the preceding column (now lost), it would have preceded the phrase. Thus, the writing that follows]ην is unlikely to be the reading the annotator is confirming. In fact, the space after]ην may indicate that what follows belongs to a second comment. In this case, αυ( ) is probably a lemma, and δ̓αί evidently an attempt to clarify pronunciation. The grave accent and brevis indicate that alpha is to be pronounced short and unaccented, while iota carries an acute accent. This might be the beginning of δαΐζω, δαΐω, δαΐφρων, etc., but it might well be the dative of δαΐς, the accentuation of which was in fact disputed. Herodian (*sch. in* Hom. *Il.* 14.387a) favors δαΐς, that is, the accentuation of the papyrus. He criticizes Ptolemaeus of Ascalon for preferring δάις (presumably in his Προσῳδία Ὁμηρική: *Sud.* π 3038 Adler). We must also, however, entertain the possibility that δαί is not an exegetic note (nor part of one), but rather a variant reading. For an example of a papyrus annotation that offers an alternate accentuation as a variant reading, see P.Oxy. V 841, Pind. *Pae.* 2.37, where κᾱι θε°, i.e, "Theon read -κᾱι" is offered as an alternative to the main text's αλκᾱι. F. Montana suggests, *per litt.*, that if δαί is, in fact, a variant, the text to its left may have begun ἔν τισιν] ἦν. But a drawback to this solution, as he notes, is that it leaves unexplained the space after]ην and the abbreviation αυ( ).

P.Oxy. XXXI 2543   saec. II^P

Marginal note on Andromache?

Prov.: Oxyrhynchus.

Cons.: Oxford, Sackler Library, Papyrology Rooms.

Edd.: Barns 1966; Diggle 1981-1984 (Π³).

Tab.: https://www.sds.ox.ac.uk/oxyrhynchus-papyri.

Comm.: MP³ 379.2; LDAB 929; TM 59824   ATHANASSIOU 1999, pp. 18-19; CARRARA 2009, pp. 308-310.

The text consists of several small fragments of a book roll containing *Andromache* 346-369, the largest piece measuring 3 x 4.9 cm. Writing, which survives only from the middle and end of lines, follows the horizontal fibers. Interlineation spaces are commodious (3-4 mm). The script is an elegant, well spaced, version of the "formal mixed" style. Barns dates it to the second century but the third (or at the earliest the late second) seems more likely. It is nearly identical to the handwriting in P.Oxy. LIII 3719 (⇒ 7), a copy of *IA* that Haslam assigns "more probably to the third than the second century." Cf. also the slightly less formal P.Oxy. VII 1016, written on the back of a document dated to either 173-174 or 195-196 C.E. (Roberts 1955 pl. 20a) and the London Bacchylides (Brit.Libr. inv. 733, MP³ 175), which Schubart 1925, p. 126, and Turner-Parsons 1987, p. 22, assign to the later second century. No accents or punctuation remain. The single correction is by the original scribe. The main text contains no interlinear notes, and the written portions have lost their margins, but a small fragment (1.1 x 1.8 cm) "found with the others and evidently in the same writing" (Barns 1966) contains parts of two words in neat, small, angular capitals of the same type. The papyrus below is blank, but the clean break above the surviving writing suggests that the note could possibly have occupied more than one line. The sample is too small for absolute identification of this scribe with that of the *Andromache*, but the forms of κ, λ, δ, and possibly ε are notably different from the shapes of those letters in the main text, and I think the note (assuming it comes from the same papyrus) was more likely by a second hand. I see no way to determine where in the text the annotator placed it (so also Athanassiou 1999); Barns assumed it came from the foot of a column. The back of the papyrus is blank.

?

]κτελει δ[

ἐ]κτελεῖ δ[ὲ?

... achieves/accomplishes ...

A loose fragment like the one containing this obscure note is prima facie likely to refer to something in the vicinity of the text with which it was found. Athanassiou 1999, pp. 18-19 doubtfully ventures ἐκτελεῖ δ[όλον, "he is pulling off a trick," an explanation of Menelaus' deception of Andromache in lines 380-383, but notes that the word combination does not occur elsewhere. It may be worth noting a possible link to *Andr.* 790-801, where the chorus apostrophizes the accomplishments of Peleus. The relevant scholia, on *Andr.* 796, quote a similar eulogy (Pind. fr. 172) in which the poet employs the word ἐκτελέcαc.

P.Oxy. LXVII 4554   saec. V^P?

Marginal note on Andromache *791-792*

Prov.: Oxyrhynchus.

Cons.: Oxford, Sackler Library, Papyrology Rooms.

Ed.: OBBINK 2001.

Tab.: https://www.sds.ox.ac.uk/oxyrhynchus-papyri.

Comm.: MP^3 379.31; LDAB 9898; TM 69627   McNAMEE 2007b, p. 253; CARRARA 2009, pp. 541-543.

The fragment is from the outer corner of the top of a papyrus codex page. The side with horizontal fibers precedes, containing the beginnings of *Andromache* 748-751. On the back are portions from the second half of lines 790-792, indicating that the pages had about 38 lines per side. Uncertainty about how the scribe divided lines in the choral passage rules out better precision. Margins are of ordinary size: at the top, 4.4 cm on the front and 5 cm on the back, with the inner (left) margin on the front 2.8 wide. On the back, where the first line of text starts lower on the page, a break in the papyrus at the end of the line prevents measurement. The text is written in a grayish brown ink. The script is unfussy angular capitals of the Coptic style, with clear differentiation between thick and thin strokes and thick serifs on the branches of τ, υ, and χ, which is graceful and rather expansive. An apostrophe in line 748 is by the original scribe. Accents, in black ink, are secondary as are two stops in lines 748 and 749. The single note, in gray ink and a smaller script in which both ει and αι are ligatured, is probably not by the original scribe, nor by the hand responsible for accents, which made a finer line. Modern editors divide lines 791-792 after the second syllable of Κενταύροιϲ; this scribe ends 791 with Κεν-. At the right of this syllable, after a lacuna of 11 mm, are the first traces of the marginal note. Below the lacuna and the note papyrus is lost.

791-792   [πείθομαι καὶ ϲὺ]ν Λαπ[ί]θ[αιϲ]ι ϲε Κεγ[-
                [ταύροιϲ ὁμιλῆϲ]αι δ[ορὶ κλ]ειν[οτάτῳ

                    ].ο εἶν[α]ι

Surviving traces are at the right of line 791, in the inner margin] . : horizontal line in the upper register above a lacuna: the crossbar of τ?   ειν[α]ι̣ after ν, a short unwritten space and then, in ink slightly lighter than the rest of the note, a curve below the line in the shape of the arc from 1 to 6 on a clock; seemingly the end of an αι ligature

———

ει̣ν[α]ι̣ Obbink

The traces possibly belong to a note (of two lines?) dealing with *Andr.* 792 ὁμιλῆcαι. Euripides uses the verb here in its hostile sense in a reference to the battle of Lapiths and Centaurs. This possibility is also mooted by Carrara. Perhaps reconstruct [ἀν]τ(ὶ) [τ]ο(ῦ) εἶναι | [. . . . (ἐν ἀγῶνι, ἐν μάχη e.g.?); cf. Hsch. ε 3241 Latte-Cunningham ἐν ὁμίλῳ· … ἐν μάχῃ; *sch. ad loc.* (792) ὁμιλῆcαι δορί: πολέμῳ. πολεμῆcαι καὶ cυγκοινωνῆcαι. A problem with this reading is that the space available for the first letter of [τ]ο(ῦ) is very small. One might also expect the ο of το(ῦ) to be suprascript, although this is not a conclusive objection (McNamee 1981, p. xii). Carrara's alternative suggestion [ἀν⁻ τ°ᵘ ν]οεῖν as a gloss on 791 πείθομαι would exceed the space available, disregard the traces following the surviving ν, and produce a gloss that does not, as expected, match inflection of its lemma (McNamee 1992, pp. 65-81). But there is, finally, a chance that those traces are merely illusory letters. Samuele Coen, on autopsy, notices offsets of ink in the upper margin that are faded like the mark following ν. If nothing was written after ν, we are left with] . οειν, for which there is no obvious interpretation.

P.Leuven Greek (P. de Langhe) s.n.   saec. VI or VII[P]

Variant reading or marginal note on Andromache *1089*

Prov.: Sinai?

Cons.: Leuven, University Library (*deperdita*).

Ed.: MOSSAY 1972; DIGGLE 1984, cod. U.

Tab.: MOSSAY 1972, pll. I-II; PORRO 1985, pl. VI.

Comm.: MP³ 382, LDAB 1005, TM 59897   WOUTERS 1973; LUPPE 1980, p. 239; PORRO
    1985, pp. 191-195 (no. 13); BOUQUIAUX-SIMON-MERTENS 1992, p. 98 (no. 382.2); ATHA-
    NASSIOU 1999, pp. 34-35; CRISCI 2000; CAVALLO 2005 (P.Ross.Georg. I 8); CRISCI 2003,
    pp. 99-100, 114; SAVIGNAGO 2008, pp. 147-149 (no. 25); CARRARA 2009, pp. 551-553 (no.
    146).

A fragmentary parchment bifolium purchased in Bethlehem from a Bed-
ouin in 1953 by Robert de Langhe, the Director of excavations in the Judaean
desert conducted that year by the University of Louvain. Because the fragment itself disintegrated and no longer existed at the time of its publication,
the ed.pr. was based on a surviving photograph of mediocre quality in which
there is no indication of scale. Script, content, and provenance suggest it
comes from the same manuscript as P.Ross.Georg. I 8, a parchment fragment
of *Andromache* in a similarly eccentric version of Alexandrine majuscule that
was found in Sinai but may have been written in Palestine (Cavallo 2005, pp.
178 n. 16, 197). One of Porro's two hypothetical reconstructions of the fragments supports the identification (although with allowance for variations in
line-spacing) and the other rules it out, but in the absence of any information
about the dimensions of P. de Langhe it is impossible to determine whether
either is correct. The fragments are treated as separate manuscripts by Diggle
1984 (cod. U; Π6), LDAB (nos. 1005 and 1007), TM (nos. 59897 and 59899), and
Carrara 2009 (nos. 145, 146). They are treated as one by Porro 1985 (guardedly,
owing to our ignorance of the dimensions of P. de Langhe) and MP³ (no. 382).
The question does not arise in Wouters 1973, which deals only with the handwriting of P. de Langhe (nor is P.Ross.Georg. among the palaeographical parallels suggested to him by Turner and Cavallo); Turner 1977, no. 66 refers only
to P.Ross.Georg.
    The text is written in single columns, with about 31 lines per side. There
are no marks of punctuation, accents, or breathings; apostrophes mark elision,

and in two cases initial iota is marked by diaeresis (1123 ἴδειν, 1124 ἵστορων). The final choral passage of the play, which starts at line 1284, is indented. Beside its first line is a speaker note that appears to differ from the usual abbreviation for χορός used for this purpose in Egyptian papyri. Here it is possible to make out χ surmounted by o, as in Egyptian texts, but a suprascript c seems also to have been written at the right (unless this is an artefact of the poor photograph). At the left below the final line of text and beside two horizontal rows of ornamental dots, is a siglum (two concentric partial circles, open at the bottom, with a mark resembling an H at the center) that presumably serves, like a coronis, to mark the end of the play. The script is variously assigned to the sixth or seventh century (seventh: Mossay 1972 and Cavallo ap. Wouters; sixth or seventh: Wouters 1973; sixth: Porro 1985; Turner ap. Wouters, noting the similarity of the marginal hand with the writing of Dioscorus, evidently favored the mid- to late sixth century).[1] There are one or two marginal entries other than speaker notes or sigla. The first is written halfway between the top of the page and the first line of fr. 1.1, in an otherwise blank upper margin, in sloping, distinct capitals. Its final words seem to be the end of *Andr.* 1089. In the main text, only a few illegible letters of line 1089 are visible (perhaps four in the middle of the column and two near the end of the line). The ed.pr. reports a second annotation beside the siglum at the end of the play, but the photograph does not allow confirmation. If present, it is more likely to be a subscription, e.g., τέλος Ἀνδρομάχης (Porro 1985).

1089   κύκλους τ᾽ ἐχώρει λαὸς οἰκήτωρ θεοῦ (ed. Diggle)

φας(ίν) ἀλ(λοι) [.] . . . ει λαὸς . . . τωρ θεοῦ

Note is in the upper marg.   ạ: lower portion of a letter resembling a triangle; ι unlikely   ᾿λ᾿: the upper part is visible above a lacuna   ς . . . : after ς, a stain or lacuna sufficient for one letter, then a very short stroke inclining toward the right in the bottom of the writing space (κ? οι quite unlikely), then a stroke high in the writing space inclining downward to the right (λ?); lastly, two dots of ink   θ: what is visible seems to be a stroke inclining steeply upward to the right, with a transverse line intersecting and inclining slightly toward the right.   ε: traces only

———

φασὶ [   ] (τινες vel ἄλλοι vel εἶναι)   λαος οι . . . τωρ θεου Athanassiou   ἐχώρει convenit spatio   fort. κλήτωρ

Others say, "The populace, (summoner?) of the god, ?stepped back…"

---

[1] In Turner 1977, no. 66 (P.Ross.Georg. I 8) is assigned to the seventh century, which tells against the hypothesis that the fragments come from one codex.

Apparently a variant reading attributed to "others," i.e., other editors of line 1089. If so, the note is unusual in three ways: Diggle reports no variant readings here; the expected word order is φασὶν ἄλλοι; and marginal variants are virtually unknown in texts from late antiquity. Because the main text is very broken, it is impossible to be certain whether the suggestion in the margin restores the traditional text or challenges it. In the latter case it is also unclear whether the reported variant offered affects the verb ἐχώρει or οἰκήτωρ, the noun that ordinarily precedes θεοῦ. If the note refers to the verb, I can offer no suggestions. If the noun, perhaps κλήτωρ (= κλητήρ), referring to the Pythia's summoning of Apollo, or alternatively to the population's witnessing of that act. Cf. Hsch. κ 2989 Latte-Cunningham κλήτωρ· κῆρυξ r. ἄγγελοc. ὑπηρέτηc. μάρτυc; Tim. κ 14 Valente κλητῆρεc· οἱ εἰc μαρτυρίαν κλητοί.

P.Schøyen I 8   saec. VI[P]

Marginal note on Bacchae *1069-1070*

Prov.: ?

Cons.: Oslo, private collection Schøyen (MS 1802/1).

Ed.: CARRARA 2005.

Tabb.: P.Schøyen I, pl. 5;

    http://www.schoyencollection.com/religionsExtinct.html#1802_01 (fr. 1 →).

Comm.: MP³ 385.01; LDAB 10509; TM 69119   AUSTIN 2005, p. 164; LUPPE 2008, p. 259;
    SAVIGNAGO 2008, pp. 153-154, no. 27; CARRARA 2009, pp. 566-568, no. 151.

Two fragments survive, coming from two non-adjacent leaves of a papyrus codex. Each has been reused as reinforcement in the binding of another
codex. Fr. 1 ↓, from the top inner corner of a page, precedes fr. 2 and contains
the beginnings of *Bacchae* 681-686. On the back (fr. 1 →, from the upper right
corner of the page), are the ends of *Bacchae* 725-730. There are no annotations
on either side. Fr. 2 →, from the outer bottom of a page, preserves the ends of
Bacchae 1032-1034, and the beginnings of *Bacchae* 1068-1071 occupy fr. 2 ↓. The
distribution of text indicates there were about 44 lines per page, with two
leaves of text lost between fr. 1 and fr. 2, but the line count must have varied
on one or two pages. For if the scribe had written exactly 44 lines per side,
Bacchae 1032 would be the last line of fr. 2 → and not *Bacchae* 1034. Margins are
broken on all sides of both pieces. About 1 cm remains of the upper margin on
fr. 1; on fr. 2 a bottom margin of 2.5 cm survives. The left (inner) margin of fr.
1 ↓ and the right (inner) margin of fr. 1 → measure about 2 cm; the right (outer)
margin of fr. 2 → is about 1.5 cm, while the left (outer) margin of fr. 2 ↓, which
contains marginalia, is about 2.5 cm. The principal text is written, without
great accuracy, in rather informal sloping capitals with cursive features. Elision is marked by apostrophe, and diaereses were added above iota. Other
punctuation is lacking. A second hand added an illegible note and a gloss in
the bottom left (outer) margin of fr. 2 ↓.

Fr. 2 ↓

1069   ἔκαμπτεν ἐc γῆν, ἔργματ' οὐχὶ θνητὰ δρῶν

. . .ν

1070   ἱδρύcαc

κατακαθίcαc

Written in the left (outer) margin

Having seated

1069   At 1069-1070 a messenger describes Dionysus bending down a tall
pine and seating Pentheus atop. For the broken note at 1069, Haslam (*per litt.*)
suggests ἔκλιν(ε), explaining ἔκαμπτεν. The exiguous traces on the published
photograph do not rule out this reading with, possibly, a suprascript ε lost at
the break above the writing. Alternatively, perhaps a gloss on the poetic word
ἔργματ' or on δρῶν (a commoner word and less likely candidate for glossing).
Cf. Hsch. δ 2462 Latte-Cunningham δρῶντεc· ποιοῦντεc; but the traces do not
seem to fit ποιῶν.

1070   κατακαθίcαc is a hapax. Glosses of ἱδρύω in scholia and elsewhere
feature uncompounded forms of καθίζω: cf. *sch. D. in* Hom. *Od.* 3.37c Pontani
ἵδρυcεν· ἐκάθιcεν; Hsch. ι 235 Latte-Cunningham (Cyril) ἵδρυε· κάθιζε; Σ ι 19
Cunningham ἱδρύcαντο· ἐκάθιcαν, ἵδρυcαν, hence *Sud.* ι 138 Adler; Phot. ι 34
Theodoridis.

P.Oxy. VI 852 saec. II^P

P.Oxy. VI 852   saec. II^P

Marginal notes on Hypsipyle *815, 1571, 1572*

Prov.: Oxyrhynchus.

Cons.: Oxford, Bodleian Library.

Edd.: Grenfell-Hunt 1908, pp. 19-106; Bond 1963; Cockle 1987; Salomons 1996; Diggle 1998; Kannicht 2004, 5.2 pp. 745-792 (TrGF Eur. 752b-759b).

Tabb.: Grenfell-Hunt 1908, pl. VI, 2, 3; Bond 1963, opposite p. 16 (partial); Donovan 1969, pl. 7-13; Cockle 1987 (full plates); Turner-Parsons 1987, no. 31 (partial); Irigoin 1984, 6 (partial).

Comm.: MP³ 438; LDAB 957; TM 59851   Hunt 1912; Italie 1923; Scatena 1934; Page 1942; Andrieu 1954, p. 268; Musso 1966; Webster 1966, p. 93; Donovan 1969, pp. 60-64 (no. 11); Görschen 1969; Lama 1991, pp. 75, 83-84; Puglia 1997, p. 57; Athanassiou 1999, pp. 22-26; Rutherford 2001, pp. 149, 186-187; Jouan-Looy 2002, pp. 177-219; Collard et al. 2004; Battezzato 2005, p. 198 and n. 116; Cavallo 2005, p. 111; McNamee 2007a; McNamee 2007b, p. 257; Houston 2007; Savignago 2008, pp. 280-297 (no. 54); Carrara 2009, pp. 345-348.

The foregoing are relevant mainly to the annotations; for additional bibliography, see Bond 1963, pp. 141-142; Cockle 1987 pp. 223-227; Kannicht 2004, 5.2, pp. 745-792.

The text consists of extensive fragments of Euripides *Hypsipyle* written on the back of a roll whose recto contains accounts of receipt and expenditure dated probably to 90 C.E. (P.Oxy. VI 985; Cockle 1987, pp. 195-218). The manuscript was tall, originally measuring 37.1 cm. An incomplete upper margin of 2.5 cm and a possibly complete lower margin of 3.8 cm survive on fr. 64. Cockle (p. 23) calculates the length of the play at about 1,742 lines that occupied over thirty columns varying between 55 and 62 lines in length. Lines are well spaced. The script is quickly written and practiced, angular capitals with a generally rightward slant.

The original scribe marked diaereses inconsistently and indicated speaker changes with paragraphi and occasional speaker notes. He also added some of the accents, breathing marks, punctuation, and corrections. A second hand, also writing in sloping angular capitals but with a finer pen and lighter ink, also contributed accents, breathings, corrections, and punctuation and added a few annotations. The text contains a few variant readings and several corrections (some accompanied by marginal ἄνω or κάτω and diagonal strokes) by both the principal scribe and the second hand.

Stichometric numerals indicate the manuscript as the work of a professional scribe, while occasional ligatures and a certain waviness in the lines (on which see Donovan 1969, p. 61) point to his preference for speed and clarity over beauty and precision. This and the fact that the play is written on recycled papyrus indicate the copy was made for a serious reader's personal use. Archaeological context reinforces this conclusion. The manuscript was discovered in January 1906 along with fourteen or fifteen other substantial fragments of literary texts (Houston 2007, p. 329 n. 7; McNamee 2007a) belonging, evidently, to a single private library. Six of that group are written on versos (Cockle 1987, p. 22), and two others (P.Oxy. V 841, Pindar *Paeans* and V 843, Plato *Symposium*) also have annotations. The scribe who added a gloss in P.Oxy. V. 843 at *Symp.* 206e had handwriting similar to that of the *Hypsipyle* scribe, and his α resembles that of the latter in its sharply pointed lower left 'loop,' but too little survives in either text to assert scribal identity. As to the *Paeans* manuscript, T.S. Pattie examined and rejected the possibility (ap. Cockle 1987, p. 174, note on lines 49-50) that the *Hypsipyle* annotator was the same as the writer or writers that Grenfell and Hunt identified (P.Oxy. V, p. 16) as S1 and S2, Rutherford 2001 as c^{s1} or c^{s2}, and McNamee 2007b as hand 2.[1] Pattie's analysis seems right. The marginal script in the *Hypsipyle* is very like that of S1, but the particular resemblances in letters-forms that one sees (in ν, θ, and perhaps κ) are not definitive, and c and η are formed differently in the two manuscripts. The intelligible notes in fr. 64, which contains an incomplete choral lyric on Dionysus, are terse and explain proper nouns; they are useful for incidental information they provide, namely, that the words Ἠδωνίσι and Πάγγαιον occurred in the lost text.

col. xiv (frr. 29 + 68 + 116)

815   πο[   ]

        ]΄ξονο( )[

]ξονᵒ pap., the accent seemingly written above ξ   Col. xiv is reconstructed from several fragments. Fr. 29 contains only the initial letters of lines 814-816. Fr. 68 provides line-ends of 803-813. Fr. 116, containing the note, has been fitted below these line-ends at the level of 815, a position that suggests that line was shorter than those preceding it and thus may have begun, or at least contained, a lyric passage.

──────

---

[1] The principal difference between S1/ c^{s1} and S2/c^{s2} is that the latter is more cursive and in the view of Grenfell and Hunt was written at a different time.

TrGF Eur. F757   n. marg. Cockle: Eurip. verba Kannicht   ]'ξονϙ( )[McNamee :]'ξον c[
Cockle, Kannicht

The acute mark may indicate that the addition is a variant reading and not exegesis.

col. xxvii (fr. 64 col. i, line 49 Kannicht = 50 Cockle)

1571 ['Ηδωνίϲι]

'Η]δωνίϲι· Θρα-
κίαιϲ

]δωνίϲι pap.   Written, with the following note, at the right of presumably lyric verses

TrGF Eur. F759a   *Hyps.* 1571 Kannicht: *Hyps.* 1570 Cockle

Edonians: Thracian women

Comments like this and the next, identifying the homelands of exotic nations and the location of mountains, are not uncommon in ancient marginalia on lyric and Hellenistic poets, and often survive in scholia and elsewhere. On the Edonians, cf. *sch. vet. in* Eur. *Hec.* 1153 Schwartz Ἠδωνοὶ γὰρ οἱ Θρᾷκεϲ; *sch. vet. in* Lycophr. 418 Scheer Ἠδωνοὶ ἔθνοϲ Θρᾴκηϲ; *sch. vet. in* Theocr. 7.111a Wendel εἴηϲ δ' Ἠδωνῶν: ἔθνοϲ Θρᾴκηϲ, 111b Wendel οἱ Ἠδωνοὶ ἔθνοϲ Θρᾳκικόν; Steph. Byz. η 3 Billerbeck-Zubler Ἠδωνοί· ἔθνοϲ Θρᾴκηϲ, ἀπὸ Ἠδωνοῦ τοῦ Μύγδονοϲ ἀδελφοῦ. καὶ τὸ ἐθνικὸν Ἠδωνοί καὶ Ἠδωνϲί. λέγεται καὶ Ἠδωνεύϲ καὶ Ἠδωνιάτηϲ. Presumably notes of this kind originated in Alexandrian collections of useful or little known facts (for examples, see McNamee 2007b, pp. 552 and 558 s.v. ἔθνοϲ, ὄροϲ).

For discussion of possible contexts for these notes see Grenfell-Hunt 1908, pp. 27-30; Cockle 1987, pp. 174-175; Bond 1963, p. 123; Battezzato 2005.

col. xxvii (fr. 64 col. i)

1572 [Πάγγαιον]

Πά]γγαιον· ὄροϲ
τῆϲ Θρᾴκηϲ

TrGF Eur. F759a   *Hyps.* 1572 Kannicht: *Hyps.* 1571 Cockle

Pangaion: a mountain of Thrace

On the nature of the note, see above on 1571 Ἠδωνίςι. The information here recurs in Euripidean and other scholia (*sch. addenda in* Eur. *Rhes.* 408 Πάγγαιον· ὄρος Θράκης; *sch. vet. in* Callim. *H.* 4.134 Πάγγαιον ὄρος Θράκης. Whether it also lies behind an entry in the Suda (π 6 Πάγγαιον· ὄνομα ὄρους) is not clear. Adler traced that definition to the lexicon compiled in the Hadrianic age (a few decades before the papyrus was copied) by Diogenianus, who drew on a mid-first-century lexicon by Pamphilus. The alternative form Παγγαῖον occasionally occurs, but ancient authors more routinely use the proparoxytone.

P.Oxy. LIII 3719 saec. III[P]

Marginal note on Iphigenia Aulidensis *919?*

Prov.: Oxyrhynchus.

Cons.: Oxford, Sackler Library, Papyrology Rooms.

Edd.: HASLAM 1986a; DIGGLE 1984 (Π³).

Tabb.: https://www.sds.ox.ac.uk/oxyrhynchus-papyri.

Comm.: MP³ 399.21; LDAB 968; TM 59862   PAGE 1934, pp. 175-180; LUPPE 1991, p. 79; ATHANASSIOU 1999, pp. 25-26; DEL CORSO 2006, p. 90 no. 146; MCNAMEE 2007b, p. 253; SAVIGNAGO 2008, pp. 198-199 no. 35; CARRARA 2009, pp. 434-435.

A small scrap (3.8 x 10.1 cm) of a medium brown papyrus roll, stained a somewhat darker brown in places. Surviving are the last four to five letters of *IA* 913-918 and the intercolumn to the right, which extends about 4.5 cm further than line 918. The top and bottom of the column are lost. The back is blank. Because the ends of lines 913-916, which are tetrameters, are roughly aligned with the ends of lines 917-918, which are trimeters, it appears the scribe indented the latter with respect to the former.

The intercolumn beside the place where *IA* 919-928 will have been written is blank, with the exception of the *nota personae* κλυˀ, which indicates an original intercolumn about 1.8 cm wide. The speaker note may have been prefixed to *IA* 977, where manuscripts LP have the beginning of Clytemnestra's response to a speech Achilles began in line 919. If the papyrus had the same version of Achilles's speech as LP, then the columns of the papyrus roll were some 50 lines long, which is unusually long but not without parallel (⇒ 6). But there is room for doubt about what followed *IA* 918 in the papyrus, since *IA* 919-1035 are thought to be post-Euripidean (Page 1934; Diggle 1984 "*vix Euripidei*").

The solitary annotation in the papyrus begins, intriguingly, just to the right of what might be *IA* 919. The note is unintelligible, however, and there is no way of knowing whether it concerned the authenticity of the passage that begins there. By comparison with most ancient marginalia, it was a bit long: it seems to have run for two lines and extended the full width of the intercolumn (traces of the last preserved letter are vertically aligned above the last letter of the *nota personae* κλυˀ two and a half cm below).

The main text is elegantly written by a professional hand in rather upright angular capitals. Upsilons are wide-branched with long descenders; theta and sigma are narrow and small; omicrons are small and round and suspended high in the writing space; mu and nu are wide. Punctuation and lectional signs do not survive. The *nota personae* is written in the same style and may be by the original scribe, but the script is so regular and formalized and the writing sample so limited that it is impossible to be certain. The single marginal note is in smaller sloping capitals and probably was written by a second hand.

?919 [ὑψηλόφρων μοι θυμὸς αἴρεται πρόσω]

]ο.ειτο[.]...τ..πε[
]   traces   [

Probably one or two letters are missing from the beginning of the note, where the fibers are stripped away.   After ο, perhaps a two-stroke λ, written quickly, its right leg just touching the lower bell of the following ε. ρ more problematic: the top loop is incomplete and will have overlapped the following ε, although the annotator's writing is not so crowded.   ο̣: or α̣?, followed by stripped papyrus   ].̣.̣.̣: two short ink strokes protrude from the extreme right edge of the lacuna: c, π? After this, a circular letter, possibly open at the right: ε, c? θ, ο less likely. Then two shallow curves open at the top: ω?   ε̣ in three strokes

———
]ολειτο̣. Haslam ("not, e.g., φ]ορεῖται")

The writing in the margin must have started just at the end of line 919, in the empty space below the longer preceding line, so probably little was lost at the beginning. Just below the transcribed line are illegible traces of a second, but whether the two lines belong to one note is unclear. In L, the unique mediaeval manuscript containing *IA*, and in its apograph P, line 919 is the start of Achilles' iambic response to a trochaic appeal of Clytemnestra begun at line 900. If Achilles' speech figured in the papyrus, then the speaker note Κλυτ(αιμηςτρα) beside the lost second column should mark the beginning of her speech at line 977; a difficulty is the absence of a speaker designation marking the chorus' response in lines 975-976. The column of writing will have been 51 lines tall: not impossible but very long. Savignago 2008, p. 199 suggests, alternatively, that the chorus's third stasimon (lines 1036-1097 in LP) might have followed line 918 instead. In that case, the surviving speaker designation marks the start of Clytemnestra's speech at line 1098, the column length remains approximately the same (a long 55 lines), and no additional speaker note is necessary. Any reconstruction must be speculative, however, given that the posthumous *IA* contains extensive interpolations of the 4th and 3rd centuries B.C.E. (on interpolation in *IA* see Page 1934, esp. pp. 122-206, Hamilton 1974, Kovacs 2003, Finglass 2015; Diggle labelled lines 919-1035 *vix Euripidei*). Scholia are lacking for *IA*.

?919   The note, if legible, should clarify whether Achilles' speech stood in the main text or not. Bastianini's suggestion φορεῖται ("is lifted up") has appeal as a gloss on *IA* 919 αἴρεται, but the reading not possible.

P.Ant. I 23 saec. V-VI[p]

Marginal notes on Medea *825, 864*

Prov.: Antinoopolis.

Cons.: Oxford, Sackler Library, Papyrology Rooms.

Edd.: Roberts 1950, no. 23; Diggle 1984 (Π[6]).

Tab.: Oxford, The Imaging Papyri Project (P.Ant. website).

Comm.: MP³ 406; LDAB 993; TM 59885   CALDERINI 1951, p. 71; PRATO 1964, pp. 33-35; DI BENEDETTO 1965; ZUNTZ 1965, pp. 31-32, 274n.; TURNER 1977, pp. 17, 105 (no. 74); McNAMEE 1981, pp. 5, 102; DIGGLE 1983; MAEHLER 1993, pp. 113-114; PONZIO 1996, p. 103 (Π[11]); ATHANASSIOU 1999, pp. 33-34; McNAMEE 2007b, p. 254; CARRARA 2009, pp. 555-560.

Six pieces of a one or more leaves from a nice papyrus codex originally measuring approximately 18 x 30 cm (Turner 1977, Group 5). In the same hand and from the same codex is P.Ant. II 73 (*Bacchae,* MP³ 387). Of the *Medea* fragment, the ed.pr. publishes only fr. 1, the most extensive piece. The papyrus is broken off at top and bottom, so there is no way to know whether it comes from top or bottom of the column. Fabric ranges in color from medium or dark brown to a grayish color. Portions show wear, especially on the side with vertical fibers (which preceded); the opposite side is relatively well preserved. The front (↓) preserves the beginnings of *Medea* 825-840 with about 1.7 cm of margin remaining at the left (inner) side. Whether this is its full extent is unknown, but since inner margins of codices can be rather narrow, it is possible that not much is lost (⟹ 3, 12). On the back (→) are line-ends of *Medea* 866-878 and part of the right (inner) margin. Fragments 2-6 are all very small and have not been placed. The main scribe wrote even, strongly sloping, cramped angular capitals in brown ink. The same writer secondarily added apostrophes, a breathing mark, and frequent accents; the diaeresis in line 825 ἴερας seems to have been made in the course of copying, as was the erroneous paragraphus that is written one line prematurely above the last line of the first strophe (ξανθὰν Ἁρμονίαν φ[υτεῦσαι]). Division of cola in the lyric passage on fr. 1 ↓ differs from that of the mediaeval manuscripts.[1] A second hand made correc-

---

[1] Cola in the papyrus are shorter. In the annotated portion of fr. 1 ↓, the line breaks after 825

tions and added marginalia in a ligatured, rounder script which is smaller than that of the main text, although not itself extremely small. This is also the hand responsible for writing surviving in frr. 2-6. There are striking verbal connections with the scholia vetera in the annotations of fr. 1. Presumably the notes derive from a condensed version of the same tradition of commentary (Maehler 1993, Athanassiou 1999).

Fr. 1 ↓

824-826   [Ἐρεχθεῖδαι τὸ παλαιὸν ὄλβιοι]
               κ[αὶ θεῶν παῖδες μακάρων]
               ἱερ[ᾶς χώρας ἀπορθήτου]

                        ] ρ..[
                        ]απotρεπ[.].[
                        ]..εια της
                        ]..αιρεϲε
               5   ].οιον
                        ] υποδεξ..[ ]

Med. 826 ἱερ[pap.   Note is written in the left, inner margin; extent of loss above and at the left unknown.

1 There may be a dot of ink of about one letter-width to the left of ρ; after ρ, conceivably o.   2 A "microscopic trace" (DC, on autopsy) before α   3 Traces, then a vertical stroke descending well below the line: ι likely, ρ just possible, although there is virtually no space for its loop; δ impossible. ν was not written between α and τ.   4]αν?   5]χ? alternatively perhaps ζ, ξ; φον- cannot be read.   It is not clear that anything was written after ν. Blank papyrus follows, then a dot high in the line.

---

1 [χο]ρο[ϲ] Roberts, McNamee 2007b: ο χο|ρο[ϲ]? McNamee   2 ἀποτρέ[π(ων)] Roberts, ἀποτρέ[πων] McNamee 2007b   3 [Μή]δειαν τῆϲ Roberts, McNamee 2007b : possis ἱ]έρεια (ἱερεία, ἱερεῖα) FaM per litt. : ἀνι]έρεια⟨ι⟩? McNamee   4 ἀναιρέϲε‖[ωϲ? McNamee: [παίδ(ων)] ἀναιρέϲε(ωϲ) Roberts, McNamee 2007b   5 [ὡϲ μια]ίφονον Roberts, McNamee 2007b : οὐ]χ οἷον? McNamee   6 [οὐχ] ὑποδέξον(ται) Roberts, McNamee 2007b   5-7 possis οἷόν | τε] ὑποδέξεϲ[θ](αι) aut ὑποδέξεϲ‖[θαι] FaM per litt.

μακάρων and 826 ἀπορθήτου, in the manuscripts after ἱερὰς and φερβόμενοι (not reproduced here).

Fr. 1 →

   864   [τέγξαι χέρα φοινίαν]

            [τλάμονι θυμῷ]

          ].[.]....[

          ]μολῦν(αι)

Right, inner margin, written at the end of the choral song. The annotator took advantage of the extra space afforded by the shorter lyric lines. Truncation of the trimeters in lines 870-871 suggests that up to 1 cm of blank margin may be lost at the right.

1].[tip of a long descender   ].... a speck of ink followed perhaps by α or ω, then possibly χ and another speck of ink   2 μολυνˢ pap.

———

1 φ[ο]νῳ χε[ρα] Roberts, McNamee 2007b

... defile (your hand with murder?)

Fr. 2 ↓

      ?

        ]κουϲτ[

        ]τερον .[

          ]..[

Fr. 2 →

      ?

        ]φωνα[

        ]ερϲιου .[

          ]μν[

Fr. 3 ↓

      ?

        ]ωϲο[

        ]εθει[

        ]..αμον.[

          ].[

Fr. 3 →

    ?

        ]χυς.[
        ].υνα[
        ].μενη.[

]ςμενη.[? McNamee

Fr. 1 ↓

The note treats the choral song that begins at line 824. Its beginning is lost, but if it started at the same point as the first words of the stasimon, which also are lost, then perhaps two lines are missing. The annotator's writing is compact and so crowded as to abut parts of the main text at the right. The compression is possibly due to the note having been written in the inner margin after the manuscript was bound; cf. McNamee 2007b, pl. XXIII (Parthenius, 4th century, parchment codex, MP³ 1338, TM 64569, LDAB 5799).

The annotation has striking verbal connections with the scholia and conveys roughly the same information. Provisionally, e.g., [ὁ χο]|ρὸς αὐτ|ὴν ἀποτρέπει | ἀνιερείᾳ τῆς | ἀναιρέσε|ως· οὐχ οἷόν | τε ὑποδέξες|θαι, "[The] chorus turn [her] away because of the blasphemy of the slaying. It is not possible that (she) will be received."

2-6   There are clear verbal echoes with scholia in line 2 ἀποτρέπ[ ) and line 6] υποδεξ..., and possibly also in line 3   ]. εια, if ρ is to be read before ε: *sch. vet. in Med.* 824 Ἐρεχθεῖδαι: μακαρίζει νῦν τοὺς Ἀθηναίους ὡς εὐδαίμονας καὶ σοφίας πάσης ἐπιστήμονας ἱεροὺς τε καὶ μύστας, ὅτι μέλλει τὰ κατὰ τὴν Μήδειαν ἐπάγειν μιάσματα. τῇ γὰρ παραθέσει βούλεται αὐτὴν ἀποτρέψαι τοῦ κατὰ τῶν παίδων φόνου. οὕτως γὰρ ἐν τοῖς ἑξῆς ἐπάγει, ὅτι οὐκ εἰκὸς τοὺς οὕτως ἱεροὺς καὶ σοφοὺς ἄνδρας σὲ μιαιφόνον γενομένην ὑποδέξεσθαι. AB.

5-6 υποδεξ.. [ ]: Given the proximity of the note to the beginnings of lines 828 and 829, the word may have been abbreviated. After .[there is a lacuna large enough for a suprascript letter or abbreviation mark. Alternatively, a short final syllable perhaps followed at the start of the next line, left of the paragraphus.

Fr. 1 →

1-2   ]μολῦν(αι) in line 2, a vivid verb, marks another strong connection with the *sch. vet. in Med.* 864: τέγξαι χεῖρα φόνου: τὸ ἑξῆς· φόνου χεῖρα φονίαν. εὖ οἶδα, φησί, ὅτι οὐ καρτερήσεις τὴν ἐργάτιν τοῦ φόνου χεῖρα μολῦναι τῷ αἵματι τῶν παίδων γονυπετούντων σε.

Frr. 2-6

Unpublished scraps containing writing apparently in the hand of the annotator, but with traces that appear not to be connected to preserved scholia.

P.Harr. I 38 (inv. 179) + P.Fitzw.Mus. inv. Add. 109 +
P.Oxy. LXVII 4550   saec. II^P

Marginal notes (?) on Medea *1282 and 1292*

Prov.: Oxyrhynchus.

Cons.: University of Birmingham, Edgbaston Campus, Main Library, Special Collec-
tions Department P. Harris 179 (stored at Orchard Learning Research Centre, Selly
Oaks Colleges Campus) + Cambridge, Fitzwilliam Museum Add. 109 + Oxford,
Sackler Library, Papyrology Rooms.

Edd.: POWELL 1936 (Π⁵ᵃ DIGGLE); PAGE 1938 (P.Fitzw.Mus. inv. Add. 109 = Π⁵ᵇ DIGGLE);
PAGE 1952 (Π⁷, Π⁸ = Π⁵ᵃ, ᵇ DIGGLE); DIGGLE 1984 (Π⁵ᵃ, ᵇ, ᶜ); ATHANASSIOU 1999, pp. 13-14;
HUGHES-NODAR 2001, pp. 26-28 (P.Oxy. LXVII 4550 = Π⁵ᶜ DIGGLE).

Comm.: MP³ 405; LDAB 918; TM 59814   LEWIS 1936; SNELL 1937, p. 75; BARBER 1938, pp.
93-94; HEICHELHEIM 1940; ANDRIEU 1954, p. 268; PRATO 1964, pp. 33-37; DI BENEDETTO
1965, p. 143; ZUNTZ 1965, pp. 29-38; AUSTIN 1968; DONOVAN 1969, p. 24; MCNAMEE
1981; MASTRONARDE-BREMER 1982, pp. 151-164; DIGGLE 1983, p. 340; DIGGLE 1984, pp.
63-65; LUPPE 1991, p. 80; PONZIO 1996, pp. 103 with n. 25, 118-124, 130-141 (Π¹⁰ PON-
ZIO); MCNAMEE 2007b, p. 254; SAVIGNAGO 2008, pp. 202-207; CARRARA 2009, pp. 292-
297; MASTRONARDE 2011, p. 196; MCNAMEE 2012.

Tabb.: POWELL 1936, pl. I (P.Harr., part); https://www.sds.ox.ac.uk/oxyrhynchus-papyri.
(P.Oxy.)

Three groups of fragments, whose provenance was established as Oxyrhynchus early enough for Diggle 1984 to take it into account, although the
third set of fragments was not published until 2011, as P.Oxy. LXVII 4550. Information about the location of the other two groups of fragments has been
spotty and confusing: "Pack says that [P.Harris] is in the Fitzwilliam Museum,
Cambridge. Only part of it is there... The rest is still in the Central Library of
the Selly Oak Colleges, Birmingham" (Diggle 1983, p. 340 n. 14). The three sets
of fragments evidently had the following trajectories. P.Oxy. was dug up in
the 1903-1904 winter, as its inventory number shows, and presumably went
straight to England. P.Harris was acquired "privately in Egypt" in 1922-1923,
according to the preface to Powell 1936. P.Fitzw.Mus. came to the Museum in
1922 as a gift of the British School of Archaeology in Egypt, presumably
through the agency of Petrie, then Director of the British School. Powell 1938
was aware that P.Harris and P.Fitz.Mus. were parts of the same manuscript
(presumably from Hunt's journals, to which he alludes at Page 1938, p. 46, n.1;
and see Barber 1938, pp. 93-94). But Powell's 1936 edition of P.Harris contains

no reference to P.Fitz.Mus. Nor does Page 1938, in his edition of P.Fitz.Mus., make any mention of P.Harris. The P.Oxy. portion, first studied by D. Hughes, was identified as part of the same manuscript by A. Nodar on grounds of palaeography and characteristic diacritical marks. For details on the history of the fragments, see McNamee 2012.

Marginal annotation is found only in P.Harr. I 38, which consists of four fragments. Fr. 1, 6.6 x 6.3 cm and labelled 'a' in its glass frame, contains *Med.* 719-723 and is shaped roughly like a backward L. At its widest point it contains the right ends of five trimeters spoken by Aegeus, plus a section 3.2 cm in breadth of the right-hand intercolumn. A vertical strip roughly a centimeter in width extends this upward from the right of this for about 13 lines. Fr. 2, 2 x 3.8 cm and labeled 'b', has *Med.* 1046-1053. Fr. 3a, 1.2 x 0.8 cm + fr. 3b 0.4 x 0.6 cm (unpublished) and labeled 'd' contain four or five disconnected letters from unplaced text.[1] Fr. 4, the most substantial fragment in the three sets of publications, is labelled 'c' and measures 22 x 21.1 cm. Its first column is the only complete one among any of the fragments. It consists of 34 lines (*Med.* 1279-1312), which occupy about 17 cm vertically; upper and lower margins of 2.2 and 3 cm respectively are probably complete. In a second column are the beginnings of *Med.* 1313-1319 and 1323-1328. Writing is regular in size except in the last three or four lines of col. i, which are slightly reduced in height, a fact that suggests the scribe may have been trying to copy the layout as well as the text of his model. P.Fitzw. Mus. inv. Add. 109 is in two pieces. Fr. 1, 5.5 by 10.3 cm, contains line-ends of *Med.* 1165-1177. Fr. 2, 10.2 cm across and 5.8 cm high, contains parts of two columns: col. i has the ends of trimeters from *Med.* 1156-1160, which were originally part of the same column as the text in fr. 1; col. ii has the beginnings of trimeters from *Med.* 1191-1199. An intercolumn of 5.5 cm survives complete at the top for a space of four lines; a narrower portion is attached to the left of col. ii at lines 1194-1199. Of P.Oxy. LXVII 4550, three fragments survive: fr. 1 (2 x 3.4 cm) containing *Med.* 748(?)-752; fr. 2 (3.9 x 2.2 cm) with *Med.* 1007-1009; and fr. 3 (7.5 x 6.4 cm) with *Med.* 1345-1346(?).

Writing is on the front. The back is blank, although the backs of P.Fitzw. Mus. and P.Oxy. have what seem to be random traces of ink. Writing in the principal text is in regular, carefully formed, round upright capitals, heavily serifed, the serifs often appearing as hooks or blobs of ink. It is very like the hand of P.Oxy. XXVI 2441 (Pindar *Paeans*, Turner-Parsons 1987, no. 22) and belongs to the same general type as both the first and second hand of P.Oxy. V 841 (Pindar *Paeans*, Roberts 1955 no. 14), although neither of those is so decorous. Indentation of lines in lyric meters is pronounced (1279-1283, 1286-1287, and 1291-1294; intervening lines in iambic trimeters, although part of the

---

[1] Fr. 3a:] ̣ ̣[|]εκ [|] ̣[(line 2 εβ Powell). Fr. 3b:] ̣ω[.

same song, are aligned with spoken portions of the play further down in the column; see Savignago 2008). Division of cola in the lyrical portion is slightly different from that found in manuscripts LPV or adopted by editors (Zuntz 1965, p. 32).[2] Iota adscript is erratically applied, sometimes in error (1282 δηι, 1288 ἀκτὴἱϲ, 1293 ἥδηι for ἤδη). In the vertical strip of intercolumn at the right of P.Harris fr. 1 are faint traces of ink, previously unnoticed, that seem to correspond to speaker notes naming Aegeus and Medea beside lines 748 and 749, where Medea extracts an oath from Aegeus.[3] Portions from the middle of these lines survive in P.Oxy.

Presumably the original scribe made these notations, for the speaker notes at lines 1295, 1306, 1308, 1314, 1317, and 1323 are all his work. This writer is also responsible for paragraphi that mark off sections and for the apostrophes marking elisions (although he also occasionally employed *scriptio plena*, e.g., in lines 1294 and 1297). The same writer also entered an erroneous correction or variant in line 1288, and some accents and the marginal note at line 1282 are his work. A second scribe using a lighter ink and a slightly finer pen but lacking the first scribe's controlled attention to form corrected text (lines 1285, 1292, 1299) and accents and added most of the numerous diacritical and punctuation marks. The accents on εμῶν and ἦλθ[ον in line 1303 give an idea of the relative flamboyance of this hand compared with the restraint and tidiness of the first scribe. This second person also wrote low and high stops, marks of quantity, hyphens, all three accents, and both breathing marks and, in the first seven lines of the choral song, he wrote six apostrophe-shaped marks between words in which elision is not present (the same mark also appears once in P.Oxy. in *Med.* 1008, a trimeter). The purpose of these latter marks is not entirely clear. One may guess that in using them the secondary writer adapted the

---

[2] Instead of breaking 1280 after τέκνων (so Diggle 1984, Page 1952), the papyrus continues with ὃν ἔτεκες; in 1290, the papyrus interrupts the final dochmiac before the last syllable, δεινόν; / ὦ; after 1292 βροτοῖς, the scribe starts a new line. Zuntz' conclusion—that the papyrus confirms that the metrical layout of mediaeval mss. goes back to Aristophanes of Byzantium—is contested by Mastronarde-Bremer 1982, pp. 151-164.

[3]]Α[ι]γ̣ε̣[υ]ϲ̣[: The remains of the supposed alpha are two convex curves that may have formed the bottom left and bottom right of a loop, plus a short diagonal stroke from northwest to southeast that is slightly below and to the right of the second curve. Of the supposed gamma, there is a dot of ink on the line, plus two unconnected parts of the cross bar, the rightmost of which seems to bend slightly downward to the right in ligature with the upward curve of the top of epsilon. A stroke that may have been the end of the top curve of epsilon is also preserved (unless this is the top of sigma). The final traces are consistent with the bottom right of the lower stroke of sigma.]Μη̣δε̣[ι]α̣[: equally difficult. The remains of the supposed mu are a short, shallow, curved stroke tilted slightly leftward in the bottom left of the writing space with a fleck of ink above the right-hand end, and the mirror opposite of the curve on the right side. In the spaces that eta and delta should occupy, only two dots remain. Epsilon may be represented by a low curve with its concave side upward, plus a short horizontal stroke above. This is followed by a short curve in the upper register, rather like an apostrophe, which may belong to alpha.

usual role of the apostrophe (which is to separate pairs of letters within a word or to mark elision) and extended it to passages in which the meter is complex, the diction elevated, or the *scriptio continua* more than usually difficult to parse. Possibly it was intended to make recitation or memorization easier. If so, in the lyric portion at least, pauses were quite frequent, and they sometimes occur where a modern reader might not be inclined to mark a break.[4] These and the abundant other diacritical marks of the papyrus indicate, in any case, that this was a book that saw use in school.

The second hand may be responsible for the possible annotation at the left of line 1293. The same scribe also added rather shapeless *chi*-sigla between lines 1191 and 1192 (P.Fitzw.Mus.), between lines 1281 and 1282 (P.Harris), at 1310 (P.Harris), and possibly also at 1294 below a speaker note, unless this is a diple as Harris reports. The purpose of all these signs is obscure. At *Med.* 1282 *chi* may mark the beginning of the antistrophe, which the *nota personae* of the first scribe wrongly indicated as starting at line 1281; it is not likely to refer to the marginal note at the right of the column, which was written by the original scribe. The *chi* or *diple* at 1294 may decorate the speaker note above it. Scholia shed no light on these or the others: apart from short glosses on *Med.* 1192 and 1281, none survive for the marked passages.

P.Harris
fr. 4 col. i

> **1282** μίαν δὴ κλύω μίαν τῶν πάρος
>
> μόναν δι( )

Text: δηι κλυώ, μίαν τῶν πάρος pap.   Note written by the first scribe at the right of the column   δι̣
Powell 1936, Page 1952, pp. 171-172, but the diagonal stroke seen by Powell above ι is no longer visible: the horizontal fibers above the note are lost, and mold at the right edge of the papyrus obscures anything that may have followed

———

δι(ορθωτέον)? McNamee, SP per litt.: δί(c) aut δι(ττῶc) aut δι(πλῆ) Powell: δί[c] McNamee 2007b: δή Snell 1937, haud verisimile : Δίδ(υμος)? Haslam per litt.

" 'Solitary,' ..."

> **1292** ἔρεξας ἤδη κακά

———

4   1279 πέτρος' η; 1279-1280 cίδη|ρος' άτις; 1280 όν' έτεκες; 1281 άροτον' αυτόχειρι; 1283 χέρα' βαλεῖν (χείρα pap.), 1284 μανεῖcαν' ε[κ, 1285 νῖν' εξέπ[εμψε.

]ο)

Text: ἔρεξας ἤδηι pap.   Note: written by the second hand at the left of the last line of a choral song   ]ο followed by a large curve twice its height which is shaped like a right-hand parenthesis

χ]ο) Powell, i.e., χ]ο(ρόϲ)

"Chorus" (?)

1282   μόνην, not μόναν, would be expected if the note were in some way exegetic. The Doric μόναν strongly suggests, rather, that it is a variant reading, albeit one without manuscript support. Codices universally have μίαν μίαν, with the exception of A, where the word is written once only; see Diggle 1983, p. 352; Diggle 1984, pp. 63-65; contra Lewis 1936, p. 6 and Snell 1937, p. 74. δι- is also obscure. An abbreviation meaning δί(ϲ) or δι(ττῶϲ) (Powell) would presumably indicate that μόναν and not μίαν should be written, twice. Haslam's suggestion that the abbreviation represents the name of Didymus, is attractive and, if correct, would mean that μόναν was Didymus' preferred reading. An abbreviation of διπλῆ, the name of the critical symbol, (Powell) is unlikely. Annotators used the symbol itself, >, not its name, to signal the existence of commentary. Lastly, it is conceivable that δι- represents a form of διορθόω (cf. McNamee 2007b, p. 350 on BKT II = MP³ 1393 and McNamee 1981), in which case μόναν δι(ορθωτέον) would mean, "μόναν (is the reading); it (i.e., the text μίαν) needs to be corrected."

1292   The addition is written in untidy script, unlike the main scribe's neatly formed monograms at the beginning of other choral passages (*pace* Powell); cf. the speaker notes at lines 1279 (not reported by Powell) and 1306. Its most likely interpretation is that it stands for χο(ρόϲ) and was written by the same person responsible for accents and punctuation, even though its location is odd: indications of speaker regularly appear beside the first, not the final, line of a speech or choral passage. It is unlikely to be exegetic; explanatory notes hardly ever appear in the left margin of book rolls.

P.Mich. inv. 3735 (ex inv. 3723)   saec. I[a]

Marginal notes on Orestes *835 and 840-841*

Prov.: Oxyrhynchus?

Cons.: Ann Arbor, University of Michigan, Hatcher Graduate Library.

Edd.: Koenen-Sijpesteijn 1989; Diggle 1994 (Π^{19}).

Tab.: https://quod.lib.umich.edu/a/apis.

Comm.: MP³ 412.01; LDAB 1010; TM 59902   Diggle 1991, pp. 116, 119, 137; Luppe 1991, p. 81; Athanassiou 1999, pp. 11-13; McNamee 2007b, p. 255; Savignago 2008, pp. 224-228 (no. 41); Carrara 2009, pp. 227-230.

Medium-brown papyrus measuring 6 x 9 cm. Writing runs along the fibers. The verso is blank. According to a report of May 2, 1925 by H.I. Bell, the papyrus was purchased by A.E.R. Boak in that year and was said to come from Behneseh (Oxyrhynchus).[1]

Parts of the ends of line from *Orestes* 835-846 survive, line 835 being almost wholly effaced. A narrow upper margin 1.8 cm remains. Script is a laboriously formed capital with a generally squarish appearance: δ, ε, c, τ, ω, and usually o are as wide as they are tall, but o is now and again more oval and α, ι, ρ, and most ν's are narrow. Bilinearity (except for φ) was intended but not consistently rendered. μ is in four strokes. The cross-bar of ε is detached and short, and in one case little more than a dot. Serifs ornament several letters. The writing resembles Cavallo-Maehler 2008, no. 70 (TM 61126, which predates 5 B.C.E.); also similar are Cavallo-Maehler nos. 68, 69, 71, and 72 (TM 60263, 59246, 65577, and 61190). The original scribe has made a single interlinear correction above line 837. Two high stops, a circumflex accent and a macron appear to be in different ink. At the right of the column are two fragmentary notes in blacker ink and written in a script more compressed both horizontally and vertically. The two lines of each note are written close together, so that neither note extends as far as the next line of text.

---

[1] See the APIS entry of this papyrus in https://quod.lib.umich.edu/a/apis.

835   [βεβάκχευ]τ̣[αι] μ̣α̣ν̣ί̣α̣ι̣ς̣

. . . [

] . . ι̣ . [

1   traces of the bottom of three letters, and horizontal fibers stripped above the remaining ink   2   In the first position, stripped horizontal fibers and a stroke of ink on a vertical fiber, then a horizontal stroke: γ? Next, a circumflex-like curve at the top with abrasion beneath and a dot of ink at the bottom: ρ conceivable, but not assured. After ι, possibly the left curve of ω, but the reading is difficult

840-841 [χρυσεοπηνήτ]ων φαρέων
         [μαστὸν ὑπε]ρ̣τ̣έλλοντ' ἐσιδ[ὼν]

χ̣ρ̣υ̣[c-
ει̣ . [

ει̣ . [: θε̣[ed.pr.

χ̣ρ̣υ̣[cοῦφῶν] | ε̣ἱ̣μ̣[ατίων]? FaM: χ̣ρ̣υ̣[cέου ὕφαν]|θ̣έ̣[ντων] Athanassiou

Garments woven of gold(?)

835 Presumably a gloss on βεβάκχευται, but scholia and glossaries offer no certain restoration. Conceivably in line 2 [ἠγ]ρ̣ίω̣[ται] was written, cf. *sch. rec. in Or.* 835 βεβάκχευται: … ἠγρίωται, ἐξεμάνη, ἐταράχθη.

840 The two lines of text in the margin are written very close together beside line 840 and the interlinear space following it, but above the end of line 841, which extends into the right intercolumn. The compactness led Koenen and Sijpesteijn to surmise that the two marginal lines probably belong to a single note. How far it extended to the right is difficult to ascertain. Line 840 is part of a lyric, with lines shorter than the trimeters in lines 844-845, parts of which survive. They will have extended at least 2 cm beyond the remains of the note at line 840, and still further to the right there will presumably have been a narrow intercolumn (as is typical in Hellenistic papyri; cf., e.g., Cavallo-Maehler 2008, nos. 41, 55, 58 etc.). The note is evidently a gloss on χρυσεοπήνητος, and the space available would easily accommodate, e.g., χ̣ρ̣υ̣[cοῦφῶν | ε̣ἱ̣μ̣[ατίων (Montana *per litt.*; cf. *sch. vet. in Or.* 841 χρυσοὐφῶν ἱματίων;) or χ̣ρ̣υ̣[cέου ὕφαν]|θ̣έ̣[ντων] (Athanassiou 1999, p. 12; cf. *sch. vet. in Or.* 840 ἐκ χρυσοῦ ὑφανθέντων and *sch. rec.* (Dindorf) *in Or.* 841 τῶν ἐκ χρυσοῦ καὶ μετάξης ὑφανθέντων (κατεσκευασμένων ἱματίων supersc. in Z). Note, however,

Athanassiou's caution against inferring links between scholia and notes dating from before Didymus).

P.Oxy. LIII 3716   saec. II-I^a

Marginal note on Orestes 946

Prov.: Oxyrhynchus.

Cons.: Oxford, Sackler Library, Papyrology Rooms.

Edd.: HASLAM 1986b; DIGGLE 1984 (Π^{13}).

Tabb.: P.Oxy. LIII pl. V; https://www.sds.ox.ac.uk/oxyrhynchus-papyri.

Comm.: MP^3 412.12; LDAB 1026; TM 59916   DIGGLE 1991, pp. 116-117, 119, 137; LUPPE 1991, p. 81; ATHANASSIOU 1999, pp. 9-11; MCNAMEE 2007b, p. 255.

This is a medium-brown, creased and worm-eaten piece of papyrus in the shape of a diamond, measuring 6.2 x 9.9 cm at its greatest breadth and height and containing parts of two columns. Writing is along the fibers and the back is blank. Top and bottom margins are missing; the intercolumn, as usual in Hellenistic books, is a fairly narrow (1.6 cm). The principal scribe wrote a somewhat informal squarish hand similar to that of Cavallo-Maehler 2008, nos. 63 and 64, dated respectively to the second to first centuries B.C.E. and the end of the second century B.C.E. Serifs are added irregularly at the foot of verticals in η, π, μ, τ. The saddle of μ has the shape of a V with a rounded point. Writing in the lines at the bottom of column i are squeezed together more tightly than the writing elsewhere. A forked paragraphus at the left between lines 981 and 982 separates antistrophe and epode of Electra's lyric, but there is no other punctuation, nor are there diacritical signs. At *Or.* 981, at the left of the paragraphus, a writer (probably the original scribe) wrote a stichometric K, representing 1,000. It is difficult to account with certainty for the variance in the numbering of lines, given the variable line-divisions in lyric passages (⇒ 9) and the opportunities for interpolation. Haslam notes that if the series of trochaic exchanges at *Or.* 774-798 has been subdivided, the figure 1,000 at *Or.* 981 would be approximately correct. Column height will have been about 31 lines if 957-959 were absent (cf. sch. *Or.* 957 ἐν ἐνίοις δὲ οὐ φέρονται οἱ τρεῖς ϲτίχοι οὗτοι). A second hand, smaller and quicker, wrote something, now illegible, in grayish ink at the right of *Or.* 944 (which does not survive) and at the right of and just above the final letter of *Or.* 946. In the ed.pr. M. Haslam describes the marginal hand "no earlier than the first century AD;" F. Maltomini, *per litt.*, prefers the first century B.C.E. or earlier.

946 [μόλις δ' ἔπεισε μὴ ?πετρουμένουc θ]ανεῖν

ζή(τει)

A supralinear ν may have been written above the α of θ]ανεῖν in the main text. Papyrus on either side is damaged.   ζ written quickly, with a long upper horizontal angled upward as if to ten on a clock. What is read as η is a slightly undulating horizontal stroke in ligature with the lower horizontal of ζ.

Check (it).

946 The note ζή(τει) generally indicates a text-critical query. Known variants, one of which may have been present in the lost text, are πετρούμενοc P.Oxy. XI 1370 and HMVᵖᶜC / πετρουμένουc *rell.* F. Montana suggests *per litt.* that]ν in the interlineation above θανεῖν may represent [πετρούμενο]ν (a previously unknown variant). In this case, the query presumably refers to this alternate reading.

P.Oxy. XI 1370   saec. V[P]

Marginal notes on Orestes *1370, 1371*

Prov.: Oxyrhynchus.

Cons.: Massachusetts, Williamstown, Williams College Library.

Edd.: GRENFELL-HUNT 1915; DONOVAN 1969, pp. 85-90 no. 23; DIGGLE 1981 (Π^9).

Comm.: MP³ 402; LDAB 992; TM 59885   SCHMIDT 1918, pp. 100-101; PASQUALI 1952, pp. 192-193; DI BENEDETTO 1965, pp. 140-143; DONOVAN 1969, pp. 85-90; TUILIER 1965, pp. 112, 125, 234; DIGGLE 1971; TURNER 1977, pp. 17, 67, 105 no. 72, Group 5; DIGGLE 1991, pp. 116, 119, 136-137, 139-140, 150 (Π^9); Ponzio 1996-1997, p. 102 (*Medea*); ATHANAS-SIOU 1999, pp. 26-28; MCNAMEE 2007b, p. 254; SAVIGNAGO 2008, pp. 217-223; CARRARA 2009, pp. 524-530.

Tabb.: GRENFELL-HUNT 1915, pl. 7 (fr. 3→, fr. 9↓); DONOVAN 1969, pll. 20-23; https://unbound.williams.edu/williamsarchives/.

Nine fragments of a papyrus codex containing *Medea* and *Orestes* (Diggle Π^2 and Π^9, respectively). The original order of the plays in the codex is uncertain. The material is golden in color, the ink a grayish brown. Grenfell and Hunt calculated that there were originally 37 or 38 lines per page, so that the two plays will have occupied about 84 pages, or 42 leaves. The upper margin, which is complete on fr. 1 and the two folios of fr. 9, ranges from 3.8 to 4.6 cm. The bottom margin, surviving on frr. 3 and 8, varies from 5.3 to 5.5 cm. Side margins vary considerably, depending on whether they are inner or outer and at the left or right of the text. A left outer margin survives only on fr. 1, where it measures 3.9 cm. Left inner margins are much smaller, running from 1.5 to about 2.1 cm. Variable line-length makes right-hand margins even more irregular; those at the inside of the codex measure about 2.7 cm to 4 cm; the sole right margin at the outside of a page (fr. 1) is 5.3 cm wide.[1] Fr. 1 contains *Medea* 20-26 and 57-63 (Diggle Π^2); no annotations are preserved. The rest of the papyrus has portions of *Orestes* (Π^9),[2] with marginalia only in fr. 9.

---

[1] Upper margins: fr. 1 ↓ 3.9 cm, → 3.8 cm., fr. 9 fol. 1 → 4.4 cm., ↓ 4.6 cm., fr. 9 fol. 2 ↓ 4.2 cm., → 4.4 cm. Lower margins: fr. 3 → 5.4 cm, ↓ 5.3 cm.; fr. 8 ↓ 5.3 cm., → 5.5 cm. Left inner margins: fr. 1 ↓ 1.5 cm, fr. 3 → 2 cm., fr. 9 fol. 1 ↓ 2 cm. Right-hand inner margins: fr. 1 → 3.5 cm, fr. 3 ↓ 3.8 cm., fr. 9 fol. 1 → 2.7 cm., fr. 9 fol. 2 ↓ 4 cm.

[2] Frr. 2 + 3: *Or.* 445-449, 469-474, 482-486, 508-512; frr. 4 + 5: *Or.* 685-690, 723-729; fr. 6: *Or.* 811-817, 850-854 (only margin is preserved at the end of line 850); frr. 7 + 8: *Or.* 896-898,

The main text is written rather loosely in competent sloping capitals assigned by Grenfell and Hunt to the fifth rather than the sixth century. The script is very like that of the main text of P.Oxy. XI 1371 (Aristophanes *Clouds*; Cavallo-Maehler 1987, pp. 40-41, no. 16a; ⇒ Aristophanes 13), with which it was found. That papyrus is dated to the first half or middle of the fifth century on the basis of its half-cursive annotation. The legible notes of the Euripides text are written in a different and quite personal half-cursive in which noteworthy features are the exaggerated flourish of the elongated top stroke of final sigma and the variable height of letters: mu appears in two sizes, one twice the other, and the pronounced vertical shaft of eta is twice the height of letters of average size and more than four times the height of short letters. Grenfell and Hunt set it "somewhat later" than the notes in P.Oxy. XI 1371, which they assign to the fifth century.

Numerous other manuscripts, mainly dramatic, were found with P.Oxy. XI 1370, and all presumably belonged to a single collection, sometimes referred to as the Byzantine library of Oxyrhynchus. They are published in P.Oxy. XI.[3] In addition to P.Oxy. XI 1370, three others in the group (apart from no. 1371, already mentioned, also nos. 1397, a copy of Hom. *Od.* 18, and 1402 ⇒ Aristophanes 32 (?)) have exegetic marginalia, sometimes lengthy. In each case, however, the notes are by different hands.

In P.Oxy. XI 1370 the responsibility for diacritical marks and punctuation differs between the *Medea* text and that of *Orestes*. In the former, the principal scribe wrote all or nearly all the paragraphi and seems to have contributed the first diaeresis in *Medea* 57. This portion also has frequent accents of three sorts, rough and smooth breathing marks, and stops in three positions by a second hand, who also supplied two missing iota adscripts and probably the second diaeresis in line 1 (this is attributed by the ed.pr. to the original scribe, but digital photos indicate the ink is different).

The *Orestes* fragments have far fewer diacritics and punctuation marks: in the twelve lines of fr. 3, which contains the longest line segments (about half to three-quarters of each line, on average, is preserved), there are only ten, compared to twenty-nine in the fourteen (admittedly complete) lines from *Medea* in fr. 1. Even given the uneven states of preservation of the two plays,

---

907-910, 934-936, 945-948; fr. 9 fol. 1: *Or.* 1246-1265, 1297-1305; fol. 2: *Or.* 1334-1345, 1369b-1371.

[3] P.Oxy. XI 1369, Soph. *OT*, MP³ 1469, LDAB 3951; 1371, Aristoph. *Nub.*, MP³ 145, LDAB 372; 1372, Aristoph. *Ran.*, MP³ 153, LDAB 383; 1373, Aristoph. *Pax, Eq.*, MP³ 151, LDAB 373; 1374, Aristoph. *Vesp.*, MP³ 155, LDAB 382; 1385, Hom. *Il.*, MP³ 654, LDAB 2193; 1391, Hom. *Il.*, MP³ 881.1, LDAB 2178; 1394, Hom. *Od.*, MP³ 1026, LDAB 2181; 1396, Hom. *Od.*, MP³ 1082, LDAB 2189; 1397, Hom. *Od.*, MP³ 1212, LDAB 2190; 1401, Aristoph.?, MP³ 1578, LDAB 377; 1402, Aristoph. *Eq.*, MP³ 1630, LDAB 370; 1403, Aristoph.?, MP³ 1627, LDAB 371.

the difference is noticeable and suggests different scribes added diacritics in each. For the *Orestes* portion, Grenfell and Hunt assigned accents, breathings, stops, and elision marks to main scribe. Certainly the ductus is similar, and most paragraphi are by that hand (a diaeresis attributed to this scribe at *Orestes* 470 is too worn to verify). But since the diacritics were added secondarily, and in grayer ink, it seems a second writer may be at work here. Whether or not this is so, at least two writers other than the main scribe are at work in the *Orestes* portion. One, possibly identical with supposed second writer who contributed diacritics, drew the paragraphi at lines 1250, 1257, and 1260, added the speaker note χορ(όc) at *Orestes* 1249, and make additional corrections at lines 511, 1334, and 1342 in gray ink. Grenfell and Hunt tentatively attribute the speaker note Τ̣υν̣δ(αρεύc) at line 470 to this hand also, but the resemblance is unclear, and I am inclined to assign it, rather, to the person who added corrections at *Or.* 897 and 909. These are written in brown ink by an altogether different scribe; the same writer may also have added the speaker note Ἠλ(έκτρα) at line 1247, unless this was the work of the original scribe. The notes are both glossographical, with verbal echoes of scholia on this play, scholia on Hellenistic authors, and Hesychius.

Damage to the papyrus over time, especially from the brown ink employed, has destroyed portions of text; as a result, the plate published in the ed.pr. provides, in places, more information than autopsy. This is most apparent at fr. 9 f. 1 ↓, where Grenfell and Hunt read ἄλ]λο̣ ἡμιχ(όριον), "Another half-chorus," beside *Or.* 1260. The ink of the adscript has now so badly damaged the papyrus surface that where the editors saw writing is now a deep crevice 2 mm wide, about 16 mm long, and deepest in its right half, which has cut right through the top layer of fibers in the left margin. Only the most doubtful traces of ink survive: one or two specks possibly, about midway along the crack, and another tiny dot in the suprascript position at the extreme right. If the reading of the ed.pr. is correct, it is unique in papyri of drama, where *notae personarum* do not otherwise indicate responsion between half-choruses.

Fr. 9

f. 2 ↓

1370   εὐμά]ρισιν

εἶδος ὑποδήματο[c

Written in the right (inner) margin

A kind of shoe

1371   [παстάδων]

ἡ παстάс
π[ε]πο[ι]κιλμένο[
[ ]κ̣[.].[..].

Right (inner) margin   3   [ ] space for one or two letters. After κ[.], a dot of ink from the top of a lost letter. Following [..]. a short stroke at a steep northwest/southeast angle, with a fleck of ink at the left: nu?

———

3 [ο]ι̣[τω]ν̣? McNamee : [οι]κ̣ο̣ς̣ Grenfell-Hunt

The bridal chamber: a decorated (bedroom?)

1370   The note corresponds to the scholia on this line, *sch. vet. in Or.* 1370, ἐν εὐμάρισιν· εὔμαρις εἶδος ὑποδήματος сανδαλώδουс· πεποίηται δὲ ἀπὸ τοῦ εὐμαρῶс ὑποδεῖсθαι. προπαροξύνεται ἐν τῇ καθόλου; *sch. rec.* ἐν ὑποδήμαси βαρβαρικοῖс· εὔμαρὶс γὰρ εἶδος ὑποδήματος βαρβαρικοῦ...; cf. *sch. vet. in* Ap.Rhod. 2.633, *sch. in* Lycophr. 855. But its terseness here suggests a lexicon may have been the immediate source. The entry in Hesychius, whose lexicon was produced about the same time as the papyrus, is nearly identical: Hsch. ε 6977 Latte-Cunningham εὐμάριδεс· εἶδος ὑποδήματος.

1371   Definitions of παстάс and related words proliferate in ancient lexicographic and exegetic works from the time of Apollonius Sophistes onward: Ap. Soph. 129.1-2 Bekker πάссε ἐπὶ μὲν τοῦ καὶ ἡμῖν νουμένου "πάссε δ᾽ ἁλὸς θείοιο" (*Il.* 9.214), ἐπὶ δὲ τοῦ ἐποίκιλλεν "πολλοὺс δ᾽ ἐνέπαссεν ἀέθλουс" (*Il.* 3.126). ἀφ᾽ οὗ καὶ παстὸν λέγομεν γαμικὸν ποικίλον ὕφαсμα κυρίωс; Hsch. π 1083 Hansen: παстάδεс· ... ἴсωс δὲ καὶ οἱ διαγεγραμμένοι οἶκοι· πάсαι γὰρ τὸ ποικίλαι (cf. Hsch. α 8451 Latte-Cunningham αὐτόπαстοι πύλαι· παстάδαс ἔχουсαι, ποικίλαι); Choer., *Epim. Ps.* 131.18 παстάс, παρὰ τὸ πάссω τὸ ποικίλλω; *sch.* Pind. *Ol.* 10.114b–f: 114b καὶ γὰρ τὸ πάссειν ποικίλλειν ἐстὶ, καὶ παстὸс διὰ τὸ πεποικίλθαι; Eustath. 1.32 Cullhed-Olsen *ad* Hom. *Od.* 1.124 πάссειν δέ, τό τε ποικίλλειν ὅθεν καὶ ἡ παстάς (cf. Eustath. *Comm. in Il.* 1.619.5-9 van der Valk). The Euripidean scholia on the passage offer more limited information, not obviously related to this tradition: ...παстάδων δὲ τῶν κοιτώνων... (ἄλλωс· *sch. rec.*) ... παстάδων γὰρ τῶν θαλάμων... .

P.Oxy. LIII 3718   saec. V^P

Marginal notes on Orestes *1406, 1408, 1625, 1652; and* Bacchae *211, 216, 223, 225, 231, 234, 257, 261*

Prov.: Oxyrhynchus.

Cons.: Papyrology Rooms, Sackler Library, Oxford.

Edd.: HASLAM 1986c; DIGGLE 1994 (Π^{18}: *Orestes*), (Π^4: *Bacchae*).

Tabb.: https://www.sds.ox.ac.uk/oxyrhynchus-papyri.

Comm.: MP³ 414.02; LDAB 988; TM 59881   MCNAMEE 1981; DIGGLE 1991, pp. 116, 117, 119, 120, 124, 140-142, 150 (Π^{18}); LUPPE 1991, p. 81; ATHANASSIOU 1999, pp. 28-32; AUSTIN 2005, pp. 162-163; MCNAMEE 2007b, pp. 255-526; SAVIGNAGO 2008, p. 317; CARRARA 2009, pp. 533-540.

The manuscript consists of several fragments from at least four folios of a codex that contained *Orestes* and *Bacchae*. Two page numbers, ρ̅ϙ̅η̅ and ρ̅ϙ̅θ̅ (198 and 199), survive on B ↓ (front) and B → (back), allowing the deduction that each page held about 29 lines, and that the pages preceding what survives will have accommodated 5510 lines of text. It is impossible to ascertain what that text might have been. One might speculate that the *Orestes* of P.Oxy. LIII 3718 rounded out the Byzantine triad, but the combined verse-count of the *Hecuba, Phoenissae,* and *Orestes* is much less (4754) than the room available. And even with allowance made for vagaries in line division and blank areas before and after each play, the space available is too extensive to be filled just by these three plays. Haslam 1986c, p. 137 considers other options (additional, even non-canonical plays, and perhaps not ordered as they appear in mediaeval manuscripts). The possibility also remains that the space was filled with something other than Euripidean tragedy, for example, ancillary material on the plays or the works of one or more other authors.

The papyrus is mottled and medium brown. The legible portion of the codex consists of parts of two single pages and a pair of joined pages. Fr. A, inv. 66 6B.3/C(1-3)c, measures 7.7 x 12.3 cm and contains parts of *Orestes* 1407-1412 and 1432-1442. The side with vertical fibers precedes, with a surviving left (inner) margin of 4 cm on the front. On the back, which contains a lyric section, some lines continue the width of the fragment. The upper edge is likely to have been the top of the page. On this assumption, Haslam calculates that *Orestes* 1407 will have been the fifth line on the front and *Orestes* 1432 the first on the back side. Fr. B, inv. 65 6B.35/C(1)a, is a bifolium reconstructed from ten fragments (one of which is incorrectly grouped with fr. C in the available digital images: see below on *Orestes* 1625). Parts of *Orestes* 1621-1635 and 1649-1660 occupy the two sides of one leaf, which presumably preceded; parts of *Bacchae* 194-222 and 223-245 were written on the other. The largest constituent piece with legible text, fr. B, comes from the center of the codex and measures 12.5 x 12.8 cm. The bifolium was not the central sheet of its gathering: two additional sheets will have been necessary for the conclusion of *Orestes* (assuming that it preceded) and the first 193 lines of *Bacchae*, plus any introductory material accompanying it. Along with fr. B Haslam includes descriptions of another eight fragments (frr. k-r) that he was not able to place because of their extreme deterioration (one, measuring 14 x 10 cm, is quite large). I was not able to inspect these or the published portions of fr. B. Fr. C, inv. 65 6B.40/D(a), is from the outer edge of a folio with portions of the outer margin. On the side with horizontal fibers, which preceded, the margin is on the right and measures 3.2 cm. On the back, it is 4 cm wide. The fragment overall is 8.2 x 13 cm. The original size of the codex, which Haslam estimates as having been about 20 x 35 cm, means it will have fit into Turner's Group 1, the largest, although this manuscript will have been one of the smallest in that group (Turner 1977, pp. 14-15).

Ink is brown and often very much abraded. The scribe writes confident, angled capitals of the standard "sloping majuscule" or "Byzantine uncial" type. The writing has a pronounced slope and alternates between thick and thin strokes. Haslam likens it to that of the cache of dramatic and Homeric texts published as P.Oxy. XI 1369-1374, although he notes that the Euripidean text in that group (P.Oxy. XI 1370, ⇒ 12) is by another scribe, and he doubts that 3718 is from the same source, as it was found in a different excavation year. In fact, the closest parallel to the script is P.Oxy. XI 1371, assigned to the first half or middle of the 5th century: Cavallo and Maehler 1987, pp. 40-41 no. 16a, ⇒ Aristophanes 13 CLGP; cf. also their nos. 15b (first half of the fifth century) and 17b (later in the fifth century). The main scribe is responsible for most accents and diacritical marks, although these were supplemented by a second writer who wrote in black ink and also restored an omitted line. The *nota personae* απ[ο]λ? was written erroneously at the left of line 1621, where a speech by Menelaus begins (απο^λ is properly written a few lines below, at 1625). Someone has crossed out the entry at 1621 and written με[ν]ε, directly above. A hand that is smaller and probably different from that of the main text has added a few marginal notes in lighter brown ink and well-spaced, sloping letters between the lines and in the margins. These are mostly terse glosses, with frequent linkages to lexica and dramatic scholia.

A ↓ (front)

Orestes

1406   [ξυνετὸς πολέμου]

᷎ἔμπειρος

Written in the left (inner) margin

Experienced

1407   προνοίας [κακοῦργος ὤν]

]. . . τι. τῳς

Text: προνοί̄ας pap.   The note is written in the left (inner) margin   Except for τ and c, the writing is nearly illegible. Before τ perhaps ο . . : possibly . . .   Before ῳc, a horizontal line like the
cross-bar of τ

φρ]οντίδος Athanassiou (*ad* προνοίας) :]. .τιcτοc? FaM: οὐκ ἀ]φροντίcτωc SP

B → (front)

1625   λ̣ῆμ[’

φρόγ[η]μα

Interlinear above λ̣ημ[

Arrogance

B ↓ (back)

1651-1652 [πά]γοιϲιν [ἐν Ἀρείοιϲιν εὐϲεβεϲτά]την
    [ψῆ]φον διοίϲ[ο]υ[ϲ']

    π(αρὰ) Ἄρει

Interlinear above διοίϲ[ο]υ[ϲ'] π' pap. ρει: bottoms of letters only, including descenders in the first and third letters

———
Ἄρει? (not Ἀθηνᾷ) Haslam

(*sc.* They will give a vote) in the presence of Ares.

B ↓ (front)

Bacchae

211 [ἐγὼ π]ροφ[ήτηϲ ϲοι λόγων γενήϲομαι]

  ].εε..[

Interlinear above π]ροφ[ήτηϲ]. : possibly η

———
εε Haslam: θε? McNamee

216 νεοχμά

  νέα [

Interlinear above νεοχμά

New

B → (back)

223   πτώccoυcαν

        ]φεῠγωcι

Written in the left (outer) margin

They run away

225   τ[ὴν δ' Ἀφροδίτην

        κ̣[

Interlinear above the place where Ἀφροδίτην should have been written
——
κ̣[οίτην? Haslam

231   ἐ]ν̣ ἄρκυcιν

        ]λήμαcι

Interlinear above ἄρκυcιν

234   [γόηc ἐ]πῳδό[c

        ]φαρμακ̣[

Interlinear above ἐ]πῳδό[c
——
ἔμπειροc] φαρμάκ̣[ων? Haslam: φάρμακ[οc? McNamee: φαρμακ[εύc? FaM

... sorcerer ...

C → (front)

257 ϲκοπεῖν πτερωτὰ κὰμπύρων μι]ϲθόν φέρειν

υ.

Written in the right (outer) margin

Text: μιϲθουϲ codd.   φέρειν P, Trˢ (corr. in L): φέρων L   Note: υ'? McNamee

261 ὅπου βότρυοϲ ἐν δαιτὶ γίγνεται γάνοϲ

πόμα

Written in the right (outer) margin

Drink

Orestes

1406 Difficult to read, but doubtless correct, given the similarity of the *sch. vet. ad loc.*: ἀντὶ τοῦ ἔμπειροϲ τοῦ πολέμου; cf. *sch. rec.* ἐπιϲτήμων, ἔμπειροϲ. Lexicographers handle ἔμπειροϲ and ϲυνετόϲ as synonyms: cf. Hsch. ε 777 Latte-Cunningham καὶ εἰδυίηϲιν· ἐμπείροιϲ, ἐπιϲτήμοϲι, ϲυνεταῖϲ, ἐπιϲταμέναιϲ (Hom. *Il.* 1.608), φ 824 Hansen-Cunningham φράδμονεϲ· ἔμπειροι, ϲυνετοί (Greg. Naz. *c.* 1, 2, 1, 555 [37, 564, 2 Migne]); *Sud.* φ 686 Adler φράδμων: ϲυνετόϲ, φρόνιμοϲ, ἢ ἔμπειροϲ.

1407 Given the annotator's inclination, the note presumably deals with a single word. κακοῦργοϲ is an unlikely candidate, since it presents no great difficulty. A gloss on πρόνοια in the context of the difficult expression ἡϲύχου / προνοίαϲ κακοῦργοϲ ὤν would be a reasonable expectation (so F. Montana). Athanassiou suggests φροντίδοϲ (Athanassiou 1999, p. 30; cf. Hsch. π 3597 Hansen πρόνοια· προενθύμηϲιϲ, ἐπιμέλεια, φροντίϲ), but although the word suits the sense, a horizontal stroke ligatured to the following letter makes the reading doubtful. S. Perrone offers οὐκ ἀ]φροντιϲτῶϲ, a phrase employed at Eur. *Med.* 914, which suits the traces better, but the remains are too damaged to confirm the reading. There is no discernible link with scholia.

1625 The tiny fragment containing the lemma, the interlineation]φρον[, and part of line 1624, has been grouped in the digital images with the fragments of C → (front). For the content, cf. *sch. rec. in Or.* 1625 λῆμα: φρόνημα. The same equivalence is fairly common in scholia (cf., e.g., the *sch. vet. in Eur.*

Med. 119, 348; *sch. rec. in* Aeschl. *Ag.* 123a; *sch. vet. in* Aristoph. *Nub.* 457b; *sch. vet. in* Pind. *N.* 3.146) and in lexica (Hsch. λ 860, 865, 866, 867 Latte-Cunningham; *Lex.Seg.* p. 290.7, 11; *Glossae in Herodotum* λ 5.1; *Sud.* λ 441, 445, 446 Adler; and Phot. λ 263 Theodoridis).

1652   π(αρὰ) Ἄρει: possibly implying that Ares presided (Haslam 1986c, p. 146). Cf. *sch. vet. ad l.*, ... ἐδίκασαν δὲ Ἀθηνᾶ καὶ Ἄρης. In earlier Roman centuries, π′ represents περί and the term for παρά is π̅. That system falls out of use after the third century, and there is no standard abbreviation for παρά in papyri of late antiquity (see McNamee 1981, pp. 77-78 and 80-81 *ss.vv.* παρά, περί).

Bacchae

211   The interlineation is presumably a gloss on προφήτηϲ. If the first ε is in fact θ, perhaps [ὡϲ? βο]ήθει[α], "(as) an aid"?

216   νεοχμόϲ in various inflections is glossed by forms of νέοϲ in dramatic scholia (e.g. the *sch. vet. in* Aeschl. *PV* 150 and *Persae* 693) and in lexica (Ael. Dion. ν 9 Erbse; Hsch. ν 368 Latte-Cunningham, Phot. ν 296.17 Theodoridis, *Sud.* ν 222 Adler; *Lex. Seg.* p. 308).

223   φεύγωϲι: I see no way to account for the subjunctive form without assuming some error. The note may be either a one-word explanation summing up the situation described in 222-223 ἄλλην δ' ἄλλοϲ' εἰϲ ἐρημίαν / πτώϲϲουϲαν, in which case we should expect φεύγουϲι. Or else the writer intended the simple gloss φεύγουϲαν (the explanation that Haslam prefers, *per litt.*). The verbs φεύγω and πτώϲϲω are in fact linked in scholia and glossaries: cf. *sch. rec. in* Eur. *Hec.* 1064 με φυγᾷ πτώϲϲουϲι: ... φεύγουϲι B.; *sch. in* Pind. *P.* 8.124b ...πτώϲϲοντι: οἷον εὐλαβοῦνται καὶ φεύγουϲι; *sch. D in* Hom. *Il.* 4.224 καταπτώϲϲοντα: ἀποδειλιῶντα, φεύγοντα; cf. Eustath. 2.69.12 comm. *in* Hom. *Il.* 5.254.

225   The name of Aphrodite is used metaphorically by Pentheus to denote sexual intercourse, hence Haslam's suggestion κ[οίτην. Another option is κοινωνίαν, used in this sense by Agave at *B.* 1276.

231   Haslam considers the marginal addition more likely a variant than a gloss, but variants are so rare in late codices (see also on line 261) that it is worth considering how this might belong to an explanatory note. He offers περιβ]λήμαϲι but notes that iron 'garments' makes an odd equivalent for ϲιδηραῖϲ... ἄρκυϲι. δικτύοιϲ is the meaning usually given for ἄρκυϲι in scholia. A solution, if περιβλήμαϲι is to be read, is to take it in the sense of περίβολοϲ (cf. LSJ s.v. περίβλημα II) and see it as referring to iron 'cages'. Athanassiou 1999, pp. 31-32 suggests λίνου περιβ]λήμαϲι: cf. *sch. vet. Or.* 1421 (ἀρκυϲτάταν μηχανάν): τοῖϲ δὲ ἐδόκει Ὀρέϲτηϲ ἐν ἀϲφαλεϲτάτῃ δικτύων μηχανῇ καὶ περιβλήματι λίνου ἐμπλέκειν καὶ ἐμβάλλειν τὴν Ἑλένην. οἷον εἰϲ ἀρκυϲτάτην μηχανὴν καὶ [ὡϲ] περίβλημα λίνων.

234 Supporting the restoration ἔμπειρος] φαρμάκ[ων, 'skilled in the use of drugs', (Haslam) is a scholion on Eur. *Hipp.* 1038 ἐπῳδὸς καὶ γόης· ἀπατεών, φαρμάκων ἔμπειρος. Other considerations favor restoring φάρμακ[ος, 'sorcerer' instead, namely, Hdn. 3.1.150 φάρμακος δὲ ὁ γόης and the exact correspondence between ἐπαοιδός and φαρμακός in the lexica: cf. Hsch. ε 4203 Latte-Cunningham ἐπαοιδοί· φαρμακοί, γόητες, Σ ε 579 Cunningham ἐπαοιδός· φαρμακός, γόης (= Phot. ε 1364 Theodoridis, *Sud.* ε 1987 Adler, *Lex.Seg.* p. 226.17); cf. *EGud.* p. 319.16 Sturz, Ps.-Zon. *Lex.* p. 446.24 Tittmann; second, the fact that a one-word gloss on ἐ]πῳδό[ς would suit this annotator's apparent inclination toward terseness; and, third, the fact that ἐπῳδός and φάρμακος are direct equivalents, like the majority of these notes, whereas ἔμπειρος] φαρμάκ[ων is a descriptive phrase. An alternative possibility is φαρμακ[εύς (F. Montana *per litt.*), based on Plat. *Symp.* 207d γόης καὶ φαρμακεύς, Cass. Dio 77.17.2 φαρμακεὺς καὶ γόης.

257 The point of the marginal addition is unknown. As Haslam notes, it is too terse to be sensible as a correction of μιсθόν to μιсθούς.

261 Haslam ventures πόμα as a variant for γάνος although, as he notes, the form attested in classical Attic, πῶμα, is metrically unacceptable (πόμα is, however, the reading of LP at *B.* 279 βότρυος ὑγρὸν πῶμ'). In view of the rarity of textual notes in late papyri and the nature of the other notes here, better to understand this annotation as explaining βότρυος... γάνος; see above on *B.* 231.

P.Oxy. LIII 3712   saec. II^P

Interlinear notes on Phoenissae 57

Prov.: Oxyrhynchus.

Cons.: Oxford, Sackler Library, Papyrology Rooms.

Edd.: Haslam 1986d; Mastronarde 1988; Diggle 1994 (Π[19]).

Comm.: MP³ 415.01; LDAB 933; TM 59828   Bremer-Worp 1986, p. 240, n. 1; Cribiore
    1996, p. 237 no. 270; Luppe 1991, p. 81; McNamee 1992; Athanassiou 1999, pp. 16-18;
    Puglia 1997, pp. 31-32; McNamee 2007b, p. 256; Carrara 2009, pp. 270-273.

Tab.: https://www.sds.ox.ac.uk/oxyrhynchus-papyri; Cribiore 1996 pl. 30.

The papyrus, which is light to medium brown and of poor quality, is in
two pieces. The first, measuring 1.9 x 4.1 cm, contains a few letters from the
center of *Phoenissae* 50-54. The second, which has cracked vertically where it
was once folded, measures 5.7 x 13.1 cm. It contains the ends of lines 53-69,
originally from the same column, which was presumably the second column
of the play's text. Another piece of papyrus was glued to the back in antiquity
and will have added an extra layer of protection, in the way that the beginning of roll was reinforced against hard use in P.Oxy. XLVIII 3369. No top or
bottom margins survive, but the larger fragment retains a bit of intercolumn
at the end of shorter lines. The back is blank.

The scribe writes along the fibers in good-sized, upright, very informal
("crude," ed.pr.) square capitals. The considerable variation in the size of letters, the numerous blunders, and the poor quality of the papyrus make it likely this is the work of a schoolchild. Space between lines is ample. The same
writer may also be responsible for the diagonal strokes at the right of lines 55
(where the mark appears to have been washed out or rubbed off), 56, and 68;
at lines 54, 60, and 69, the papyrus is too damaged to be sure whether similar
strokes appeared there; the other line-ends are lost. Parsons (ap. Haslam
1986d) suggested that every line may have ended with such a mark. Its purpose is not, however, obvious. At line 56 it may be related to the fact that the
verse evidently ended prematurely (the papyrus breaks off after πολυνεικου /,
and line 57 is displaced to the right for a distance suitable to accommodate
βίαν, the last word of 56). Alternatively, the strokes may be associated with a
student's exercise in separating text into trimeters, either from dictation or by

copying from a text that was not divided into verses. An exercise of the latter sort survives in P.Mil. I.2 15, a papyrus of the second century B.C.E. in which the prologue of Euripides' *Telephus* has been written twice: in the first column, trimeters are separated by short spaces; in the second, each trimeter occupies a separate line (MP³ 447, Cribiore 1996, p. 231, no. 246).

How much of the play was copied is unknown. Since the text comes from the beginning of the tragedy, it is conceivable that all or part of the prologue (*Phoenissae* 1-87) was reproduced. Comparably long passages used as copying exercises include TM 61028 (Cribiore 1996, pp. 250-251, no. 315; Hom. *Il.* 96 lines), TM 59946 (Cribiore 1996 no. 265: tragic speech, 3 columns), and TM 63922 (Cribiore 1996 no. 288: life of Secundus, 3 columns); see also TM 60909, 60963, 62310, and 59430 (Cribiore 1996 nos. 291, 296, 297, and 303). In this papyrus, the text may have occupied a single largish sheet. On the other hand, the deliberate reinforcement on the back suggests the fragment may come from a book roll meant for hard use (or from an already damaged roll reused for exercises). If so, the text might be the first of a series of exercises (cf. the *Livre d'écolier*, P.Cair. inv. 65445, MP³ 2642, Cribiore 1996, p. 269, McNamee 2007b, p. 256 no. 379; Puglia 1997, p. 30). Given the writer's skill level and difficulty getting the text right it is doubtful, however, that he was capable of filling a whole roll with either exercises or an entire play. On the difficulty of identifying long student exercises see Cribiore 1996, pp. 47-49. Above line 57, possibly in the hand of the first scribe, are two insertions that may be short explanatory notes. The papyrus is too damaged for certainty, however, both about what was written and about who was responsible for it.

Note a

57   [κόρας τε διccά]c

δύ]ο̣ ΄

Written above the final letter of διccάc
___
A slanted stroke (΄) like that in the next note presumably preceded the annotation (ed.pr.)

Two

Note b

57   τὴν μὲν Ἰcμήνη[ν

΄θυγ . . ερ[

Text: ειϲμηνη[pap.   The note starts above the μ of ειϲμηνη. As in the preceding annotation, it presumably concluded with a slanted mark (').

ˋθυγ . . ερ[*possis* Haslam per litt. (. θ . . . . ρ[ed.pr.); ˋθ . . . . ρ[Athanassiou 1999

(?)... daughter

Note b: There is some textual confusion at the end of line 56, where the scribe has written πολυνεικου / and not the expected πολυνείκουϲ βίαν. Immediately below the end of πολυνεικου /, approximately where Note b begins, there seems to be washed-out ink. But whether it is associated with the supposed error or with the note is not apparent. Haslam assumed the interlineation is θυγατέρα, but the writing is too damaged to verify. Athanassiou 1999, p. 17 proposes ˋθυγατέρ[α νεωτέρανˊ], anticipating line 58 τὴν δὲ πρόϲθεν Ἀντιγόνην (cf. *sch. vet. ad loc.*: τὴν προγενεϲτέραν, τὴν μείζονα Mᵍ). On the coordination in case between gloss and word glossed see McNamee 1992, pp. 65-81.

MPER N.S. III 21 (P.Vindob. inv. G 29769)   saec. VI^{p in.}

Marginal notes on Phoenissae *340, 341?*

Prov.: ?

Cons.: Vienna, Nationalbibliothek.

Edd.: OELLACHER 1939; DIGGLE 1994, p. 101 (Π⁸).

Tab.: CAVALLO 2005, pl. 49b (recto); https://www.onb.ac.at/.

Comm.: MP³ 418; LDAB 1001; TM 59894   TUILIER 1965, p. 112; DIGGLE 1971; TURNER
    1977, pp. 15, 105 (no. 77; Group 3); MASTRONARDE-BREMER 1982 (Π⁸); PORRO 1985, pp.
    174-175; BREMER-WORP, 1986, pp. 246-248; ATHANASSIOU 1999, pp. 36-37; CRISCI 2000,
    p. 9 n. 27; CAVALLO 2005, pp. 195, 199; CRISCI 2006, p. 114; MCNAMEE 2007b, p. 256;
    CARRARA 2009, pp. 510-512.

The bottom outside corner of a papyrus codex, 7.3 cm wide and 5.5 cm
high, containing line-ends of *Phoenissae* 306-310 and perhaps 337-342 (see below). The material is golden brown, the ink reddish-brown. The side with
horizontal fibers preceded. There were about thirty lines to the page, although
the variable line-divisions in the lyric passage on the back make precision
impossible. A lower margin of 2.3 cm is preserved on the front and 2.4 on the
back, and small portions of the right-hand margin (the outer margin on the
front, the inner on the back) survive at the end of most lines. Iota adscript is
sometimes included, sometimes omitted. Most of the few remaining words of
the text carry accents, which were added secondarily in a darker ink and
sharper pen, and are generally written a little to the right of the affected letters. A rough-breathing mark, presumably by the same second hand, appears
at the beginning of the one word where it might be expected, and another is
written internally in a compound word (α]μφἕπειν, *Phoenissae* 340). There is a
high stop at the end of *Phoenissae* 310. The script is Alexandrian majuscule (see
Cavallo 1975, 2005 and Porro 1985). ε, ο, and c are narrow. The horizontal or
diagonal portions of wide letters (γ, μ, π, τ) are connected by 'pseudo-liga-
tures' to the letters following. Diagonals drawn from upper left to lower right
in δ, λ, and χ start with a curve at the top. The ed.pr. dated the hand to the
sixth-seventh century; Turner 1977 pushed this back to the sixth century, and
Cavallo 2005 to the beginning of that century. The hand is in fact very like that
of the Paschal letter of 577 C.E. in P.Grenf. II 112: see Cavallo-Maehler 1987,
pp. 82-83 (no. 37), and their description of the type at p. 5.

The papyrus contains line-ends of *Phoenissae* 306-310 and 338a-342, but the text and line divisions vary too much from tradition, especially on the back, for certain restorations. Traces of two or three letters of an illegible marginal note survive on the back at the right of *Phoenissae* 340. In the lower margin on the same side is another annotation in a smaller and more carelessly formed hand than that of the main text. Porro, the ed.pr., and McNamee 2007b, p. 256 considered it the work of the main scribe but (with Bremer-Worp 1986) I now think this unlikely. The annotator's ν is slightly slanted, whereas those in the text are strictly upright, and curves characteristic of the diagonals in the main text are missing here in χ and δ. The marginal scribe adds trema over an initial ι, but otherwise no diacritical marks or punctuation.

340   [?ξενὸν δὲ κῆδος ἀ]μφέπειν

[. .] . χ[. . ?]

Inner (right) margin

Text: ἔπειν pap.   The original extent of the note is unknown, since the vertical fibers of the surface are stripped or damaged for a space of about two letters at the left of γ and two or three at the right, after which is the broken right edge of the papyrus.

341   [?ἄλαστα ματρὶ τᾷδε] Λαΐωι [τ] τῷ πάλαι γέν[ει]

] . ἔχω τοῦ ἰδεῖν τὰ τέκνα
] . ς

The note is written in the bottom margin, beneath *Phoenissae* 342   ] . : a curve as from 5 to 8 o'clock, with a short vertical line arising from the bottom right (ν possible, π not)   ἰδειν pap.

Text: ἄλαστα ματρὶ τᾷδε Λαΐου τε τοῦ πάλαι γένει Diggle, with line division at Λαΐου   τω pap.   Note: ἀ]πέχω Oellacher, McNamee 2007b : πόθο]ν e.g. Bremer-Worp

I have a longing(?) to see your children...

340   Probably a gloss on κῆδος employing either a form of γάμος (cf. *sch. in Ph.* 340 τὸ ἑξῆς· ξένον δὲ κῆδος ἀμφέπειν γάμων· ποῖον κῆδος· τὴν ἄτην ἣν ἐπηγάγου ἡμῖν· διὰ γὰρ τοῦ γάμου πολεμεῖς τὴν πατρίδα MᶠTAB; cf. also *sch. in Eur. Or.* 1081 κῆδος δὲ τοὐμόν· τὸ διὰ τοῦ γάμου· μὴ γαμηθείςης γὰρ αὐτῆς οὐκ ἔμελλε κῆδος εἶναι MTABⁱ) or a synonym for κῆδος such as ἐπιγαμία, ςυναλλαγή, or ςυγγένεια; cf.

Poll. *Onom.* 3.30.5 κῆδος ἡ ἐπιγαμία κατὰ Θουκυδίδην (2.29.3); Σ κ 314 Cunningham (Cyril) = Phot. κ 653 Theodoridis = *Sud.* κ 1494 Adler κῆδος· ἡ συναλλαγὴ τοῦ γάμου; *EGud.* p. 318.59 Sturz = *EM.* p. 509.51 Gaisford κῆδος δὲ εἴρηται (*EM.* γάρ ἐστιν) ἡ κατ᾽ ἐπιγαμίαν συγγένεια.

341? The note perhaps pertains to this passage, although, since it is written in the bottom margin, this is not absolutely certain. If it refers to line 341, it seems to develop Jocasta's line of thought to a point further than Euripides takes us, so as to illustrate the extent of the ruinous family cleavage that Polyneices' marriage, and thus her separation from his children, has introduced. The scholia to *Phoen.* 337-341, in addition to glosses, metaphrases, and a comment on delivery, discuss consequences of the marriage, but not the enforced separation named in the annotation.

P.Würzb. 1   saec. VI[P]

Comments on Phoenissae

Prov.: Hermopolis?

Cons.: Würzburg, University Library, inv. 18.

Edd.: WILCKEN 1934, pp. 7-22 (repr. WILCKEN 1970, vol. 2, pp. 47-62); ATHANASSIOU 1999, p. 191; ESSLER-MASTRONARDE-MCNAMEE 2013.

Tabb.: WILCKEN 1934, Taf. 1-2; WILCKEN 1970, Taf. 1-2 following p. 112; http://papyri-wuerzburg.dl.uni-leipzig.de/receive/WrzPapyri_schrift_00000040.

Comm.: MP³ 419; CPP 98; LDAB 1002; TM 59895   DINDORF 1864; SCHWARTZ 1887-1891; MAYSER 1906; DEUBNER 1942; BLASS-DEBRUNNER-FUNK 1961; TUILIER 1968, pp. 219-220; TURNER 1977, pp. 17, 105; DEL FABBRO 1979, p. 115; DIGGLE 1981-1994, vol. 3; MASTRONARDE-BREMER 1982; BREMER 1983; BREMER-WORP 1986, pp. 240-246; CAVALLO-MAEHLER 1987; TURNER-PARSONS 1987; MASTRONARDE 1988; MAEHLER 1993, pp. 109-111, 133-136; MCNAMEE 1994; ATHANASSIOU 1999, pp. 44-58; MAEHLER 2000, pp. 32-34; CAMERON 2004; CRIBIORE 2001; FOURNET 2007; MCNAMEE 2007b; STROPPA 2008, pp. 58-60; CARRARA 2009, p. 584; FOURNET 2009; PERRONE 2009b, pp. 236-238; ESSLER 2009; STROPPA 2009; MASTRONARDE 2010-; MONTANA 2011; MCNAMEE 2012; ESSLER-MASTRONARDE-MCNAMEE 2013; MASTRONARDE 2017, pp. 9-10; FOURNET 2020.

The papyrus was purchased at Hermopolis in 1903 by Otto Rubensohn for the Deutsches Papyruskartell (Essler 2009). Ulrich Wilcken published the ed.pr. in 1934 with assistance from Eduard Schwartz, the editor of the still-standard edition of the *scholia vetera* on Euripides (Schwartz 1897). Since 1934, detailed studies of the lemmata were conducted in the 1980s (Mastronarde-Bremer 1982, Bremer 1983, Bremer-Worp 1986, pp. 240-246); and Herwig Maehler used the evidence of the papyrus in arguing for the late origin of marginal corpora of scholia (Maehler 1994, Maehler 2000). Nikolaos Athanassiou devoted a chapter of his unpublished dissertation (Athanassiou 1999) to the Würzburg scholia and suggested new readings in some of the most damaged and obscure parts of the text. The first complete edition since 1934 is Essler-Mastronarde-McNamee 2013[1], which is adapted here and augmented

---

[1] The latest edition was facilitated through the kindness of Dr H.-G. Schmidt of the manuscripts department of Würzburg University Library. It also was advanced by the helpful intercession of Dr D. Obbink, who made available the Oxford University multi-spectral imaging facilities, and of Dr W.B. Henry, who kindly read the manuscript and suggested important changes. Quotations of mediaeval scholia that appear here are from the new edition of the Euripidean scholia by Donald

with suggestions by Michael Haslam (*per litt.*). From the beginning, the deplorable condition of the papyrus has hindered accurate decipherment. Wilcken himself lamented, "Ich habe selten meine Augen so angestrengt wie bei diesem Stück und habe selten so viel Zeit auf einen Text verwendet wie auf diesen, und doch ist das Ergebnis noch sehr verbesserungsbedürftig." The present edition was produced with the aid of autopsy (Essler, McNamee), various photographic images (Wilcken's plates; a large-format slide made probably in the 1970s that was available to Bremer, Mastronarde, and Worp; TIFF images from 2003, 2007, and 2009; and multi-spectral images made in 2010).

P.Würzb. 1 offers the most extensive group of annotations on a Greek tragedy to be preserved from the time before the mediaeval scholia. It contains at least 27 lemmata and associated comments on *Phoenissae,* which in antiquity was the single most widely read play by Euripides (Cribiore 2001, pp. 198-199). The lemmata represent an irregular scattering of passages from *Ph.* 24 to *Ph.* 1108. Most, but not all, follow the order of their occurrence in the text. The information they provide is primarily antiquarian and mythological, and in general is highly reminiscent of the mythological compendia that were popular during the centuries of high empire and in late antiquity (Cameron 2004). Explanations of ancient customs dominate on the papyrological verso ($\downarrow$), where the phrase εἰώθεcαν οἱ ἀρχαῖοι figures certainly at least twice and probably actually four times. On the other side ($\rightarrow$), mythological explanations predominate. An especially striking feature of the recto is the frequency with which the commentator supplies multiple versions of a particular myth (five notes out of seven). A few glosses and simple interpretations also appear on this side (the verso has only a single such note, in line 22). But with the exception of a single grammatical note (lines 40-43), none of the material here reflects any interest in language or in textual or literary criticism. In this want of critical scholarship the commentary is very much a product of late antiquity, although it must be said that serious scholarship lies somewhere deep in the long exegetic tradition from which it was culled (see below and also, e.g., the commentary on lines 48-51).

The papyrus itself is a single sheet measuring 17.1 by 31 cm and written on both sides. The lower right of the paypyrological recto looks as if it may preserve the right and bottom edges of the original sheet, and it is likely that the top edge is also close to its original state. With one exception, margins are very narrow: about 1 cm at the top on both sides and at the bottom of the papyrological recto, and 1 cm at most at the right edge of the recto. The bottom mar-

Mastronarde (Mastronarde 2010-), now in progress; see EuripidesScholia.org. Sigla are those used in modern editions of Euripides and on EuripidesScholia.org and therefore differ in some cases from those used in the editions of Schwartz or Dindorf 1863.

gin on the papyrological verso by contrast is nearly 6 cm deep. The left edge on the papyrological recto and both the left and right edges of the verso are lost, although lines 1, 19, and 20 on the verso contain the very beginning of the lines. Turner 1977 estimated the full width of the page as 18.5 cm, which seems right, and he classified the papyrus in his group 5 (18 x 30 cm). The material is in rather deteriorated condition, particularly on the side with vertical fibers, where abrasion and fading of the ink have rendered the text indecipherable in parts.

The writing, assigned to the 6th century, is an informal sloping script with some cursive features and ligatures. Useful comparanda are TM 62355 (Cavallo-Maehler 1987 no. 21b, 5th-6th c.) and TM 59893 (Cavallo-Maehler 1987 no. 27b, first half of the 6th c.). Finer versions of the same general script are nos. 23b (early 6th c.), and 33b (mid- or late-6th c.). Iota adscript is written with one or two possible exceptions (see commentary on lines 6 and 18), and the scribe writes *scriptio plena* in lines 49 and 50 within a comment (and possibly also in a lemma in line 6). Punctuation consists of a high stop in lines 16, 46, 55, 56; diaeresis in lines 3, 61, 63, 64, 74, 75; and apostrophes marking elision in lines 18, 21 (within comments), and 60 (within a lemma). Elision without apostrophe is found in lines 8 and 19 (comments). A cross is written at the top center of the recto. The writer uses the rough breathing mark frequently but not consistently, and a few smooth breathings serve to forestall ambiguities. On diphthongs, breathings are written between the two letters (printed here, for practical reasons, over the second letter (lines 4, 8, 11, 38, 55, 56, 73, and 81). Breathing marks are also found on single vowels (variously ὁ, ἡ, ὁν; also over ἡ and ἡcαν) in lines 8, 9, 13, 16, 19, 20, 21, 23, 30, 37, 39 (twice), 42, 47, 52 (twice), 54 (twice), 59, 61, 63, 66, 69, 71, 73 (twice), 74, 78, 82, 85. There is a horizontal stroke above the name Γῆ in line 37. Ordinarily a new lemma is introduced by a pair of marks in the shape of space-fillers (>>), but in lines 10, 13, 38, and 48 triple caret-marks occur (Turner-Parsons 1987, p. 15 n. 76). A double stroke (//, sometimes nearly horizontal) separates lemmata from their comments and marks the end of comments (there is no other graphic distinction between lemmata and explanations). Exceptions occur in lines 57 and 59, where the end is marked by double and triple (respectively), nearly vertical strokes, in each case with a single long horizontal line following and the rest of the line left blank. The original scribe added material above lines 6, 30 (twice), 45, 53, 56, 58, 59, 78, 81, and 82; where legible, these are all corrections or omissions made good; in line 78, the correction was clearly made *currente calamo*. He also added some words below line 43 that uncharacteristically refer to the text above them; presumably the addition is also a supplement, since exegetic annotations do not appear.

The text is written on both sides of a papyrus sheet (or half-sheet from a

codex or notebook: see below). Line spacing is inconsistent, and script varies
in both spacing and size: near the top of the recto, lines 38-59 are crowded
more tightly and written smaller than either of the two preceding lines on the
page or lines 60 and following. The reason is unclear. The scribe may have
thought he was going to run out of room and therefore wrote in a smaller
hand, or he may have left this space blank at first and gone on to write material further down the page but then found, upon returning to fill the blank
(from a different source?), that it was insufficient. In favor of the latter view
are a repeated lemma (see on lines 36-39), disorder in the sequence of the lemmata in lines 48-60, and a different mode of punctuation in lines 57 and 59.
Also, but for no clear reason, line 57 is left half empty, with a new lemma
starting at the left of line 58, and line 59 ends considerably short of the right
edge of the writing space. At line 80 a comment breaks off abruptly after ὅτι,
which is followed by a black space.

The intended order of the two sides and whether the papyrus was a loose
sheet or came from a codex are open questions. Wilcken 1933 saw it as part of
a codex. This explained why, in his view, the scribe used the side with vertical
fibers (which is of decidedly poorer quality) before that with horizontal fibers.
His assumption was premised, though, on his reading θ at the top center of
the codicological recto, and interpreting it as a page number. Under magnifi-
cation and with autopsy, the traces are better resolved as a cross of the sort
that scribes in late antiquity often place at the beginning of a text. No such
trace survives above the first line of the papyrological verso, so the cross on
the recto suggests *prima facie* that the scribe started on that side. The fact that
he wrote right to the bottom of the page on that side, whereas he stopped
much farther from the bottom edge on the verso, also seems to support this.
The prevalence of glosses on the papyrological recto and their almost complete absence on the verso may be a further sign that the writer, having set out
to collect useful information from various sources, began with the recto but
after turning the page over switched to a single, consecutive, source.

Other features suggest, rather, that the verso was written first. The considerable disorder in the lemmata of the recto suggests it was written second. For
lemmata on the verso run consecutively from *Ph.* 344 onward, and continue in
order, although the order soon breaks down. Following the note on *Ph.* 807 are
comments on *Ph.* 606, 24, 43, 982, and 90. Thereafter normal order resumes
with the lemma from *Ph.* 1019. It is difficult to see why the writer would have
started his work at the top of the recto with notes on *Ph.* 683, 687, 730, and 807,
then interrupted the consecutive pattern for twelve lines, then returned to
consecutive order with notes on *Ph.* 1019, 1023, 1028, 1033, 1043, 1046, and
1108—left unfinished—, and then turned the sheet over and started the verso
with a consecutive series of notes on *Ph.* 344-659. Conceivably, while he was

working he left a gap on the recto between the notes on *Ph.* 807 and 1019 so that he could later add something particular, then decided against that entry and filled the unused space with non-sequential, random notes on *Ph.* 606, 24, 43, 982, and 90; but there are other possibilities.

If the papyrus was a single sheet, another factor that favors seeing the verso as the side written first is the custom, re-adopted in late antiquity, of writing documents and letters *transversa charta*.[2] If so, the writer may have started out only intending to copy notes on *Ph.* 344 to 807. Then, upon seeing that this left most of the recto empty, he took that occasion to add several more miscellaneous comments. In the end, neither scenario is entirely satisfactory: one does not account for the disorder of lines on the recto, and the other does not explain why the scribe left so much blank space at the bottom of the verso. See Essler-Mastronarde-McNamee 2013, p. 85 n. 30, for further possibilities.

But the issue of the order of the sides is complicated by the question whether the papyrus was in fact a loose sheet or part of a codex. Curiously, an argument might be made that either side continues text begun on an earlier page. On the recto (→), the text at the top left is now lost in lacuna and is arguably a continuation of material written on a lost preceding leaf (see commentary). Certainly it is not a continuation of material from the bottom of the verso, for the final comment there is complete. On the verso (↓), something similar applies, although there are perhaps better arguments in support. The lemma in line 1 of the verso ought properly (as Haslam points out) to be ἐγὼ δ᾽ οὔδε coι πυρός, as in the *sch. vet.* on *Ph.* 344, and not simply οὔδε coι πυρός. As a matter of fact, the commentator routinely supplies lemmata that are considerably more explicit than those in scholia; in fact, that for *Ph.* 344 adds ἀνῆψα φῶc after πυρός. The possibility, then, that the missing ἐγὼ δ(ὲ) in fact appeared at the bottom of a previous, and now lost, page, seems rather good. And this, if true, means that the commentary occupied more than one sheet of papyrus, either loose or bound into a codex. If, in fact, the letters λα in the top margin of the verso are a page number and not a form of λαμπάc (see commentary), then thirty pages preceded this one.

The text has been adduced in the longstanding dispute about the date at which 'scholia' were compiled in the margins of literary texts (cf. Montana 2011). The contents of P.Würzb. 1 contribute no clear evidence to either side of the debate, and the issue remains unsettled. The papyrus does in fact have some coincidences in content and language with some extant scholia, but the

---

[2] This entails the assumption that practice of writing *transversa charta* may, by the date of P. Würzb., have crept into literary and paraliterary scribal practice. Possibly favoring this explanation is P.Oslo inv. 1662 (→ 17), which is written across the fibers and has no writing on the back, a fact that seems to indicate that it was originally a single sheet and not part of a codex. See Fournet 2007 and 2009.

connections are not very close. Although the exact nature and purpose of this collection of notes remain unclear, the likeliest hypothesis, to judge from the content, is that it is a compilation made for private use either by a mid-level schoolteacher or by a somewhat ambitious student. Notes appear to fall into three or four clusters, each one starting with a group of comments on closely spaced lines from lyric passages: (a) *Ph.* 344, 347 (end of a lyric passage sung by Jocasta); (b) *Ph.* 638, 640 (the very beginning of a choral lyric); (c) *Ph.* 683, 687 (from the epode of the same choral song); (d) *Ph.* 1019-1020 (the beginning of the third chorus). Attached to the notes in each cluster are other lemmata introducing comments about content and background information. Comments evince the strong interest in mythography and genealogy that characterized both ancient schooling and the more learned commentaries on poetry. In fact, twenty-four of the about thirty notes are connected to gods or to mythography or to both. Because of the general character of the notes, Wilcken and Schwartz were rather contemptuous of the author. Maehler and Athanassiou have tried to rehabilitate him and to show that his interests reflect some scholarly practices that we might associate with more learned hypomnemata, and that his information has more connections with other known sources than Wilcken and Schwartz had mentioned (Maehler 1994, pp. 109-111; Athanassiou 1999, pp. 45-58). In some details, rehabilitation seems correct. While there are coincidences in content and sometimes language with some of the extant learned scholia in six different notes (*Ph.* 606, 90, 807, 982, 1019-1029, and cf. 1108, 683, and possibly 687), and while the author is conscious of divergent interpretations such as might appear in scholarly commentaries,[3] he does not champion one view over another. Explanations are simply juxtaposed, as often happens in scholia drawn from multiple sources (see Montana 2011, pp. 127-128 on a possible explanation for this phenomenon). There is no mention of variant readings (but this is normal in an Egyptian papyrus of this date). Nor are scholars or commentators named, and quotations of other poets are lacking. Even the abundant paraphrasing or metaphrastic comments in the mediaeval scholia go unrepresented here. The note on *Ph.* 347, for example, says nothing about the recherché syntax, as the scholia do, but goes straight to the explanation of the custom; and the note on *Ph.* 638 makes no effort to disentangle the syntax and clausal structure but starts immediately with the narration of the myth. The closest thing to a para-

---

[3] Such as presumably could be found, for example, in τὰ μικτά ⟨ὑπομνήματα⟩, which are mentioned in the subscription to the scholia on *Orestes* (although there is apparently no reference in the *Phoenissae* scholia to the alternative interpretation of the epithet πυροφόρους as "grain-bearing" (cιτοφόρουc) instead of "fire-bearing": *sch. vet.* in *Ph.* 687 πυροφόρουc δὲ εἶπε Δήμητρα καὶ Κόρην, ἐπεὶ δᾳδουχίαι αὐταῖc γίνονται τοῦ φωτὸc ἐμφαίνοντος τὴν ἐκ τῶν καρπῶν τοῖc ἀνθρώποιc ζωήν. ἢ τὰc cιτοφόρουc λέγει. ἔcτι δὲ ταὐτό MBCVMnRfS).

phrase is in lines 52-53 on *Ph.* 43. The notes bear comparison to some known scholia but it is doubtful they were carefully copied from a thorough hypomnema. The surviving older scholia generally display a decided ambition to employ learned Greek, usually in Attic dialect, but P.Würzb. 1 incorporates naïve features that betray a lower level of ambition or competence. Examples include the use of rather imprecise verbs in προβαλεῖν in line 4 and βαλόντες in line 11; the fourfold repetition of ἐκεῖ in lines 19-21; the repetitious ring-composition in the short explanation of the derivation of ἰάλεμος in lines 66-68; the repetition κυνηγέτις οὖσα, κυνηγέτης ὤν, κυνηγέτις οὖσα (lines 79-83); and the echoing of συνήγοντο, which makes good sense as a plural, by the singular συνήχθη, which makes less sense (lines 81-83). Another oddity is the curious assimilation of Oedipus' inquiry to the oracle to that made by Laius: each goes to Delphi to find out whether the other is alive (lines 70, 73). Also, the phrase 'by the man of Laius' (ὑπὸ τοῦ ἀνδρὸς τοῦ Λαΐου, line 75) involves a usage of ἀνήρ (as "servant, attendant") for which no clear parallel has emerged (although it is impossible to check all the instances of such a common word). Finally, there is the mystery of what the author was thinking of when he mentioned ἱμάτια twice in connection with the dedication of spoils (lines 8-10): was he merely ignorant of or confused about the ancient custom, or is he describing a ritual not otherwise known?

Maehler 1994, p. 111 speculated that the author of the notes was transcribing them from an old commentary on a papyrus roll that was in fragments. He suggested the disorder of the comments resulted from the fact that the loose pieces were in the wrong order. Alternatively the disorder, the tighter format of some of the notes on the recto, the blank spaces left in lines 57 and 59, and the different appearance of the punctuation marks in those lines (vertical rather than oblique or horizontal) may be signs that these are occasional jottings for private use, not all recorded at the same time. The complete lack of information about scribal intention, or the intended purpose of the text, or the circumstances of its discovery seriously complicate efforts to explain its peculiarities.

Verso (↓)

a   λα

1   οὐδέ coι πυρὸc ἀνῆψα φῶc εἰω[θ-   21-24   ]   **344**

   [ ] ἐ[ξ]άξαι καὶ προηγεῖcθαι τοῦ νυμφίου[19-22   ]

   [4-6].. υ... ἀνυμέναια δ' ἐκ[η]δεύθη Ἰcμηνὸc [λουτροφόρου]   **347**

   [χλιδᾶc] εἰώθα[c]ιν οἱ ἀρχαῖοι προβ[α]λεῖν ἀπὸ τῶν ἐπιχ[ωρίων ποταμῶν]

5   [ἢ ἀπὸ πη]γῆc ὕδατα καὶ λοῦcαι τὸ[ν] νυμφίον καὶ παιδ[οποιίαν εὐ-]

   [χεcθαι ἐκ τῶν] γάμων. **κᾷτα δ[ὲ] ἦλθεν αὖ φυγάc** ἦλθ[εν] [ὁ Τ]υ[δεὺc ποι-]   **417** [ἥϲαϲ φό]νον ἐν τῆι πατρίδι αὐτοῦ καὶ τούτου χάριν φυγὰϲ γε[νόμε-]

[νοϲ   4-6   ] **καὶ ϲκῦλα [γ]ράψειϲ** εἰώθαϲιν οἱ ἀρχαῖοι ὅτε πορί[ζ[ουϲι]   574

[νίκην ἐπιγρ]άφε[ι]ν ἱματίοιϲ ὅτι ὁ δεῖνα ἐπόρι[ϲ]εν τ . . . . [3-5   ]

10 [7-9   τὰ ἱμ]άτια τοῖϲ θεοῖϲ ἀνατιθέναι. **καὶ ϲὺ Φοῖβε ἄγ[αξ]**   631

[Ἀγυιεῦ 3-5] . [.]αν οἱ ἀρχαῖοι βαλόντεϲ ἐν τοῖϲ προθύρο[ιϲ] αὐτ[ῶν   0-1]

[10-12   τ]οῦ Ἀπόλλ[ω]νοϲ ἐκάλουν αὐτὸν Φοῖβον Ἀγυ[ιέα. οὗ-]

[τοϲ γὰρ ἦν φύλα]ξ τῆϲ ὁδοῦ. **Κάδμοϲ ἔμολε τάνδε [γ]ᾶν Τ̣ύ[ριοϲ ὧι τε-]**   638

[τραϲκελὴϲ μόϲ]χο̣ϲ ἀδά[μ]α̣ϲ̣τον πέϲημα Κάδμοϲ βουλόμενοϲ κτίϲα[ι πό-]

15 [λιν ἠρώτηϲ]εν καὶ ἔ[λ]αβεν χρηϲμὸν ἐκ τοῦ Ἀπόλλωνοϲ ποῦ ἂν κ̣[τί-]

[ϲαι πόλι]ν καὶ ἔχρηϲεν αὐτῶι ὁ Ἀπόλλων χρηϲμὸν τοιοῦτον· . [.] . [2-3   ]

[6-8   π]ρ̣ὸ̣ϲ β[ο]υ̣κόλον Πελάγοντα καὶ ἐξ αὐτοῦ βοῦν αἴ[τηϲαι φακοὺϲ]

[ἔχ]ου[ϲαν ἐ]ν τῷ ν̣ώτω[ι ϲ]τρογγύλο[υ]ϲ. καὶ ὅπου χ᾽ ἂν πέϲη[ι]η . . [4-5   ]

ἡ βοῦϲ ἀφ᾽ ἑαυτῆϲ, ἀπανιϲτὰϲ ἐκεῖ κτίϲον πόλιν. εἶτα λαβὼν τὸν χρ[ηϲμὸν]

20 ἦλθεν ε[ἰ]ϲ τὰϲ Θήβαϲ τῆϲ Βοιωτίαϲ καὶ ἐκεῖ ἔπεϲεν ἡ βοῦϲ καὶ ἔκτ[ιϲεν].

[ἐκ]εῖ τὰϲ Θήβαϲ. Βοιωτία δ᾽ ἐκλήθη ὁ τόποϲ ἐκεῖνοϲ διὰ τὸ ἐκεῖ π[εϲεῖν]

[3-4   ] . τὴν βοῦ[ν]. **ἀδάμαϲτον πέϲημα** οἷον [ἄ]δμητον [5-7   ]   640

[αὐ]τομάτωϲ . . . ν . π . . . ου. **κιϲϲὸϲ ὃν περιϲτεφή[ϲ]** [.] . . . [5-7   ]   651

[1-2] . [. . . .]ην[.]ερ[.] . ν[.] . . κ̣η̣ρομε . . . . . . [10-12   ]

25 [1-2] . οϲ . . . . ϲαπ . . κιϲϲὸϲ καὶ ϲκεπάϲαι τὸν Δι[όνυϲον   4-6   ]

[7-9   ] . δα . . . . **καὶ γυναιξὶν εὐίο[ιϲ** Βάκχαιϲ.]   656

[αἱ μαινάδε]ϲ ἐκαλοῦντο Βάκχαι, ἐπειδὴ ἐχόρευον ὑπ[ὲρ τοῦ Διο-]

[νύϲου. εὐο]ῖ εὐὰν ἦν ὁ ὕμνοϲ αὐτῶν. **Ἄρεο[ϲ**   7-9   ]   658

[6-8   ] . . . . ον τοῦ κτίϲαι τὰϲ Θήβαϲ αυ . [7-9   ]

30 [6-8   ]ν δράκων. ἦν δὲ ἐκεῖ δράκων ὃϲ `ἐ᾽ φύλαϲϲε τὴν [5-7   ]

[5-7   ] . α . αυτ . . . . [. .] . α . . . [5-7   ]   659?

[5-7   ] . . δε τ[ο]ῦτο ἀλλὰ καὶ Καδμ . . . . . ο . δ . . . . [5-7   ]

[1-2] Καδμ . . . . ἀπὸ τ[ο]ῦ δράκ[ο]ντοϲ τον . . . . [5-7   ]

[ἀ]πολαβὼν τοὺϲ ὀδ[ό]ντα̣ϲ

35   δράκω̣ν̣

Recto (→)

+

[5-9   **αἱ διώνυμοι θεαὶ Πε]ρϲέφαϲϲα καὶ φίλα Δαμάτηρ θεά**   683-684

[διώνυμοι λέγονται, ὅτι ἡ Δημήτηρ] ἐκλήθη Γῆ καὶ Δημήτηρ καὶ ἡ Π[ερ-]

[ϲεφόνη ἐκλή]θη Κόρη κ̣α̣ὶ Περϲεφόνη. **αἱ διώνυμοι θε[αί]**   683

[ὅτι οὕτωϲ ἐν] τ̣α̣ῖϲ Θήβαιϲ ἐτιμῶντο ἡ Δημήτηρ καὶ ἡ [Πε]ρ̣ϲ[εφόνη.]

40 [　2-4　**πέμπε**] **πυρφόρους θεὰς** τὴν Περσεφόνην καὶ Δήμητρα. πυ[　　6-8]　687

　　[　8-10　].[.].ιν....[.]... ἵνα συνεκδοχικὸν ἦι· τὸ σχῆμα θηλυκὸν..[7-9]

　　[　7-9　]........ ἐξ ἑτέρου μὲν οἷον ἡ Δημήτηρ.[..]..[.]...[　6-8　]

　　[　8-10　]..... **πυρφορους** ....α λαμπαδηφόροι λάμπαδ[ας 6-8] 687?

43a　　　　　　　　ἄλλαι λαμπαδηφοροῦσι (*inter lin.*)

　　[**βαθύς γέ τοι**] **Δ**[**ι**]**ρκαῖος ἀναχωρεῖν πόρος** Δίρκη κρ[ή]γη ἐς[τίν,　5-7　]　　730

45 [ἔστι δ]ὲ καὶ ποταμὸς Δίρκη ἐκεῖ `καὶ ο[ὗ]τ[ος ὁ]´ [π]όρος καλεῖται Διρκαῖος. [**ἀμουσοτά-**] 807

　　[**ταις**]**ι σὺν ᾠδαῖς** ταῖς αἰνιγματώδεσιν ᾠδαῖς· ἔλεγεν [ἐμμέτρως ἐ-]

　　[ρωτῶ]σα ἡ Σφίγξ· τίς δίπους, τίς τρ[ίπ]ους τίς τετράπ[ους. ἀμουσοτάταισι]

　　[ὡς]ανεὶ ταῖς κακομούσοις. **καὶ θεῶν τῶν λευκ**[**οπώλων δώμα-**]　　　　606

　　[**τα**] τοῦ Ζήθου καὶ τοῦ Ἀμφίονος, οὗτοι δὲ ἐτιμῶν[το ἐν Θήβαις]

50 [**ἢ κα**]**ὶ** τοῦ Κάστορος καὶ τοῦ Πολυδεύκους, οὗτοι δὲ ἐτιμῶντ[ο ἐν Λακεδαίμο-]

　　[νι.] **λειμῶνα ἐς Ἥρας** τόπος ἐστὶν ἐν τῶι Κιθαιρῶ[ν]ι [ἀλσώδης τῆι Ἥραι]　24

　　[ἀν]ακείμενος. **ὅθεν τί τἀκτός** τὰ περιττά, θυραῖα. πῶς ὃ π[εριττόν ἐστι]　43

　　[λέ]γω; **σεμνὰ Δωδώνης βάθρα** ἐν τῆι Δωδώνηι. ἔστι δὲ τό[πος τις τῆς Ἠ-]　982

　　[πεί]ρου χώρας ἡ Δωδώνη. ἔστιν ἐκεῖ ἱερόν, [ἔ]νθα ἦσαν τρεῖ[ς πελειά-]

55 [δες μα]ντευόμεναι ἐπάνω τῆς δρυός· οἱ δὲ λέγουσιν ὅτι τρ[ε]ῖ[ς γρ]αῖ[ας]

　　[ἐκάλουν π]ερ[ι]στερὰς τῆς προφήτιδος τῆς Πελείας ὀνόματι, αἵτινες επ[4-5]

　　[　6-8　].ο.ῳ[..]. μαντείας.　　　　　*vacat*

　　[**ἐς δ**]**ϊῆρες ἔσχατον** εἰς τὸν ὑψηλὸν τόπον καὶ ἀπὸ [τ]ῶν ἄλλων δ[ιηιρη-]　90

　　[μένον ἢ τ]ὸ δ[ί]στεγον, τὸ ὑπὲρ τοῦτον ἐν τῆι δευτέραι στέγηι.

60 [**ἔ**]**βας ἔβας, ὦ πτερ**[**ο**]**ῦσα, γᾶς λόχευμα νερτέρου δ' Ἐχίδνης**　　　1019-1020

　　[τινὲ]ς λέγουσιν ὅτι ἡ Σφίγξ γέγονεν ἐκ τοῦ αἵματος τοῦ Λαΐου, ἄλλοι

　　[δὲ ὅ]τι ἐκ τ[ῆ]ς Γῆς ἐγεννήθη, ἄλλοι ὅτι ἐκ τοῦ Τυφῶνος καὶ τῆς Ἐχίδνης.

　　[**μ**]**ιξοπάρθενος, δάϊον τέρας** ὅτι ἡ Σφίγξ εἶχεν τὸ ἥμισυ αὐτῆς　　　1023

　　[ἀπὸ παρθ]ένου καὶ [τ]ὸ ἄλ[λ]ο ἥμισυ ἀπὸ λέοντος, λέγεται δάϊον τέρας δ[2-4]

65 [　6-8　]...[.]αι. **ἄλυρον** [**ἀ**]**μφὶ μοῦσ**[**α**]**ν** τὸ αἴνιγμα λέγει.　　　1028

　　[**ἰάλεμοι δὲ ματ**]**έρων** Ἰάλεμος λέγεται ὁ θρῆνος ἐντεῦθεν· Ἰα-　　　1033

　　[λέμου πρὸ τοῦ] ἱεροῦ γάμους ἀποτελοῦντος ἔπεσε[ν] ἐπάνω αὐτοῦ

　　[　8-10　　καὶ] ἐτελεύτησεν καὶ ἐντεῦθεν ἰάλεμος ἐκαλεῖτ[ο ὁ θρ]ῆνο[ς.]

　　[**χρόνωι δ' ἔ**]**βα Πυθίαις ἀποστολαῖς Οἰδίπους ὁ τλάμων** [ὁ Οἰδίπους] 1043-1044

70 [πευσόμενος] εἰ ζῆι ὁ πατὴρ αὐτοῦ ἀπῆλθεν εἰς τὸ μαντεῖον, τ[ὸ δ' εἶπεν]

　　[ὅτι κτανεῖ αὐ]τόν. εἶτα ἐρχόμενος ἀπὸ τοῦ μαντείου ὁ Οἰδ[ίπους ὑπήν-]

　　[τησε τῶι Λαΐ]ωι ἀπερχομένωι καὶ [α]ὐτῶι ἐπὶ τὸ μαντεῖον τοῦ [θεοῦ]

　　[πευσομένω]ι, εἰ ζῆι ὁ υἱὸς αὐτοῦ Οἰδίπους ἢ οὔ. εἶτα ἀπαντῶν [κατὰ τὴν]

　　[σχιστὴν ὁ]δὸν ὁ Οἰδίπους ἀναιρεῖ Λάϊον τὸν αὑ[τ]οῦ πατέρα δι[ὰ τὸ τετύ-]

75 [φθαι αὐτὸ]ϲ ὑπὸ τοῦ ἀνδρὸϲ τοῦ Λαΐου. **τότε μὲν ἀϲμένοιϲ** [ὅτι αὐ-]   1046
[τοῖϲ τὸ αἴν]ιγμα ἔλυϲεν τῆϲ Cφιγγὸϲ τότε. **ἐκηβόλοιϲ τόξοιϲιν Ἀτα-**   1108
[λάντην κάπ]ρον χειρουμένην Αἰτωλόν τοῦ Οἰνέωϲ θύϲαντοϲ πᾶ-
[ϲι τοῖϲ θεοῖϲ] `καὶ´ ἐάϲαντοϲ τὴν Ἄρτεμιν χωρὶϲ θυμάτων ὀργιϲθεῖϲα ἡ Ἄρτε-
[μιϲ ἀφῆκεν] ὡϲ κυνηγέτιϲ οὖϲα κάπρον κατὰ τῆϲ Αἰτωλίαϲ. Καλυδώνι-
80 [οϲ δ᾽ οὗτοϲ ἐ]κλήθη ὅτι   *vacat* 14-17   εἶτα τοῦ κάπρου ἐλθόντοϲ εἰϲ
[7-9   ] [.] . τα . . . . . η καὶ λυμηναμένου τὴν γῆν ϲυνήγοντο οἱ κυ-
[νηγετοῦντε]ϲ καὶ ὁ Μελέαγροϲ υἱὸϲ τοῦ Οἰνέωϲ καὐτὸϲ κυνηγέτηϲ
[ὤν. καὶ ἡ Ἀταλ]άντη κυνηγέτιϲ οὖϲα ϲυνή{γ}χθη καὶ ϲυνέβαλεν τὸν κάπρον
[6-9   Α]ἰτωλίοιϲ, καί τινεϲ μὲν λέγουϲιν ὅτι αὐτὴ ἐφόνε[υ]ϲεν τὸν κά-
85 [προν, οἱ δ᾽ ὅτι] ὁ Μελέαγροϲ ἦν ὁ φονεύϲαϲ αὐτὸν καὶ ἐραϲθεὶϲ τῆϲ Ἀταλάντηϲ
[αὐτῆι ἆθλα] τῆϲ νίκηϲ τὴν κεφαλὴν καὶ τὸ δέρμα τοῦ κάπρου ἔ[δωκε].

Verso
a λα[: slightly right of the presumed center of the page, above the beginning of the comment on
Ph. 344, and closer to the text than the cross at the top of the recto   1 //ʼʼ ουδε, φωϲ //   2 ηγειϲ
. . . . . . `. . .´νυμφι . [    3 . υ . //ʼʼ    ϊϲμηνοϲ    4 οι    6 γαμων //ʼʼ    φυγαϲ //`ηλθ´
8 [γ]ραψειϲ //   οι pap.   ὁτ (only the vertical stroke remaining)   9 ὁ pap.   10 ανατιθεναι
//ʼʼ   11 οι pap.   13 οδου//ʼʼ   14 πεϲημα //   16 ὁ τοιουτον· pap.   18 γ´ pap.   19 ἡ
pap.   20 ἡ pap.   21 δ᾽ pap.   ὁ pap.   22 βου[ν] //ʼʼ   πεϲημα //   οιον: a twisted fiber above
the first o gives the impression of a breathing mark, but confirmation is impossible.   23 ου //ʼʼ   περιϲτεφη[ϲ]//   26 . . . ʼʼ και   28 αυτων//ʼʼ   29 `του´ κτιϲαι
30 δρακων `//´    οϲ`ε´φ   31 [.] //ʼʼ   34 οδοντας // Clear signs of writing as far as the punctuation strokes; possible traces of ink across the rest of the line   35 δρακων centered below the
column; no longer visible on the papyrus and in images very faint

Recto
Upper margin: +, centered. Above and beside it, two lines of writing (erased?) across most of the
page:
line a:]ζ . . . . [
line b (at right of +): . ι[3-5]εχ . . . . . ι   36 θεα//   37 horizontal stroke written above γη
pap.   ἡ pap.   38 περϲεφονη//ʼʼʼ   αἱ pap.   39 ἡ pap.   ἡ[pap.   40 θεαϲ//   42 ἡ? The
letter may be overwritten.   44 πoροϲ//   45 εκει ` . . . [.] . [. . .]´   διρκαιοϲ//   46 ωδαιϲ//,
ωδαιϲ·   47 ἡ pap.   48 κακομουϲοιϲ//ʼʼ   51 init.]·   ηραϲ//   52]ακειμενοϲ//ʼʼ   ὅθεν
pap.   τακτοϲ//   ὁ pap.   53]ηω`//´ʼʼ   βαθρα//   54 ἡ pap.   ἦϲαν pap.   55 δρυοϲ·οι pap.
56 προφητιδοϲ`τηϲ´   ονοματι·αιτινεϲ pap.   57 μαντειαϲ||———, the rest of the line blank   58
εϲχατον//   το`ν´    59 δ[ . ]`ϲ´ pap.   ὑπερ pap.   ϲτεγνι|||———   60 εχιδνηϲ//   61 ἡ pap.   λαϊου
pap.   62 εχιδνηϲ//   63 δαϊον pap.   τεραϲ//   ἡ pap.   64 δαϊον pap.   65]αι//ʼʼ
]ν//   λεγει//   66]ερων//   ὁ pap.   69 ὁ pap.   71]τον apparently corrected from]του   ὁ
pap.   73 ὁ pap., breathing mark perhaps added subsequently   ἠ οὐ pap.   74 ὁ pap.   λαϊον
pap.   75 λαϊου//ʼʼ   76 τοτε//ʼʼ   77 αιτωλον//   78 [[και]]   εἴαϲεν corrected *currente calamo*
to ἐάϲαντοϲ: [[ει]]`ε´αϲ[[ε]]`α´ν`τοϲ´ (ει deleted, ε added above the line; second ε converted to α; τοϲ
added above the line after ϲαν).   ἡ pap.   81 τα ` . ´: two strokes resembling the arms of υ, then
indecipherable   οι pap.   82 ὁ μελεαγρο[[υ]] `ϲ´: υ altered to ϲ   85 ὁ pap.   86]// about 1.4
cm to the right of the final letter of καπρου; possible traces of ink after καπρου

———

Verso
a λα[μπα . .] Wilcken   1 εἰώ[θαϲιν Essler : εἰώ[θεν ἡ μήτηρ τοῦ ἀνδρὸϲ τὴν νύμ[φην]

McNamee 2 ἐ[ξ]άξαι McNamee : εἰc]άξαι Wilcken προηγεισθαι Henry τοῦ νυμφίου Henry :
καὶ `τῶι´ νυμφίωι [δοῦναι McNamee 3 ἀνυμέναια δ᾽ ἐκ[η]δεύθη Ἰcμηνὸc Wilcken : ἀ. δ᾽ Ἰcμηνὸc
ἐκηδεύθη codd., Π¹³ 3-4 [λουτροφόρου | χλιδᾶc//] Wilcken e codd. : [// ἀνυμεναίωc ἀχο|ρεύτωc]
McNamee 4 εἰώθα[c]ιν οἱ Schwartz εἰcβαλεῖν Wilcken ἐπιχ[ωρίων ποταμῶν] Wilcken :
ἐπιχ[ωρίων κρηνῶν] possis 5 [ἢ ἀπὸ πη]γῆc Schwartz 5-6 παιδ[οποιίαν εὔχεc|θαι ἀπὸ τῶν] γάμων
Schwartz : ἐκ τῶν πο]ταμῶν Essler 6 ἐπ[ῆ]λθεν Wilcken `ἦλθ[εν´ alterum McNamee 6-7 [ὁ
Τ]υ[δεὺc Essler et ποι|ήcαc φό]νον ἐν Henry : δ[ρᾶν μηχα|νώμενόc τι παρά]νομον
Schwartz 7 γε[νόμενοc] Wilcken 8 post γε[νόμε|[νοc, [ᾤχετο] Essler [γρ]άψειc
Wilcken ὅτ᾽ἐποίο[υν cκύλευcιν] Schwartz : ἐπόριζ[ον | νίκην Essler ὅτε πορίζ[ουcι Haslam 9 [τὴν
νίκην Haslam, ergo propter spatium γρ]άφε[ι]ν? McNamee [καταγράψ]αι ἐ[ν] Schwartz : ἐπιγρ]άφε[ι]ν
Essler ἐπόρι[c]εν Essler : ἐποίη[c]εν Wilcken 9-10 τὴν νείκ[ην ἀπο|λαβών, καὶ τὰ ἱμ]άτια
Wilcken : τὸν ἆθλ[ον καὶ ἐν | ἱεροῖc τὰ ἱμ]άτια McNamee 10 ἄγ[αξ Ἀγυιεῦ] Wilcken e codd. 11 [//
cτήλην ὀξ]ε[ῖ]αν Schwartz : [κίονα ἵcτ]α[c]αν McNamee : εἰώθ]ε[c]αν Mastronarde 11-12 αὐτ[ῶν
Wilcken : αὐτ[ῶν ἵc|ταντεc κίονα τ]οῦ e.g. Essler : κί|ονα cτῆcαι ὡc τ]οῦ Mastronarde 12-13 ἀγυ[ιέα·
ἀγυιὰ δὲ | ὄνομα ἀρχαῖο]ν Schwartz : Ἀγυ[ιέα, | ὅτι ἦν καὶ φύλα]ξ e.g. Essler : οὗ]τοc γὰρ ἦν φύλα]ξ
Mastronarde 13-14 Τ[ύριοc ὧι τε|τρασκελὴc μόc]χ[ο]c, ἀδά[μ]αc[τ]ον Wilcken e codd. 14-
15 disposuit Mastronarde : κτίcα[ι πόλιν τὸν | θεὸν ἠρώτηc]εν Schwartz : ἦλθ]εν Essler κ[α]ὶ ἔλ[α]βεν
Wilcken 15-16 ποῦ ἂν κ[τί|cαι πόλι]ν Henry, ποῦ ἂν iam McNamee : ποῦ ἡ πό[λιc κτί|ζητα]ι
Wilcken 16-17 ἄ[π]ι[θι ἐν|θένδε . . . . π]ρὸc Schwartz 17 β[ου]κό[λ]ον Wilcken ἀ[γόρacον
cῆμα] Wilcken : cημεῖον] Schwartz : αἴ[τηcαι leg. et suppl. Mastronarde φακούc suppl.
McNamee 18 [ἔχ]ου[cαν ἐ]πὶ τῶν ⟨ν⟩ώτω[ν dub. Wilcken πέcηι ἡγ[ηcαμένη cοι] Schwartz : fin.
αὐ[τομάτωc] dub. McNamee : πέcη[ι] ἢ κα[θίζηι] Essler, κλ[ίθηι Haslam 19 χ[ρηcμὸν]
Wilcken 20 ε[ἰ]c Wilcken ἔκτι[cεν] Wilcken 21 [ἐκ]εῖ Wilcken π[εcεῖν] Wilcken 21-
22 π[ρῶτον | πεcεῖ]ν Haslam 22 [αὐτὴ]ν McNamee [ἄ]δραcτον Wilcken : ἄδραcτοc Athanassiou
: [ἄ]δμητον vel [ἀ]δάμητον dub. McNamee 23 αὐ]τομάτωc … αὐτοῦ McNamee : αὐ]τόματον vel.
sim. Athanassiou : αὐ]τομάτωc γὰρ πίπτει, αὐ]τομάτωc πεcούcηc? Haslam, *exempli gratia* 24 ὁ μὲ[ν]
Ἑρμῆc [dub. Wilcken 25 κιccὸc καὶ cκεπάcαι τὸν Δι[όνυcον Athanassiou : τα κέρατα τοῦ δ[
Wilcken 26 καὶ γυναιξὶν εὑίο[ιc Athanassiou Βάκχαιc] McNamee 27 leg. McNamee, fin.
etiam Βάκχου| possis :] ἐκαλοῦντο ἔξι Βάκχαι ἐπειδὴ ἀκολούθου[Athanassiou 27-28 Βάκχου | καὶ
τὸ εὐο]ῖ e.g. Essler Ἄρεο[c Athanassiou 28-29 Ἄρεο[c φύλαξ// τῆc | Δίρκηc· τῶι] Κάδμωι e.g.
McNamee 29 cύμβολον? Haslam : ἐμπόδιον ad serpentem spectans susp. Mastronarde]κα[
] . . ει . τον κτιcαι τας θηβαc . cλε Athanassiou 29-30 [>> φόνιοc ἦν δρά|κων Ἄρε]οc υἱόc//
Wilcken 30 ὃc `ἐ´φύλαccε leg. McNamee : ὃν εἶαcεν Athanassiou 30-31 τὴν [κρήνην πρὸc | τὸ
μηδέ]να ἀπ᾽ αὐτῆc ὑδρεύcαcθαι e.g. McNamee :] . . cε αυτ . [πα]ρ[αι]νέcει τῆc Ἀθηνᾶc ὁ Κάδμοc ἀπεκ[
Athanassiou 32 leg. McNamee : τῶι Κάδ(μ)ῳ τῶν ὀδόντω[ν Wilcken : δὲ αὐτοῦ τοὺc vac. τῶι
Κάδμωι ἵνα οἴκωciν ο[Athanassiou 33 leg. McNamee :] Κάδμοc εδ . η ὑπὸ Athanassiou 34 leg.
McNamee *fin.* και α Athanassiou

Recto
36 αἱ ex 38 Essler-Mastronarde-McNamee 37 fin.-38 ἡ Π[ερ|cεφόνη καὶ Κόρη] Wilcken: cett. leg.
et suppl. McNamee 38 θε[αί Athanassiou : ἢ κ[αί] Wilcken αἱ διώνυμοι pap. : αι διώνυμοι
maxima pars codd. quae αἱ aut ἅι interpretantur scholia : καὶ Major 39 [ὅτι οὕτωc] Haslam :
[οὕτωc γὰρ ἐν] et ἡ [Πε]ρc[εφόνη//] e.g. McNamee, cetera iam legit Athanassiou 40 [>> πέμπε] e
codd. McNamee 41]πύρινα susp. Mastronarde ἵνα cυνεκδοχικὸν ἦι Henry cχῆμα θε . . . . [
Wilcken : cχῆμα cυνεκδ . χ[Athanassiou : cχῆμα θηλυκὸν? McNamee : cχῆμα θεαὶ καὶ Henry 42 μέν
dub. McNamee : ἑτέρου α . . ιο . ἠ Δ. Wilcken :]δοκου . . ἑτέρωc . υ . ἑτέρου τὰc ἄρτον ἡ Δημήτηρ
Athanassiou 43 dub. leg. McNamee : λαμπαδηφόρουc? Haslam : θεαc επ[et λαμπαδηφ[
Athanassiou supplementum interl. legit et ad lineam 43 referendum censuit
McNamee 44 Wilcken e codd. 45 καὶ ο 46-47 [ἐμμέτρωc] | ἐρ[ωτῶ]cα Wilcken : [ἐμμελῶc]?
McNamee 47-48 τετράπ[ουc ἀμουcοτά|ταιcι cημ]αίνει Wilcken : δια|ανεῖ Essler : ἰcοδυν]αμεῖ?
McNamee 48-49 λευκ[|οπώλων δώμαθ//] e codd. Wilcken : δώμα[τ᾽] vel δώμα|τα] McNamee 49-
50 ᾤικ[ιcαν Θή|βαc ἢ κα]ὶ Wilcken : δὲ ἐτιμῶν[το Henry et [ἐν Θήβαιc] Essler 50 ἐτιμῶντ[ο ἐν
Λακεδαίμονι] Henry Λακεδ[αίμο|νι] iam Wilcken 51 init. [//>]> McNamee fin. ἀλcώδηc Essler
: ὅc ἐcτι (ἔcτι δὲ?) Haslam 51-52 [τῆι Ἥραι | ἀνα]κείμενοc Wilcken 52 θυραῖα Henry : c[ο]βαρά

Wilcken, Essler-Mastronarde-McNamee   52-53   π[εριττόν ἐcτι] McNamee : ὃ π[εριττόν, λέ|γω]//>>
Wilcken   53-56   suppl. Wilcken   53 fin.   τιc add. Essler   56 fin.   επ[leg. Essler-Mastronarde-
McNamee : ἀπ[Wilcken   56-57   ἀπ[ὸ τῆc | δρυὸc ἔc]χον τ[ὰ]c μαντείαc Wilcken   58   et εἰc δ]
possis   58-59 suppl. Wilcken   59   ὑπὲρ τοῦτον Essler-Mastronarde-McNamee : ὑπερ . . τον
Wilcken   60-64 suppl. Wilcken   62   [δὲ ὅ]τι McNamee : [ὅτι ἐ]κ Wilcken   63   et με]ιξ-
possis   64-65   δ[άϊον | γὰρ Henry : δ[ιὰ τὸ | πολλοὺc ἀ]πολ[έc]αι Haslam   65   ]δον[ω]ν//
Wilcken   65-68 suppl. Wilcken   67   πρὸ τοῦ] ἱεροῦ Henry   68 in.   [μέροc ὀροφῆc καὶ] Schwartz
spatio longius   69-71 suppl. Wilcken   70 init.   οὐκ εἰδώc Haslam   fin.   τ[οῦτο suppl. Haslam
et ἔφη (δ')? suppl. McNamee   71-72 suppl. McNamee   Οἰδ[ίπουc | ὑπήντηcε Λαΐ]ωι Wilcken   72
fin.   [θεοῦ Wilcken : [θεοῦ καὶ Essler : [Ἀπόλλωνοc McNamee   73-74   [αὐτῶι | κατὰ cχιcτὴν ὁ]δὸν
Wilcken : [κατὰ τὴν | c. ὁ. Mastronarde   74-77 suppl. Wilcken   78   [cι τοῖc θεοῖc ˋκαὶˊ] Essler-
Mastronarde-McNamee : [cι θεοῖc ἀλλὰ] Henry : [cιν τοῖc θεοῖc] Wilcken   ἐάcαντοc Essler-Mastronarde-
McNamee : ⟦ ᵃ ⟧αc⟦ε⟧ˋαˊνˋτοˊ Wilcken   79   ἀφῆκεν McNamee : ἐφῆκεν Haslam : ἔπεμψεν
Wilcken   79-80   Καλυδώνι|[οc δ' οὗτοc ἐ]κλήθη Mastronarde : Καλυδώνι|[οc δὲ ὁ cῦc ἐ]κλήθη Essler
: Καλυδώνι|[ον, οὕτωc δ' ἐκ]λήθη Wilcken   81   [κα]τ' [ὄρη?] Haslam   82-83   κυ|[νηγέται πάντε]c
Wilcken : κυ|[νηγετοῦντε]c Mastronarde   84   [τοῖc ἄλλοιc Α]ἰτ. Henry : [ἐν τοῖc ὁρίοιc vel ἀγροῖc Α]
ἰτ. Schwartz : [ἐφεῖcα vel ἀφεῖcα τοῖc Α]ἰτ. Mastronarde : [ἡ θεὰ τοῖc Α]ἰτ. Essler   84-85   κά|[προν
Wilcken   85   οἱ δ' ὅτι] Mastronarde : ἄλλοι δ' ὅτ]ι Wilcken   86   [ἔδωκεν ἀριcτεῖα] Wilcken : τὰ
ἀριcτεῖα] iam Schwartz : [αὐτῆι ἀπὸ] vel ἆθλα] Mastronarde : γέραc] vel ἆθλον] McNamee   fin.
ἐ[φῆκε] Essler : ἔ[δωκε] Haslam

Verso

(344) Nor did I kindle the light of fire for you: they are / were accustomed to
bring out … and lead the way … the bridegroom … **(347) And Ismenus was
given a relationship by marriage without wedding song and without the
luxury of bearing the ritual bath:** the ancients had the custom of putting forth
water from local rivers or from a (local) spring and of bathing the bridegroom
and praying for offspring from the marriage. **(417) and then in turn came an
exile:** Tydeus came, [having committed a murder] in his homeland and having become an exile because of this … **(574) and (how) will you inscribe the
spoils:** the ancients customarily, when they provide [a victory, inscribe] upon
clothes (*himatia*) that so-and-so provided … to dedicate the clothes to the gods.
(631) and you, lord Phoebus [Agyieus]: … the ancients, placing at their door-
ways [an image] of Apollo, used to call him Phoebus Agyieus [for this god
was guardian?] of the street. **(638) Tyrian Cadmus came to this land, for
whom a four-legged heifer an unforced fall:** Cadmus, wanting to found [a
city, enquired] and obtained an oracle from Apollo about where to found a
city, and Apollo proclaimed to him an oracle like this: [go]… to a cowherd
named Pelagon and [ask for / buy] a cow from him that has on its back circular
[marks], and wherever the cow might fall by itself, make it get up again and
in that place found a city. Then after getting this oracle he came to Thebes in
Boeotia and there the cow fell and he founded there Thebes. That place was
called Boeotia because the cow (Greek *bous*) [fell …] there. **(640) unforced fall:**
as if to say ?not subdued … of its own accord … **(651) whom an encircling
crown of ivy:** … ivy and to cover Di[onysus?] … **(656) and to women of the
evoi cry:** [bacchants. The maenads?] used to be called bacchants, since they

danced for [Dionysus, and *evo]i evan* was their hymn. **(658) Ares [(blood-thirsty?) guardian:]**... of founding Thebes ... **(657) [there there was a murder-ous] serpent:** there was in that place a serpent which was guarding the... **(659?) ... :** ... this but also Cadm[us] ... Cadm[us]... from the serpent ... taking away the teeth. ... serpent

Recto

(683-684) [... goddesses of twin names,] Persephassa and dear goddess De-meter: [they are/were called of twin names because Demeter] was called Ge and Demeter, and P[ersephone was call]ed Kore and Persephone. **(683) the goddesses of twin names:** [for thus in] Thebes Demeter and [Persephone] used to be honored ... **(687) [send the] fire-bearing goddesses:** Persephone and Demeter: ...wheat? ... in order that it be synecdochic. The form is femi-nine ... from the other, on the one hand, as if to say, Demeter ... **(687?) fire-bear-ing:** ... torchbearers ... torches: ..., (*added below the line*) ?other women/god-desses carry torches ... **(730) deep, as you know, is the ford of Dirce to retreat across:** Dirce is a spring; and there is also a river Dirce there: and this ford is called Dircaean. **(807) with [most unmusical] songs:** riddling songs; the Sphinx spoke [in meter asking] what creature [is] two-footed, what three-foot-ed, what four-footed. Most unmusical, as if to say, the (songs) of evil music. **(606) and the [houses] of the white[-horsed] gods:** of Zethus and Amphion; these two were honored in Thebes; or else of Castor and Polydeuces; these two (were honored) in Lacedaemon. ... **(24) to the meadow of Hera:** it is a [woodland?] place on Cithaeron dedicated [to Hera]. **(43) wherefore, why the things outside:** the extraneous, pertaining to other things; how am I to say what [is extraneous]? **(982) hallowed ground of Dodone:** in Dodone; and Do-done is [a place in] the region [Epi]rus; there is there a shrine where there were three [doves (*peleiades*)] giving prophecies upon the oak tree; some say that [they used to call] three [old women] doves (*peristerai*) by the name of the prophetess, Dove (*Peleia*); (women) who... prophecies. **(90) to the outermost upper storey:** to the high place and one [separated from] the others, [or] the second storey, the one above this (place?) in the second storey. **(1019-1020) you came, you came, O winged maiden, offspring of Earth and Echidna below:** [some] say that the Sphinx was born from the blood of Laius, others that she was born from Earth, others that (she was born) from Typho and Echidna. **(1023) part maiden, destructive monster:** Because the Sphinx had half of it(-self) from a maiden and the other half from a lion it is called destructive mon-ster ... **(1028) with lyreless song:** he means the riddle. **(1033) [*ialemoi* (mourn-ing songs)] of mothers:** the dirge is termed *ialemos* for the following reason. When Ia[lemos] was completing his marriage rites [in front of the(?)] shrine (?), a ... fell on top of him [and] he died, and hence the dirge was called *iale-*

mos. **(1043) [in time] there came, sent by Pythian oracles, Oedipus the wretched:** [Oedipus, intending to find out] whether his father was alive, went to the oracle, [and it said that he would kill h]im. Then proceeding from the oracle Oedipus [met up with Lai]us, who was himself too going to the oracle of the [god to find out] whether his son Oedipus was alive or not. Then meeting (him) [along the Split] Road Oedipus kills Laius, his (own?) father, because [he had been struck] by the man of Laius. **(1046) at that time to their relief:** [because for them] he solved the riddle of the Sphinx at that time. **(1108) Ata[lante], with far-shooting arrows overcoming the Aetolian boar:** Oeneus having sacrificed to al[l the gods and] having left Artemis without sacrifices, [[and]] Artemis, becoming angry, [sent], since she was a huntress, a boar against Aetolia. [This boar] was called Calydonian because [*space of 14-16 letters left blank, for filling in explanation later*]. Then, when the boar had come to ... and had ravaged the land, [the hunters] were gathering together; and Meleager, son of Oeneus, [being] himself too a hunter, (joined them) [and Atal]ante, who was a huntress, joined them, and [...] set to fight (or engaged in battle?) [...] the boar [...] Aetolians. And some say that she herself killed the bo[ar, but others (say) tha]t Meleager was the one who killed it, and, because he had fallen in love with Atalante, as[signed to her the prize] of the victory, the head and hide of the boar.

Verso

1-3 (on *Ph.* 344). Cf. *sch. vet. ad l.* ἐγὼ δ' οὔτι cοι· ἔθος γὰρ ἦν τὴν νύμφην ὑπὸ τῆς μητρὸς τοῦ γαμοῦντος μετὰ λαμπάδων εἰсάγεсθαι.

a   If the note in the upper margin is not a page numeral (31), it may supply a word λαμπα- missing from the explanation. More plausibly (since corrections of this kind do not appear elsewhere in the text), it indicates the subject matter of lines 1-2, namely, discussion of Jocasta's regret not to have carried a wedding torch. As an indication of contents, it would serve the same function as δράκων at the foot of the page. If this was its purpose, it resembles indications of contents found (usually at the top of the text) in several papyri of the Roman and late antique periods. The practice is most prevalent in prose, in which the undifferentiated blocks of text made it difficult to locate a particular passage: so in MP³ 339 (Did. on Dem., 2ⁿᵈ c. C.E.), 536 (Hierocl., 2ⁿᵈ c. C.E.), 543 (Hp., 3ʳᵈ c. C.E.), 543.3 (Hp., 6ᵗʰ c. C.E.), 1327 (comm. on Nic., 1ˢᵗ c. C.E.), 1505 (Thuc., 1ˢᵗ c. C.E.), but also in 60 (Alc., 1ˢᵗ-2ⁿᵈ c. C.E.) and 1857.1 (anthology of epigrams, 3ʳᵈ c. C.E.). By contrast, mediaeval scholia tend to use more generic labels (ἱcτορία, cύνταξιc, ἀπορία, λύcιc) for this purpose. In Byzantine manuscripts of Euripides scholia, content labels sometimes occur, especially indicating the names of mythological characters whose stories are discussed in the notes, but they seem to be rather late additions. In Ms. B of the early 11ᵗʰ century, for example, such labels are later by several centuries (so Donald Mastronarde *per litt.*).

1   εἰῴ[θ-: cf. line 4. If the subject is the bride's mother, perhaps restore δοῦναι at the end of line 2.

2   Read νυμφίωι or νυμφίου. After line 1 εἰῴ[θασιν, the scribe's style leads one to expect the καί following ἐ[ξ]άξαι to connect with a second infinitive. For προηγεῖσθαι in the context of a torch-lit procession as in the lemma, cf. Timaeus, *FGrHist* 566 F 26a … ὧν ποιησάντων τὸ προσταχθέν, καθ' ὃν καιρὸν ἤγετο ἡ νύμφη, προηγουμένων πολλῶν τῶν τὰς δᾷδας φερόντων, ἡ μὲν πόλις ἔγεμε φωτός, τὸ δὲ συνακολουθοῦν πλῆθος.

3-6   (on *Ph.* 347). The *sch. vet. ad l.* give a lemma followed by glosses of ἀνυμέναια and then, after ἄλλως, a metaphrase of the text and explanation of the custom: ἀνυμέναια δ' Ἰσμηνός· ἀνυμεναίως ἀχορεύτως. ἄλλως· οὐ μετέσχε τῶν σῶν ὑμεναίων οὐδὲ συνήσθη τῇ σῇ πρὸς τὸν Ἄδραστον ἐπιγαμβρίᾳ· οὐ γὰρ ἐδέξω τὰ παρ' αὐτοῦ λουτρά. εἰώθεσαν δὲ οἱ νυμφίοι τὸ παλαιὸν ἀπολούεσθαι ἐπὶ τοῖς ἐγχωρίοις ποταμοῖς καὶ περιρραίνεσθαι λαμβάνοντες ὕδωρ τῶν ποταμῶν καὶ πηγῶν συμβολικῶς παιδοποιίαν εὐχόμενοι, ἐπεὶ ζῳοποιὸν τὸ ὕδωρ καὶ γόνιμον. If Wilcken is correct in assuming that the lemma extended into line 4, it presumably ended with χλιδᾶς, which would make εἰώθα[c]ιν the first word of the comment (cf. lines 1 and 8). A lemma of such length is not out of the question: that for *Ph.* 638 (lines 13-14) is also much longer than the lemma in the scholia for the line. Alternatively, if the lemma on *Ph.* 347 concluded with Ἰσμηνός, the end of line 3 and beginning of line 4 were presumably occupied by glosses on ἀνυμέναια. Something akin to what is offered in the scholia would fit the space available.

4   Cf. lines 1 and 8 for other explanations beginning εἰώθασιν. εἰσβαλεῖν may be preferable in sense, but autopsy and the image based on the original negative support reading προ-.

5-6   For εὔχομαι in proximity to γάμος in the genitive, cf. *Lib. Decl.* 42.1.6 παῖδας ηὐξάμην ὁ δυστυχὴς ἐκ τούτων μοι γενέσθαι τῶν γάμων.

6-8   (on *Ph.* 417). Very likely the note began by identifying the fugitive as Tydeus. Cf. *sch. vet. ad l.* κᾆτά γ' ἦλθεν ἄλλος· ὁ Τυδεύς· φασὶ γὰρ ὅτι τὰ τέκνα Ἀγρίου ἐφόνευσεν Ἀλκάθουν καὶ Λυκωπέα· διὸ ἔφυγεν.

6   The older Mss. and some recentiores have κᾆτά γ' ἦλθεν ἄλλος αὖ φυγάς, which recent editors approve. The lemma here matches the text κᾆτα δ' ἦλθεν attested in some recentiores. (For errors shared by ancient papyri and *recentiores* see Mastronarde-Bremer 1982, pp. 66-69.) There is no room for the π reported by Wilcken, who may have been unduly influenced by Nauck's edition (ἐπῆλθεν is Nauck's conjecture, but Nauck's critical notes are not printed beneath his text). The scribe's κατα instead of καιτα leaves open the possibility that he intended κατά, in which case we should understand the following verb

as κατῆλθε in tmesis; the reading has no manuscript authority, however. The translation assumes the traditional κᾷτα, which will in any case have been the writer's intention if he was aware of the meter of what he wrote. The suprascript ηλθ[at the end of the line is problematic. Given its position to the right of the punctuation marks, it presumably belongs to the explanatory note. This is at the basis of the restoration suggested. A comment such as this, however, would be more likely to start with a simple identification, e.g., (οὗτος) ὁ Τυδεύς, as in the *sch. vet. in Ph.* 417 (quoted above ad 6-8).

7 For ποι|ήϲαϲ φό]νον, cf. Bas. *Ep.* 188, 11 ὁ δὲ τὸν ἀκούϲιον ποιήϲαϲ φόνον ἀρκούντωϲ ἐξεπλήρωϲε τὴν δίκην ἐν τοῖϲ ἔνδεκα ἔτεϲι, and *sch. vet. in Ph.* 417 (thus in Schwartz's edition, but properly referring to *Ph.* 419 Τυδεὺϲ ὃν Οἰνέωϲ) οὗτοϲ ἔφυγε διὰ τὸν φόνον τῶν ϲυγγενῶν †Ἀλθαίαϲ.

8-10 (on *Ph.* 574). The comment discusses inscribed clothing dedicated to the gods. πορίζ[ουϲι | νίκην ἐπιγρ]άφε[ι]ν in lines 8-9 is preferable to Schwartz's ἐποίο[υν ϲκύλευϲιν καταγρ]άψαι, which entails three problems. First, the space at the end of line 8 and the beginning of line 9 seems insufficient for ϲκύλευϲιν | καταγράψαι. Second, καταγράφω does not appear in scholia with the meaning intended, namely, "inscribe on cloth" (the word used is ἐπιγράφω); the choice of καταγράφω presumably necessitated the restoration of ἐν, which cannot be read here, after the verb. Finally, a phrase like πορίζειν (or ποιεῖν) ϲκύλευϲιν is evidently unparalleled. πορίζειν νίκην, for its part, is a fairly rare expression, but its pedigree is good: in Aristoph. *Eq.* 593-594 (πορίϲαι ϲε νίκην), Ios. *AJ* 5.42 (νίκην αὐτοῖϲ ἀεὶ πορίζεϲθαι), Lib. *Thes.* 2.7 (πορίϲαϲθαι νίκην), *sch. ex. in* Hom. *Il.* 7.284 (ἑαυτῷ πορίζει νίκην), and some later writers. In lines 9-10, Wilcken's ἀπολα]|[βών also is too long for the space available and not necessary to the construction. The idea of a student recalling what the teacher has said might also be invoked for the strange statement about ἱμάτια and other somewhat deficient or inaccurate remarks; but if we are talking about the sixth century in Egypt, such errors are not necessarily impossible for a mid-level schoolmaster himself.

9 The absence of iotacistic spelling elsewhere in the papyrus makes Wilcken's νείκ[ην improbable; and although it would be satisfying to restore ἐπόριϲεν τὴν νίκην (cf. the examples cited above), neither this nor the plural fits the traces well (the αϲ of τάϲ would need to be squeezed into a space sufficient only for a little more than one letter, and νικαϲ cannot be read). Although θλ is a plausible reading in the last two positions, a form of ἀθλ- preceded by the appropriate article is also impossible to confirm. The papyrus explanation is extremely odd, perhaps an ignorant guess. It diverges from explanations in the scholia, which locate such inscriptions on the weapons themselves: *sch. vet. in Ph.* 572 τὸ δὲ καὶ ϲκῦλα γράψειϲ ἀντὶ τοῦ· τὰ ὅπλα ἐπιγράψειϲ ἤτοι τὰ ἀναθήματα τῶν πεφονευμένων; *sch.* Thom. *in Ph.* 572 τὰϲ ἀϲπίδαϲ τῶν πολεμίων ϲκυλεύοντεϲ τοῖϲ θεοῖϲ ἀνετίθουν ὡϲ αἰτίοιϲ τῆϲ νίκηϲ, ἐπιγράφοντεϲ εἰϲ αὐτὰϲ ἃ καὶ

ἐν τοῖς τροπαίοις.

10-13   (on *Ph.* 631). The *sch. vet. ad l.* give Ἀγυιεῦ: προπύλαιε. τὸν ἀγυιέα πρὸ
τῶν πυλῶν ἵcτacαν. κίων δὲ οὗτος ἦν εἰς ὀξὺ ἀπολήγων. ἐπεὶ πρὸ τῶν πυλῶν ἵcτacαν
ἀγάλματα τοῦ Ἀπόλλωνος ὡς ἀλεξικάκου καὶ φύλακος τῶν ὁδῶν. διὰ γὰρ τοῦτο
Ἀγυιεύc.

11   The writer's βαλόντες is a curious choice for describing the setting up
of a column (a form of ἵcτημι or τίθημι would be expected). Perhaps the lost
object of βαλόντες (presumably represented by]ᾳν at the beginning of line 11)
was not in fact a stele or column? A possible alternative, however, is to recon-
struct the note by beginning with εἰώθεcαν and assuming an object and infinitive are lost in the lacuna at lines 11-12; in this case the sentence ends with
Ἀπόλλωνος in line 12, and a new sentence begins in asyndeton with ἐκάλουν
(compare perhaps the asyndeton in 46, 47, 52 and assumed in 27).

13-22   (on *Ph.* 638-639). With lemma drawn from 638 only, the *sch. vet. ad*
l. supplies parallel information, in more detail: Κάδμος ἔμολε τάνδε γᾶν: Κάδμος
ζητῶν τὴν ἀδελφὴν Εὐρώπην μαντεῖον ἔλαβε περὶ τῆς ἀδελφῆς οὐδὲν αὐτῷ σημαῖνον,
ἀλλ' ὥστε αὐτὸν ἐξελθόντα ἕπεσθαι βοΐ καὶ οὗ ἂν αὐτόματος πέcῃ κτίζειν πόλιν. ἔχει
δὲ ὁ χρησμὸς τοῦ Πυθίου θεοῦ οὕτως·

> φράζεο δὴ τὸν μῦθον, Ἀγήνορος ἔκγονε Κάδμε·
> ἠοῦς ἐγρόμενος προλιπὼν ἴθι Πυθὼ δῖαν
> ἠθάδ' ἔχων ἐcθῆτα καὶ αἰγανέην μετὰ χερcὶ
> τὴν διά τε Φλεγυῶν καὶ Φωκίδος, ἔcτ' ἂν ἵκηαι
> βουκόλον ἠδὲ βόας κηριτρεφέος Πελάγοντος.
> ἔνθα δὲ προσπελάcας cυλλάμβανε βοῦν ἐρίμυκον
> τὴν ἥ κεν νώτοιcιν ἐπ' ἀμφοτέροιcιν ἔχηcι
> λευκὸν cῆμ' ἑκάτερθε περίτροχον ἠύτε μήνης·
> τήνδε cὺ ἡγεμόνα cχὲ περιτρέπτοιο κελεύθου.
> cῆμα δέ τοι ἐρέω μάλ' ἀριφραδὲς, οὐδέ cε λήcει·
> ἔνθα κέ τοι πρώτιcτα βοὸς κέρας ἀγραύλοιο
> ἵζηται κλίνη τε πέδῳ γόνυ ποιήεντι,
> καὶ τότε τὴν μὲν † ἔπειτα μελαμφύλλῳ χθονὶ ῥέζειν
> ἁγνῶς καὶ καθαρῶς· Γαίη δ' ὅταν ἱερὰ ῥέξῃς,
> ὄχθῳ ἐπ' ἀκροτάτῳ κτίζειν πόλιν εὐρυάγυιαν
> δεινὸν Ἐνυαλίου πέμψας φύλακ' Ἄϊδος εἴcω.
> καὶ cύ γ' ἐπ' ἀνθρώπους ὀνομάκλυτος ἔccεαι αὖθις
> ἀθανάτων λεχέων ἀντήcας, ὄλβιε Κάδμε.

ταῦτα ἀκούcας ὁ Κάδμος ἀφίκετο εἰς τὸ βουκόλιον τοῦ Πελάγοντος τοῦ Ἀμφιδάμαντος,
παρ' οὗ ἀγοράcας βοῦν καὶ ἡγεμόνα ταύτην τῆς ὁδοῦ ποιηcάμενος κτίζει τὰς Θήβας
ὁμωνύμους τῶν Αἰγυπτίων Θηβῶν, ἐπεὶ τὸ ἀνέκαθεν Αἰγύπτιος ἦν ὁ Κάδμος. καὶ ἡ
Βοιωτία δὲ ἀπὸ τῆς βοὸς ἐκλήθη.

In his dissertation, Athanassiou remarked upon some instances in which he found the wording used by the author and the language of Palaeologan-era scholia or prefatory material so strikingly similar that he speculated there may have been a continuous tradition accounting for it. The narrative about Cadmus in lines 13-22 is one such instance (the others are lines 40-43 and 69-75). The text in lines 13-22 is similar to prefatory item 10e in the Teubner edition of *Phoenissae*: Κάδμος πεμφθεὶς ὑπὸ τοῦ πατρὸς Ἀγήνορος ζητῆσαι τὴν ἀδελφὴν αὐτοῦ Εὐρώπην σὺν τοῖς ἀδελφοῖς καὶ μὴ εὑρὼν αὐτὴν εἰς τὸ μαντεῖον τοῦ Ἀπόλλωνος ἐν Πυθοῖ παραγίνεται πυνθανόμενος ποῦ ὀφείλει κατοικεῖν· ὁ δὲ ἔφη 'ὅπου καθίσει ἡ βοῦς αὕτη, ἐκεῖ κτίσον πόλιν'. καὶ δὴ ἐξελθὼν τοῦ μαντείου εὑρε βοῦν, καὶ ἠκολούθησεν αὐτῇ, καὶ εἰς Θήβας †ἔθηκε† καὶ ἐκεῖ ᾠκοδόμησε τὰς Θήβας. This seems to be a case of old commentary material or mythographic material surfacing in some of the recentiores of Euripides, but the stylistic similarity perhaps reflects the similar educational level for which these notes were intended rather than direct dependence on the same source. In conclusion, only this similarity seems to be significant, not for a genetic relationship, but as evidence of a less polished style used in notes aimed at a less advanced audience.

16-19   A paraphrase of the oracle. The traces in line 16 do not favor Schwartz's ἄ[π]ι̣[θι, but it seems an imperative of some verb must have been present in the lacuna to be associated with line 19 κτίσον. At the end of line 17 an imperative is again needed, followed by the plural masculine direct object modified by c]τρογγύλο[υ]ς (line 18). The traces favor reading αἴ[τησαι or αἴτησον rather than λα[βέ. As object, φακούς, e.g., would suit the sense (see below on 18 c]τρογγύλο[υ]c). Although it is a little too long for the space available it might have been squeezed in, and if the verb was αἴ[τησαι the fit will have been easier.

18   ἐ]ν τῷ νώτω[ι: reading ἐν, which suits the traces better, entails the assumption that the scribe omitted iota adscript here, against his normal practice (but see ωδαιc in line 46 (twice); and κατα in line 6 is another case, if καιτα was intended). Wilcken's reading of ἐπί induced him to see τωνωτω as an error of haplography, with the second ν omitted.

c]τρογγύλο[υ]c καὶ: the space between the second ο and και is too broad to have been filled only by ν (στρόγγυλον Wilcken); the scholia quoted above also discourage reading a singular here, as they record a verse oracle mentioning at least two marks as being νώτοιcιν ἐπ' ἀμφοτέροιcι and ἑκάτερθε. A plural cτρογγύλο[υ]c indicates that there was a plural masculine noun at the end of line 17 for it to modify. If, after βοῦν, we read αἴ[τησαι, the remaining space in line 17 could accommodate about six letters: φακούς, perhaps, as suggested. cπίλουc would be a more difficult fit. One might also expect the oracle to have mentioned a specific number of spots, but there hardly seems room for a numeral as well. Scholiasts use ὅπου γε (at *sch. vet. in* Eur. *Ph.* 100,

402, e.g.), although more often in a non-topographic sense.

]η˳˳[: of]η the right-hand vertical and part of the crossbar remain. Following this an unwritten space, and then a curve in the lower part of the writing space, as from 5 to 9 o'clock, conceivably the right-hand, lower stroke of κ. After this, only the extreme top of the writing space is preserved. Here, about one letter-space to the right of the curved stroke, are traces of a tall letter (or letters). What remains are two diagonal lines converging as they descend. These might be the right-hand stroke of λ followed by ι. Less likely either the top of β (for the top of the loop has uncharacteristically been left open) or the top of υ (for they form a much narrower angle than usual for that letter, and υ ordinarily does not project above the line of writing). There are three approaches to πέϲη[ι] η˳˳[: the subjunctive might be followed by either the feminine article or by ἤ ("or") or by a word that begins with eta (which would account for Wilcken's wish to restore ἡγηϲαμένη).

If the word following]η began with β one might restore ἡ β[οῦϲ, although this would leave the curved stroke preceding it unexplained, and the recurrence of the same word at the start of line 19 seems awkward. The 5-to-9 curve might, alternatively, belong to the loop of alpha, but normally this has a more oval shape, sloping up from its lower extremity (although the scribe's practice is not uniform, and an alpha with a similarly flattened bottom loop may be seen, e.g., in line 77 Αἰτωλόν). If in fact the letter is α and is followed by υ, αὐ̣[τομάτωϲ] is possible, and this would also fit the space available at the end of the line (for the adverb cf. *sch.* Thom. *in Ph.* 658 ... ὅπη ἂν ἐκείνη αὐτομάτωϲ καὶ μηδενὸϲ δαμάϲαντοϲ πεϲεῖται...). If instead we read πέϲη[ι] ἤ, Essler's proposal κα̣[θίζηι] or Haslam's κλ̣[ίθηι], "falls or sits (lies) down" makes sense. The latter is perhaps to be preferred. Ps.-Apollodorus also uses a form of κλίνω at *Bibl.* 3.22 to describe the cow's action (ἡ δὲ διεξιοῦϲα Βοιωτίαν ἐκλίθη), as do the *sch. vet. in Ph.* 638 ἵζηται κλίνη τε πέδῳ γόνυ (see above on lines 13-22).

21-22   Haslam's π[ρῶτον | πεϲεῖ]ν is attractive, and would be still more appealing if πρῶτον could also be read at the end of line 18, but there is not sufficient room.

22-23   (on *Ph.* 640). Cf. *sch. vet. ad l.* ἀδάμαϲτον πέϲημα· τὸ μὴ ὑπό τινοϲ ἠναγκαϲμένον πτῶμα, ἀλλ' αὐτορριφέϲ. πέϲημα δὲ τὸ ϲῶμα ἀπὸ τοῦ παρεπομένου. ἄλλωϲ· ἀδάμαϲτον· ἀντὶ τοῦ· αὐτόματον ἔβαλε τὸ ϲῶμα ἐπὶ τὴν γῆν. δίκειν γὰρ τὸ βάλλειν, ὅθεν καὶ δίϲκοϲ. τινὲϲ δὲ ἀδάμαϲτον πέϲημα τὸ μηδέπω δαμαϲθὲν ζεύγλῃ ϲῶμα. ἐμφαίνει δὲ τὸν νέον μόϲχον.

22   The lemma partially repeats that of lines 13-14. For similar occurrences, see below on lines 38-39 and on lines 40 and 43.

23   [αὐ]τομάτω̣ϲ ˳˳˳ν˳˳π˳˳˳ου //>>: at the beginning, apparently not αὐτορριφέϲ (offered, in addition to αὐτόματον, by the *sch. vet.*). At the end, per-

haps αὐτοῦ, but between τομ and ου the writing is too damaged to confirm any of this. Haslam's suggestions αὐ]τομάτως γὰρ πίπτει, αὐ]τομάτως πεςούςης are all but untestable for the same reason.

After ου, which ends an explanation, the symbol // (not read by Wilcken) should appear, followed by >> before the next lemma. Either the symbols were written very close together, or the scribe omitted one of them, for the available space is rather narrow to hold both. Because the ink is smudged and a long crack begins above ου and cuts horizontally through the place where the symbols should be written, however, neither possibility can be confirmed.

23-26   (on *Ph.* 651). The comment perhaps begins with an explanation of the protective ivy which, after the palace of Cadmus was struck by lightning, twined around the infant Dionysus to protect him. Cf. *sch. vet. ad l.* κιccὸc ὃν περιcτεφής: ὁ πανταχόθεν αὐτὸν cτέψαc. τοῦ γὰρ οἴκου κεραυνωθέντος ἐξήμβλωcεν αὐτὸν ἡ μήτηρ φοβηθεῖcα, κιccὸc δὲ περιέλιξεν. ἄλλωc· ὄντινα, Διόνυcον, κιccὸc ἔξωθεν περιπλακεὶc ἔτι βρέφος ὄντα κατὰ τοῦ νώτου ἐκάλυψεν. ἱcτορεῖ γὰρ Μναcέαc (Mnaseas fr. 21 Cappelletto) ὅτι τῶν Καδμείων βαcιλείων κεραυνωθέντων κιccὸc περὶ τοὺc κίονας φυεὶc ἐκάλυψεν αὐτὸν, ὅπωc μὴ αὐθημερὸν καὶ ἐν μηδενὶ τὸ βρέφοc διαφθαρῇ [καλυφθὲν κιccῷ]· διὸ καὶ Περικιόνιος ὁ θεὸς ἐκλήθη παρὰ Θηβαίοιc.

24   κηρομε: following these letters there is no more discernible ink. If the commentary here is dealing with protection of the infant Dionysus by ivy, a form of κρύπτω or the scholia's περιελίccω or καλύπτω (see on line 23) might be appropriate to the context, but none of these words is legible in the next traces. If Wilcken's reading is correct, line 24 perhaps contained a reference to Hermes, who saved Dionysus from Semele's corpse (D.S. 4.2.3, Luc. *D.Deor.* 12, Nonn. *D.* 8.406; *EGen.* s.v. Βρόμιος Lasserre-Livadaras = *EM.* p. 214.40 Gaisford).

25   The last phrase of *sch. vet.* quoted above suggests restoring [περικιό|ν]ιοc δὲ ἐκλήθη, but the traces hardly support it.

26-28   (on *Ph.* 656?). Cf. *sch. rec.* (Thom.?) in *Ph.* 656 ἤγουν ταῖc βάκχαιc; also *sch.* Thom. *in Ph.* 649 at end, διὰ τοῦτο οὖν αἱ βάκχαι πρὸc τιμὴν τοῦ θεοῦ κιccοῦ κλάδουc ἔφερον χορεύουcαι περὶ τὸν θεὸν καὶ βοῶcαι· εὖ οἶ· οἶ εὖ υἶιc, ἤγουν υἱὲ τοῦ Διόc. τοῦτο γάρ ἐcτι τὸ εὐίοιc; and *sch. vet. in Ph.* 651 ταῖc περὶ τὸν Διόνυcον χορευούcαιc καὶ τὸ εὐοῖ εὐάν ἐπιφθεγγομέναιc; μυcτικαῖc.

26   καὶ γυναιξὶν εὐίοιc (*Ph.* 656), a new lemma. There is nearly room for the entire phrase, but it cannot certainly be made out.

28-29   (on *Ph.* 658). The *sch. vet.* dealing directly with *Ph.* 658 are not relevant, but the *sch. vet. in Ph.* 662 may contain a parallel. See also the *sch. vet. in Ph.* 657 ἔνθα φόνιος ἦν <u>δράκων</u>: ἔνθα, παρὰ τῇ Δίρκῃ, δεινὸc ὑπῆρχε <u>δράκων</u>, ὠμὸc τὴν φύcιν, <u>φύλαξ</u> ὑπὸ τοῦ <u>Ἄρεως</u> καταcταθεὶc τῆc Δίρκηc πρὸc τὸ μηδένα ἀπ' αὐτῆc ὑδρεύcαcθαι. The *sch.* Mosch. *in Ph.* 657-669 seems less relevant but, like the commentary, more concise: ἔνθα φόνιος: ἔνθα <u>δράκων ἦν</u> τοῦ Ἄρεος φονικὸς ἄγριος ἀπηνὴς <u>φύλαξ</u>, τῆς πηγῆς δηλονότι, τὰ νάματα τὰ εὔυδρα καὶ τὰ ὑγρὰ ῥεῖθρα ἐφορῶν ὀφθαλμοῖς ἐπὶ πολλὰ διάγουσι τὸ βλέμμα καὶ σκοπούμενοις.

29   (or 30)-31. Haslam rejects Wilcken's suggestion that a lemma is found here from *Ph.* 657, on two grounds. First, it would be slightly out of order (by one line) in the otherwise orderly progression of lemmata that we have on the verso (disruption of a much more radical sort does appear on the recto). More importantly, the explanatory note following the supposed lemma would need to begin, anomalously, with ἦν <u>δὲ</u>. Note, nevertheless, that ἐκεῖ in line 30 may correspond to *Ph.* 657 ἔνθα. The condition of the text is too poor to verify Haslam's <u>ϲύμβολον</u> or Mastronarde's <u>ἐμπόδιον</u>.

31-35 treat one or more new lemmata.

31   A new lemma, just possibly from *Ph.* 659, begins in the second half of the line. The poor condition of the papyrus makes it impossible to know whether there were other lemmata in lines 32-35.

35   Possibly δράκων, written by itself in the middle of line 35, was intended as a place-marker, indicating the subject of an eventual note to be added at the bottom of the verso, where a generous amount of unwritten remains. On the order of the sides, see the introduction.

Recto

a   The initial staurogram (†,ϼ) is frequently found at the left of the first line of text in documentary papyri of late antiquity. In literary and paraliterary texts, it is less frequent and may be centered in the top margin (TM 68861, at the top of a letter) or, more often, written at the left of the first line of text (TM 59717, encomium by Dioscorus; TM 64766, medical prescription). I know of only two other cases of the simple cross (+) being used in a literary papyrus. In P.Herc. 1148, where it appears at the left of col. xl, its function is unclear (Leone 1984, p. 24); in ⇒ Aratus 2 (TM 59218), it is written above and to the left of an annotation in the left margin.

36-38   (on *Ph.* 683-684). Cf. *sch. vet. ad l.* διώνυμοι δὲ παρόϲον ἡ μὲν Κόρη καὶ Περϲεφόνη, ἡ δὲ Δημήτηρ καὶ Γῆ ὀνομάζεται.

36   What was written at the beginning of this line has ramifications for the question of which side of the papyrus preceded (see the introduction). Certainly some of it was occupied by the start of a lemma from *Ph.* 683-684, but its exact form is unknown: αἱ (or καί) may have been present, and either >> or >>> will have preceded. With so much text missing and a script so variable, greater precision is useless. That said, the lacuna appears to be sufficient to hold something on the order of 23 to 26 letters. If it contained the longest possible combination of lemma and punctuation (>>> καὶ διώνυμοι θεαὶ Πε]ρϲέφαϲϲα), the space would be nearly but not completely filled. As many as

3-6 letter-spaces will have remained. Eisthesis could account for this, but if there was no eisthesis, and if the lemma began with >> διώνυμοι, a substantial space (as many as 7-10 letters) still remained. (If eisthesis is considered as a possibility, one might also ponder whether lines 51 and 60 might have provided further instances.) The space is unlikely to have been blank, but it is too short for another whole lemma plus comment. Thus there are at least four possibilities for its contents: (1) an eccentric lemma; (2) a false start by the writer, subsequently crossed out; (3) a word finishing a note from a previous page; (4) a longer lemma than the one we have in scholia. On the whole, the latter is likeliest, because the lemmata of the papyrus almost always are longer than those of the scholia. (I owe this information Donald Mastronarde, who is preparing a collation and edition of scholia to the *Phoenissae* that will appear at EuripidesScholia.org.)

37   The supralineation above Γῆ indicates that the word is here a proper noun (Fournet 2020, pp. 161-162). Despite its presence above the name of a god, it presumably is not the marker of a *nomen sacrum* which, in any case, would typically entail internal abbreviation. Fournet 2020, pp. 154-157 surveys the documentary and paraliterary contexts in which scribes employed supralinear strokes, for example, to highlight important names or terms, as in TM 61270 (catechism on the Hom. *Il.*, 5th cent.), TM 10528 (memorandum and notes for an advocate, 342 C.E.?), and TM 32944 (judicial protocol, 4th cent.).

38-39   (on *Ph.* 683). The presence of two lemmata and two comments dealing with διώνυμοι θεαί is unusual, especially as the comments apparently treat material that a single commentator would probably have consolidated (first, identification of the two names of each goddess that warrant their being called διώνυμοι and, second, the information that διώνυμοι was their cult title at Thebes). Either the writer or his source is evidently juxtaposing material from two sources. Similar repetitions of whole or partial lemmata occur in the comments at lines 13-14 and 22 and in those at lines 40 and 43. Each of the three pairs also involves at least one lemma that is introduced by a triple angle mark instead of the usual double, but there is no discernible pattern in play: at line 13 >>> introduces the first lemma and >> the second; in lines 36 and 38 the beginning of the first lemma is missing and >>> introduces the second; in lines 40 and 43 the same apparently occurs. On these marks see also, in general, the comments in the introduction.

38   The new lemma may repeat part of *Ph.* 683-684, already quoted in line 36. ἇι would not be excluded, but since αἱ is more to be expected than ἇι, it might be odd if the scribe troubled to add a breathing mark, but not to clarify that the word was not the article. Wilcken interpreted as νται some or all of the dividing signs that end the previous lemma and begin this one; this was then

followed by αἱ διώνυμοι ἢ [καί. In his commentary he notes the presence here of a second explanation for διώνυμοι, but the presence of the second, reduplicative lemma evidently eluded him.

39 Whether text continued in line 39 after [Πε]ρ̣ς̣[εφόνη is unknown.

40-43 (on *Ph.* 687, perhaps with additional lemmata for same line?) These lines are remarkable for containing the solitary grammatical comment in the text. The commentator begins by identifying the πυρφόρους θεάς as Demeter and Persephone and then explains the adjective as an instance of synecdoche. What is synecdochic about it? The commentator may see it as deriving from the word for wheat, πυρός, and take that as the 'part' of which the implied 'whole' is all the kinds of grain associated with the goddesses. With this in mind, Haslam suggests restoring lines 41-42 with, e.g., πυ[ροφόρους | (οἶον) ϲιτοφόρο]υ̣[ϲ] τινὲ̣ϲ ..[.]..., ἵνα ϲυνεκδοχικὸ̣ν ᾖ τὸ ϲχῆμα, "Some (understand) 'wheat-bearing' (in the sense of) 'grain-bearing', so that the figure is a synecdoche." The phrase ϲχῆμα ϲυνεκδοχικόν appears in *sch. in* Soph. *Aj.* 7e, and similar expressions are found in *sch. in* Aristoph. *Nub.* 106c β and *sch. in* Lycophr. 150.17 *bis*. ϲυνεκδοχικόν alone describes figures in *sch. in* Theocr. 7.5-9l and 10.15-16b and in *sch. in* Soph. *Aj.* 7f. Alternatively, the commentator may take πυρφόρους as deriving from πῦρ and identify fire as the synecdochic whole of which a part is the torch-fire associated with Demeter's rites. Torchbearers are in fact discussed in lines 43-43a. The *sch. vet.* conflate the two ideas: πυροφόρους δὲ εἶπε Δήμητρα καὶ Κόρην, ἐπειδὴ δᾳδουχίαι αὐταῖς γίνονται. The *sch.* Thom. offer only the fire-based explanation: πυρφόρους δὲ καλεῖ, ἐπειδὴ ἐν νυκτὶ γινομένων τῶν μυστηρίων οἱ μυούμενοι πῦρ ἔφερον, ὅθεν ταύτας πυρφόρους εἰκόνιζον. At the end of line 41, the author seemingly identifies the gender of πυρφόρους as feminine. Reconstruction of line 42 is difficult. Haslam observes that (ἕτερον?) ἐξ ἑτέρου suggests a definition, and οἶον Δημήτηρ... an example; the phrase does not figure in definitions of synecdoche. Line 43 apparently repeats part of the lemma just discussed and adds an explanation, which is supplemented by an interlinear note beneath the line.

41 It is not clear where the ἵνα clause ends. The writer may have intended ἵνα ϲυνεκδοχικὸν ᾖ τὸ ϲχῆμα, "in order that the (grammatical) form be synecdochic," with a new clause starting at the supposed θηλυκόν. Alternatively, the punctuation belongs after ᾖ, giving "in order that it be synecdochic," with a new clause (although without conjunction) following: "the (grammatical) form (is) feminine."

If θηλυκόν was in fact written, it presumably refers to the gender of πυρφόρους, although there seems no great need for such a comment, given that it is adjacent to the obviously feminine θεάς, and given that compound epithets normally have a common masculine and feminine form. In making explicit that which should be obvious, this note has the quality of a schoolteacher's observation.

42   New lemma or continuation of the previous comment? οἷον presumably introduces a longer paraphrase, e.g., "that is to say / in other words" (supply "let Demeter and Persephone come bearing torches" or "with torchbearers"?).

43-43a   Before λαμπαδηφόροι perhaps read πυρφόρ[ο]υς >>> . . . . α. If so, then line 43 repeats the lemma of line 40, at least in part; cf. similar repetition of lemmata in lines 13 and 22 and in lines 36 and 38. The note concerns the chorus' appeal to Epaphus, "πέμπε πυρφόρους θεάς." The writer perhaps is pedantically explaining that the goddesses do not themselves carry torches, e.g., (οὐ θεαὶ) ἀλλὰ λαμπαδηφόροι λαμπάδ[ας φεροῦσι, "(Not goddesses—) rather, torchbearers bear torches." The interlineation directly below stipulates, then, the gender of the torchbearers: "Other women carry torches." Haslam suggests, rather, that the writer may here be stating explicitly that πυρφόρους implies πῦρ and not πυρός and suggests, e.g., οὐ σιτοφόροι (-ους) ἀλλὰ λαμπαδηφόροι (-ους) λαμπάδ[ας φέρουσαι (φερούσας), "Not grain-bearers but torch-bearers carrying torches." Cf. Hsch. s.v. π 4473 Hansen πυρσοφόρος· ... ἢ ὁ τὸ πῦρ φέρων ... σημαίνει δὲ τὴν λαμπαδηφόρον.

44-45   (on *Ph.* 730). *Sch. vet. ad l.* Δίρκη δὲ ποταμὸς ὁμώνυμος τῇ κρήνῃ.

45-48   (on *Ph.* 807). A two-part comment – factual (providing the terms of the riddle) and lexical (glossing a rare word). It combines information and language also found in the *sch. vet.* and the argument to the play. Cf. the *sch. vet. ad l.* σφιγγὸς ἀμουσοτάταισι: σὺν κακομούσοις προβλήμασι καὶ σοφίσμασι τῆς σφιγγός. ᾠδὴν δὲ κακόμουσον τὸ αἴνιγμά φησιν, ἐπεὶ ἐμμελῶς τε καὶ ἐμμέτρως ἐλέγετο, ἀπώλλυε δὲ πολλοὺς τῶν Θηβαίων· μὴ εὑρίσκοντες γὰρ τὸ αἴνιγμα κατησθίοντο, and *sch.* Thom. *in Ph.* 801-817 ἐν ᾠδαῖς ἀμουσοτάταις καὶ κακαῖς; cf. also *sch. vet. in Ph.* 50; Arg. *Ph.* (e) Diggle = 5 Mastronarde τὸ τῆς Σφιγγὸς αἴνιγμα: ἔστι δίπουν ἐπὶ γῆς καὶ τετράπον, οὗ μία φωνή, καὶ τρίπον.

κακομούσοις reflects ancient doctrine: ancient glossaries and lexica recognized that in poetry some alpha-privative adjectives were equivalent to a compound adjective with κακο-/δυς-. For the doctrine, see *sch. ex. in* Hom. *Il.* 22.428b δεδιπλασίακε πρὸς τὴν ἐπίτασιν· τὸ γὰρ δυς καὶ α ταὐτὸν δηλοῦσιν, *sch. in* D.T. (*Gramm.Gr.* 1.3 p. 502.6-10).

48-59   On the tight spacing and smaller writing in these lines, see the introduction. In line 48, the lemma from *Ph.* 606 follows a note on *Ph.* 807 and introduces a series of five comments that interrupt the Euripidean line sequence of the hypomnema. A bit of pattern emerges within the disorder, however. After this first disruptive note come comments on passages even earlier in the play (*Ph.* 24 and 43). Then follows a note on *Ph.* 982 which, at first, appears to resume the commentary's normal sequence. It can also be seen however as interrupting, itself, the interruption. For the lemma that begins in line

58 treats *Ph.* 90 and thus continues the sequence of the previous interventions that dealt with *Ph.* 24 and 43. Layout contributes to the impression that the writer wanted to squeeze in this one additional note on *Ph.* 90, presumably from a secondary source, before returning to the order of the rest of the hypomnema. For the writer ends the note on *Ph.* 982 halfway through line 57 and leaves the rest of the line blank. The note on *Ph.* 90 starts a new line and itself terminates considerably short of the end of the line after which (in line 60) the commentary resumes its normal sequence with a lemma from *Ph.* 1019-1020.

48-51   (on *Ph.* 606). Zethus and Amphion of the white steeds: Eur. *HF* 31, Hsch. δ 1929 Latte-Cunningham. The same information is presented in papyrus and scholia, the former being a little more fully expressed: *sch. vet. ad l.* Κάϲτοροc καὶ Πολυδεύκουc. ἢ Ζήθου καὶ Ἀμφίονοc, ὅπερ ἄμεινον.

51-52   *Ph.* 24 is treated, out of order.

51   [7-9   ]: the extent of the lacuna at the end of the line is unclear. It must certainly have contained the name of Hera, cf. *sch.* Mosch. *in Ph.* 24 λειμῶν᾽ ἐc Ἥραc] εἰc τὸν λειμῶνα τὸν ἀνατεθειμένον τῆι Ἥραι. But since τῆι Ἥραι by itself would make a very short line (47 letters), an epithet may also have been attached. ἀλcώδηc (referring to τόποc), which the *sch.* Thom. *in Ph.* 24 and some other passages suggest, would fit although, as Haslam notes, it would be unlikely in this position. He plausibly proposes a simple phrase such as ὅc ἐcτι or ἔcτι δὲ. Κιθαιρωνίαι (referring to Hera), which the *sch. vet. in Ph.* 24 offer, is probably too long.

52-53   (on *Ph.* 43, out of order). The contents of the note correspond to the metaphrase in the *sch. vet. ad l.*, ἄλλωc: τί οὖν, φηcί, ταῦτα τὰ περιττὰ καὶ τὰ ἐκτὸc τῶν παθῶν λέγω, but not to an explanatory note on the articulation of the line in the Mss. MCV. For Henry's reading θυραῖα cf. the Laurentianus scholion on Soph. *Phil.* 158 (p. 355.25-6 Papageorgius) ἔναυλον ἢ θυραῖον] ἐντὸc ἢ ἐκτόc. ἐγγὺc ἢ μακράν.

53-57   (on *Ph.* 982, out of order). The comment relays information provided in greater detail in the *sch. vet. in* Soph. *Trach.* 171-172 Xenis Δωδώνι διccῶν ἐκ πελειάδων: τὴν ἐν Δωδώνῃ τῆc Θεcπρωτίαc φηγὸν ἐφ᾽ ᾗ δύο περιcτεραὶ καθήμεναι ἐμαντεύοντο; *sch. vet. in* Soph. *Trach.* 172 Xenis ὑπεράνω τοῦ ἐν Δωδώνῃ μαντείου δύο ἦcαν πέλειαι δι᾽ ὧν ἐμαντεύετο ὁ Ζεύc, ὡc Ἀπόλλων ἀπὸ τρίποδοc· οἱ μὲν οὕτω λέγουcι θεcπίζειν, οἱ δὲ οὕτω τὰc ἱερείαc γραίαc οὔcαc·... Ἡρόδοτοc δὲ ἐν β΄ φηcὶ (Hdt. 2.57) "Πελειάδεc δέ μοι δοκέουcι κεκλῆcθαι πρὸc Δωδωναίων αἱ γυναῖκεc, διότι βάρβαροι οὖcαι ἐδόκουν ὁμοίωc ὄρνιcι φθέγγεcθαι, μετὰ δὲ χρόνον δοκοῦcιν ἀνθρωπίνη φωνῇ φθέγξαcθαι [ἐπείπερ ἐκ Θηβῶν Αἰγυπτίων ἦcαν]." Εὐριπίδηc (fr. 1021 Kannicht) τρεῖc γεγονέναι φηcὶν αὐτάc, οἱ δὲ δύο (at 2.55, Herodotus identifies three Peleiades by name). The subject of the mantic doves was also addressed by the mythographer Asclepiades (4th c. B.C.E.) ἐν τραγῳδουμένοιc (fr.

3 = *FHG* 3, p. 298 Müller), quoted in the *sch. vet. in* Ap.Rhod. *Argon.* 2.328. The story of the Peleiades is actually irrelevant in this context: at Eur. *Ph.* 982, Menoeceus simply asks his father where he should go as an exile and is told "Dodona." The claim of the commentator in P.Würzb. 1 that the name of the prophetess was Peleia seems to be unique to the papyrus, and the factual detail suggests an underlying learned source; Euripidean scholia provide only metaphrases and an explanation of Θεϲπρωτόν and are silent about the Peleiades. Another late papyrus intended for school use, a copy of Pind. *P.* 1 with annotations (MPER I 23, MP³ 1356, 6ᵗʰ c. C.E.; McNamee 1994), also contains an unnecessary mythological digression taken from tragedy, in that case Soph. *Phil.*

56-57   The somewhat tighter line spacing and smaller letter sizes here, as well as the empty half line in 57 and the unusual punctuation at the end of comments (long horizontal strokes in addition to two and three apparently vertical bars in lines 57 and 59, respectively) suggest that this material was added after the rest, in a space left blank on purpose, and that here the space turned out to be larger than needed.

58-59   (on *Ph.* 90, out of order). On the spacing, see previous note. This entry, which is complete, may also be a secondary addition. Its lemma is wildly out of order (but see above on lines 48-59), the writing is notably smaller than in most of the text, the second line is shorter by about five letters than typical lines, and the comment terminates with the same unusual horizontal stroke seen at the end of line 57. Why the scribe did not begin the note in the empty space in the second half of line 57 is unknown.

Although the Mss. unanimously attest ἐϲ in *Ph.* 24, it is generally true that both manuscripts and papyri have εἰϲ in most places where modern editors print ἐϲ, so it is possible that ειϲ was written in the lacuna here, perhaps because of anticipation of the following εἰϲ in line 58. Scholia and glossaries have comparable interpretations of the phrase. Restoration is based on *sch. vet. ad l.* ἐϲ διῆρεϲ ἔϲχατον: τὸ διῃρημένον καὶ ὑπερκείμενον, τὸ ὑπερῷον. ἢ τὸ δίϲτεγον; *EM.* p. 274.27 Gaisford διήρηϲ: ὁ ὑπερῷοϲ οἶκοϲ. Εὐριπίδηϲ ἐν Φοινίϲϲαιϲ, μεθῆκε μελάθρων ἐϲ διῆρεϲ ἔϲχατον. ἀπὸ τοῦ δὶϲ, διήρηϲ· ἵν' ᾖ ὁ διϲτεγήϲ; Poll. 1.82.6; cf. 4.129.7 ἡ δὲ διϲτεγία ποτὲ μὲν ἐν οἴκῳ βαϲιλείῳ διῆρεϲ δωμάτιον, οἷον ἀφ' οὗ ἐν Φοινίϲϲαιϲ ἡ Ἀντιγόνη βλέπει τὸν ϲτρατόν; cf. Ps.-Zon. *Lex.* p. 509.9 Tittmann.

59   τὸ ὑπὲρ τοῦτον: the Greek is possibly problematic. In the first place, in educated Greek style ὑπέρ with the accusative ordinarily means "beyond" in a horizontal, not a vertical sense (possible exceptions in literature are few: Hom. *Il.* 24.13 ἠὼϲ φαινομένη ...ὑπεὶρ ἅλα; Plu. *Arist.* 10.5 οὔθ' ὑπὲρ γῆν οὔθ' ὑπὸ γῆν). In documentary papyri, however, a vertical relationship is implied in physical descriptions from the Hellenistic period through at least the second century C.E., e.g., in P.Petr. 1.14 lines 15-16 οὐλὴ ἐπὶ μήλου παρ' ὀφρῦν |

[ἀριστερὰν] καὶ ἄλλη μετώπωι μέσωι καὶ ἄλλη \μετώπωι/ ὑπὲρ ὀφρῦν δεξιάν; see Mayser, *GGP* II.2.461, §124 and Blass-Debrunner-Funk 1961, p. 121 §230. Secondly, the phrase τὸν ὑψηλὸν τόπον to which τοῦτον presumably refers is vague enough to suggest the writer may have been uncertain about the topographical features he was explaining. The "high place" of which he speaks is plausibly the roof. Something that is above it would be a structure on the roof. The word he uses for this structure is the rare noun δίστεγον, which glosses διῆρες ἔσχατον in the scholia too: cf. the passages quoted above and also the *sch. D in* Hom. *Il.* 2.514, where it is used in a similar way to gloss ὑπερώιον, "upper chamber."

60-62 treat *Ph.* 1019-1120.

60   A relatively short line, only about 45 letters long. Here the normal sequence of lemmata resumes and the cramped appearance of the preceding lines is gone.

61-62   ἄλλοι δὲ … ἄλλοι ὅτι … . In scholia, the statement "Some understand x, others y" is ordinarily expressed by τινες (alone or with μέν or δέ) … ἄλλοι δὲ … . Only occasionally is ἄλλοι used without connective particle, as in fact occurs further on in this line; a parallel may be found in *sch. in* Arat. 16 where, as here, ἄλλοι introduces the third of three options; in *sch. vet. in* Pind. *P.* 7.4b and *sch. rec. in* Pi. *O.* 7.25, ἄλλοι without δέ introduces the second of two options. The comment is mythographic, offering three accounts of the birth of the Sphinx: she arose from the blood of Laius, or from the earth, or from the union of Typhon and Echidna. The scholia on this and the preceding line offer only the second and third possibilities: the *sch. vet. in Ph.* 1019 have a simple gloss, Γᾶς λόχευμα· γέννημα· ἐκ γῆς γὰρ ἀνεδόθη, but the *sch. rec.* try to rationalize the same information, γᾶς λόχευμα: παρόσον ἐν ὄρεσι διατρίβουσα τὸ πρὶν καὶ μὴ φαινομένη ἐξαίφνης ἐπέστη τοῖς Θηβαίοις, διὰ τοῦτο ἔδοξεν οἷον ἐκ γῆς ἀναδοθῆναι. Old and new scholia agree in the information they give for *Ph.* 1020: *sch. vet.* γέγονε γὰρ ἡ σφὶγξ Ἐχίδνης καὶ Τυφῶνος … ἡ δὲ σφὶγξ γέγονεν Ἐχίδνης καὶ Τυφῶνος; *sch.* Mosch. ἐκ Τυφῶνος γὰρ καὶ Ἐχίδνης ἡ σφίγξ (cf. [Apollod.] *Bibl.* 3.52). The *sch.* Thom. *in Ph.* 46 (… λέγοντες θυγατέρα εἶναι Τυφῶνος καὶ Ἐχίδνης, ἄλλοι δὲ Χιμαίρας) also mentions the Chimaera as a possible parent. Laius is claimed to be the father of the Sphinx in the *sch. vet. in Ph.* 26, on the authority of the paradoxographer Lysimachus (4th-3rd c. B.C.E.; fr. 5 = FHG 3, p. 336 Müller: Θηβαϊκὰ παράδοξα), τινὲς δὲ καὶ Λαΐου τὴν σφίγγα παραδιδόασιν ὡς Λυσίμαχος; so also the *sch. in* Lyc. 7 αὕτη ἡ σφὶγξ θυγάτηρ γέγονε Λαΐου (for a discussion of the myth see Deubner 1942, p. 12 with n. 4).

63-65   (on *Ph.* 1023). Haslam thinks ὅτι (line 63) is likely used here as the conventional scholiastic formulation for introducing explanations, in this case, of μιξοπάρθενος. If so, it is the unique example of this common usage in the papyrus. The syntactical complexity entailed in subordinating a ὅτι-clause to a verb that follows it at a considerable distance (i.e., λέγεται) would be un-characteristically artful for this writer. λέγεται in line 64, then, must introduce a second gloss, e.g., λέγεται δάϊον τέρας δ[ιὰ τὸ | πολλοὺς ἀ]πολ[έc]αι (Haslam), "She is called 'destructive monster' because of her killing many people." The scholia deal separately or not at all with μιξοπάρθενος and δάϊον τέρας: Arg. *Ph.* 11 Mastronarde, lines 4-5 (= *sch. in Ph.* 1760) ἦν δὲ ἡ cφίγξ, ὥσπερ γράφεται, παρθένου μὲν ἔχουcα πρόcωπον, οὐρὰν δὲ δρακαίνης καὶ τὰ λοιπὰ λέοντος; *sch. rec. in Ph.* 1023 μιξοπάρθενος] ἐπειδὴ τὰ μὲν παρθένου εἶχε, τὰ δὲ θηρός; *sch.* Mosch. *in Ph.* 1019-1031 ἐκ θηρίου καὶ γυναικὸς cυντεθειμένη, ζῷον ξένης καὶ παρὰ φύcιν διαπλάcεως; *sch.* Thom. *in Ph.* 1019-1066 μιξοπάρθενος καὶ τὸ ἥμιcυ παρθένου ἔχουcα (note the use of ἥμιcυ).

65 (on *Ph.* 1028). Cf. *sch. vet. ad l.* λέγει δὲ τὸ αἴνιγμα. ἢ διὰ τοὺς γενομένους θρήνους ἢ διὰ τὰ αἰνίγματα. Cf. *sch. vet. in Ph.* 1024 ἄλλως: ... ἡ cφὶγξ, ... ἁρπάζουcα ... τοὺς νέους διὰ τὴν ἄλυρον ... μοῦcαν, ἤτοι διὰ τὸ αἴνιγμά cου. The papyrus commentary omits the scholia's metaphrase and explanation of sense and offers only the same interpretation as the *sch. vet.*

66-68 (on *Ph.* 1043). The attribution of Ialemus' death to an accident on his wedding day is new. In Pindar, he died from disease and it was his brother Hymenaeus who died while lying with his wife; the commentator has trans-ferred that fate to Ialemus: Pind. fr. 128c.6-12 Maehler = fr. 56 Cannatà Fera (*Threnoi*) ἁ μὲν ἀχέταν Λίνον αἴλινον ὕμνει, / ἁ δ' Ὑμέναιον, ⟨ὃν⟩ ἐν γάμοιcι χροϊζόμενον [Μοῖρα] cύμπρωτον λάβεν, / ἐcχάτοις ὕμνοιcιν· ἁ δ' Ἰάλεμον ὠμοβόλῳ / νούcῳ {ὅτι} πεδαθέντα cθένος. Schwartz ap. Wilcken 1934, p. 20, adduces the version of Hymenaeus' death found in Servius' comment on Verg. *Aen.* 1. 651, where the cause of death on the marriage bed is spelled out: *Hymenaeus autem ... quidam iuvenis fuit, qui die nuptiarum oppressus ruina est.* Haslam, thinking of Servius' *oppressus ruina,* speculates about restoring, e.g., ἐρείπιά τινα or ἡ ὀροφή at the beginning of line 68. The scholia on this line metaphrase and interpret the text but say nothing about the myth: *sch. vet. in Ph.* 1033 ἰάλεμοι: οἱ δὲ θρῆνοι ἐcτενάζον⟨το⟩ ἐν τοῖc οἴκοις. ἔνιοι δὲ οὕτως· αἱ δὲ ἰάλεμοι τῶν παρθένων καὶ τῶν μητέρων ἐcτέναζον ἐν τοῖc οἴκοις πενθοῦcαι αἱ μὲν τὰ τέκνα, αἱ δὲ τοὺς ἀδελφούς; *sch.* Thom. *in Ph.* 1034 ἰάλεμοι δὲ παρθένων: ... ἢ πρὸς τὸ παρθένων cτικτέον, ἢ τὸ ἰάλεμοι πρὸς τὸ ἐcτέναζον cυντακτέον. καὶ μὴ ξενιcθῇς ἀκούων τὸ ἐcτέναζον ἰάλεμοι· πολλὰ γὰρ τοιαῦτα παρὰ ποιηταῖς εὕρηται. Glossaries and scholia on other works also explain ἰάλεμος as θρῆνος; cf., e.g., Moer. ι 1.1, Hsch. ι 27 Latte-Cunning-ham (cf. idem ι 28 Ἰάλεμος· υἱὸς Καλλιόπης), *sch. vet. in* Eur. *Or.* 1388, *sch. in* Lucian 51.24.2. The gloss survives in later etymologica as well.

69-75 (on *Ph.* 1043-1044). Both lemma and comment on *Ph.* 1043-1044 are more extensive in P.Würzb. 1 than in the scholia, and the information provid-ed is different and, in the case of the papyrus, intriguingly divergent from tradition: Oedipus goes to Thebes to find out if his father is alive, and Laius to find out the same about "his son Oedipus." The source of this version (if we assume it is not just a student's mangled version of the conventional story) is unknown. For a comparison of this version with Arg. *Ph.* 11 Mastronarde (in which Laius travels to Delphi to learn whether a son—whom he had engendered although warned by a curse that such a son would kill him—was alive or not), see Deubner 1942, pp. 13-14. The more concise scholia gloss Πυθίαις ἀποστολαῖσιν and explain that Oedipus was headed for Thebes because of an oracle: *sch. vet. ad l.* Πυθίαις ἀποστολαῖσιν: ἀντὶ τοῦ ὑπὸ Πυθίου ἀπεσταλμένος. κατὰ χρησμὸν γὰρ τούτου ἦλθεν εἰς Θήβας. ταῖς τοῦ Ἀπόλλωνος παραπομπαῖς. The narrative about Oedipus in lines 69-76 has some similarities with the verbose Thoman synopsis (arg. 12 in the Teubner edition), but parallel interests in mythography do not require dependency on one source for similar content, and Thomas is here closely following the traditional content of the myth and the information provided in the texts of Sophocles' *Oedipus Tyrannus* and Euripides' *Phoenissae* (both members of the Byzantine triad for their authors).

70   Haslam, questioning the grammar of τ[ὸ δ' εἶπεν], offers the alternative τ[οῦτο, which gives the line the sense, "Oedipus, intending to find out whether his father was alive, went to *this* oracle" (i.e., that which summoned him by Πυθίαις ἀποστολαῖς). After τ[οῦτο, perhaps ἔφη (δ')] | [ὅτι κτανεῖ αὐ]τόν, Apollo presumably being the speaker.

72   If the dative article preceded Λαίωι, then ὑπήντησε was probably divided between lines 71 and 72. ὑπήν|τησε best suits the limited space at the beginning of line 72. The end of line 72 can accommodate more letters than the four of θεοῦ. Although the writer did not necessarily always use all the available space, θεοῦ καὶ or Ἀπόλλωνος might also be considered as restorations.

74   It is uncertain whether the author intended αὐτοῦ or αὑτοῦ. Here (unlike line 63), αυτου is in attributive position, in contrast to ὁ πατὴρ αὐτοῦ and ὁ υἱὸς αὐτοῦ earlier in the note. Given this difference in position and given the emphasis that might be expected in connection with patricide, the intended meaning may have been "his own father" with the disyllabic reflexive; but in later Greek it is also possible to use the non-reflexive αὐτοῦ in this position.

75-76   (on *Ph.* 1046). ὑπὸ τοῦ ἀνδρὸς τοῦ Λαΐου is striking, θεράποντος being the expected noun: a case of earlier usage being supplanted by colloquial diction? The papyrus here offers less information than the scholia, but has echoes of their language: *sch. vet. ad l.* τότ' ἀσμένοις: διὰ τὸ λῦσαι τὸ αἴνιγμα. πάλιν δὲ ἄχη συνάπτει διὰ τὸν γάμον τῆς μητρὸς καὶ τὰ λοιπά. ... οὐ γὰρ εὐθὺς ὡς ἐπεδήμησεν ἄσμενοι αὐτὸν εἶδον, ἀλλ' ὅτε ἔλυσε τὸ αἴνιγμα. λείπει δὲ τὸ ἦλθεν.

76-86   (on *Ph.* 1108). The *sch.* Thom. *in Ph.* 1108 covers some of the same ground: κάπρον: ὃν ἐπήγαγεν Αἰτωλοῖς ποτὲ Ἄρτεμις λυμαίνεσθαι τὴν σφῶν χώραν, ὀργιζομένη Οἰνεῖ θύσαντι τοῖς ἄλλοις θεοῖς καὶ οὐ τῇ Ἀρτέμιδι. ἀπέκτεινε δὲ τὸν κάπρον τοῦτον ὁ Μελέαγρος; cf. *sch. rec. in Ph.* 1108 οὗτος ὁ κάπρος ἐλέγετο

Καλυδώνιος· Καλυδὼν δὲ ὄρος Αἰτωλίας. ἱστορεῖται δὲ ὡς τοῦτον τὸν κάπρον ἡ Ἄρτεμις ἐτόξευσε, Μελέαγρος δὲ τῷ cυοκτόνῳ δόρατι περὶ τὸ μέτωπον πλήξας ἀνεῖλεν Gu (copied by this 14th c. scribe from *sch. in* Lyc. *Alexandra* 492 or from Tz. *Chil.* 7.102.67, which correctly have Atalante where Gu carelessly names Artemis). More detailed versions of the story are in [Apollod.] *Bibl.* 1.66-67 (1st-2nd c. C.E.); Zen. 5.33 (2nd c. C.E.); Ioannes Malalas *Chronogr.* 6.21 (5th-6th c. C.E.).

77-79 πᾶcι θεοῖc … ἀφῆκεν: cf. *sch. vet. in* Aristoph. *Ran.* 1253 Οἰνεὺc δὲ τῆc αὑτοῦ γῆc εὐφορηcάcηc ἀπαρχὰc πᾶcι θεοῖc θύcαc, Ἀρτέμιδι οὐκ ἔθυcεν ὅθεν ὀργιcθεῖcα cὺν μέγαν κατὰ τῆc χώραc αὐτοῦ ἀφῆκεν, ἵνα ταύτην λυμήνηται.

78 The scribe originally wrote the indicative εἴαcε. Once he altered this to ἐάcαντοc, an additional conjunction (e.g. καί or perhaps ἀλλά) was needed to link the two participles. This he must have inserted in the lacuna at the beginning of the line, presumably in the interlinear space. The corrected syntax suggests the writer was not writing from dictation. Possibly he was trying to reduce or simplify material from his source.

79-80 Wilcken's restoration Κᾳλυδώνι|[ον· οὕτωc δ' ἐκ]λήθη is questionable, as ancient sources always use the article in writing about the Calydonian boar (i.e. ὁ Καλυδώνιοc κάπροc or cῦc; cf. Str. 8.6.22, [Apollod.] *Bibl.* 2.133; 3.106; 3.163, Lucian *Ind.* 14; Paus. 8.45.6; Ath. 401b-d = 9.64 Kaibel; Eust. *in Il.* 1.67.34, and scholia on several authors.

Athanassiou was impressed by the verbal similarity between lines 79-80, giving the reason for the name "Calydonian boar," and the wording of a scholion in Gu (see above on lines 76-86), which he assumed to be Thoman. Most Gu scholia in Dindorf's edition are indeed Thoman, but not all of them, and this note is in fact found in Gu alone and is one of those due solely to the personal efforts of the Gu-scribe, who copied this note (a little carelessly) from the tradition of commentary on Lycophron. The details found in the P.Würzb. 1 scholion are actually comparable to those in Ps.-Apollodorus and other sources and have no special affinity to this last annotation.

80 Space left for filling later, as perhaps occurred at lines 55-59. If so, the fact to be supplied is possibly an explanation for the epithet Καλυδώνιος, as in the *sch. rec. in Ph.* 1108, οὗτος ὁ κάπρος ἐλέγετο Καλυδώνιος· Καλυδὼν δὲ ὄρος Αἰτωλίας (but note that this scribe has identified Calydon as a mountain rather than a city, a claim confirmed by no ancient source). Alternatively, Maehler suggests the blank may be due to damage in the scribe's original (Maehler 1993, pp. 111, 135).

81 What is needed here is either the destination of the boar in the accusative or the destination plus a genitive participle and possibly an object (presumably the word that appears to end in -ρη, which in such a case would be neuter plural). But there hardly seems room for the latter.

83-84 The reading of the accusative τὸν κάπρον seems clear in the original, but the meaning of the whole clause cυνέβαλεν … A]ἰτωλίοιc is not unproblematic. Mastronarde points out that cυμβάλλω of setting parties into conflict usually has as its subject someone directing events (e.g., the gods set these heroes against each other), not a participant like Atalante. Thus restoring, e.g., τοῖc ἄλλοιc A]ἰτωλίοιc in line 84 is undesirable, and in any case begs an explanation about the identity of these other Aetolians (not Meleager?), since Atalanta herself is variously said to be Arcadian or Boeotian. Alternatively, the beginning of line 84 may have contained a participle governing the accusative κάπρον, with cυνέβαλεν being used absolutely in the sense "engage in battle" (LSJ s.v.II.1.c); but there are few choices of short verbs. Possibilities include ἐφεῖcα or ἀφεῖcα, which would give e.g., καὶ cυνέβαλεν τὸν κάπρον | [ἐφεῖcα τοῖc A]ἰτωλίοιc, "And (Atalante) engaged in battle, sending the boar forward against the Aetolians". Or we might instead, as Essler suggests, restore a subject for cυνέβαλεν in the lacuna, e.g., καὶ cυνέβαλεν τὸν κάπρον [ἡ θεὰ τοῖc A]ἰτωλίοιc, "And the goddess (i.e., Artemis) set the boar to fight with the Aetolians." This allows a normal meaning of the verb, but makes the return to Atalante as subject in the next sentence very awkward or even unidiomatic, even if demonstrative αὕτη is assumed in line 84. Finally, one might consider that the accusative κάπρον is an error for the dative, and that something like Schwartz's cυνέβαλεν τῶι κάπρωι | [ἐν τοῖc ὁρίοιc A]ἰτωλίοιc was written, "She (i.e., Atalante) engaged with the boar in the Aetolian territories" (cf. LSJ s.v. cυμβάλλω II c). But such an assumption seems wrong for a text with rather few errors and, as Henry notes, the adjective would need to go between the article and the substantive.

P.Oslo inv. 1662   saec. VI[p]

Excerpt from a commentary on Troades *9*

Prov.: ?

Cons.: Oslo, University Library.

Edd.: Eitrem-Amundsen 1957.

Tab.: https://ub-baser.uio.no/opes/record/184.

Comm.: MP³ 429; CPP 241; LDAB 987; TM 59880   Hombert 1965; Tuilier 1968, pp. 219-220 and 276; Diggle 1971; Del Fabbro 1979, pp. 120-123; McNamee 1981, p. 118; Maehler 1993, pp. 112-113; Athanassiou 1999, pp. 146, 150, 174-175; Maehler 2000, p. 32; Costa 2007, pp. 247-254; Stroppa 2008, pp. 60-61; Carrara 2009, pp. 583-584; Fournet 2009; Johnson 2009; Perrone 2009b, pp. 236-238; Stroppa 2009, pp. 302, 307, 314, 320; Jones 2016; Mastronarde 2017, p. 10.

According to the first editors, the text was purchased in Egypt in 1910. Its precise findspot is unknown (*pace* Pack², which gives the provenance as Upper Egypt). What survives is a nearly rectangular piece of papyrus measuring 4.8 x 8.4 cm, cut fairly straight at the left, right, and bottom edges. A collesis crosses through and above line 6 of the text and runs across the fibers in the same direction as the script. All four margins are missing. On the front, where the writing survives, the fibers are vertical and the papyrus is a medium to dark brown and uniform in texture and color. The back is blank, although splotchy offsets of ink, darker than that of the text, are visible. The fabric of this side is coarse: three horizontal strips of papyrus remain, which vary in color and are poorer in quality and decidedly less suitable as a writing surface than the front surface. In a few large patches, this surface layer is missing and the layer of vertical fibers from the written side is visible in the gaps. Both sides of the papyrus also have traces of an unidentified reddish or golden substance; if the papyrus was cut down to be used in a book binding, this might be glue. The ink is generally dark black, although here and there it has worn away or flecked off. In such places, however, the letter traces remain clearly legible and brown in color. The brown color, the absence of fading in the black ink, and its particulate appearance suggest that the scribe used a "mixed ink" compounded from both carbon and copper or iron sulfates (Christiansen 2017, pp. 169-170). Writing, which runs across the vertical fibers, is a clear and confidently written example of the sloping majuscule style. ε, ι, o, and c are narrow. δ, θ, κ, λ, μ, π, τ, υ, and φ are typically quite wide. Space between final ν and a following letter is usually also wide, and the scribe left more than the usual amount of space in a few other places. The occasionally uneven size or orientation of letters gives the impression that the scribe wrote quickly. The dating to Vᵖ by the original editors was accepted by Maehler 1993 and 2000 and by Athanassiou 1999 and Stroppa 2009, p. 302. Stroppa 2008, p. 60 assigns the papyrus to VIᵖ, and comparisons make this more likely. The writing resembles that of P.Cairo Masp. 67055, an encomium of Dioscorus dated to 550-570, in the outsized κ and λ with curved lower branch at the right, the β that looms above and below the line, and the θ with its crossbar extending wide on either side of the oval. Similarly the writer's oversized φ resembles that of P.Vindob. G 25949, a copy of a Psalm assigned to the same period (Cavallo-Maehler 1987, pl. 31a and 31b). On the very broad writing space (about 28 cm wide), see below. Interlinear space is ample but not generous.

The original scribe wrote a cursive, i.e., ligatured, trema at line 3 ἱεροῦ (cf. P.Oxy. LXXIII 4933 ↓ line 11 and Fournet 2020, p. 148). At the end of the same word, he also added a high stop that is hard to explain, given the absence of punctuation at major breaks. There is a suprascript horizontal stroke to mark a numeral in line 4, but no other lectional signs or punctuation. An ornamental monogram is used in abbreviating the name of Philochorus (line 4)—a mode of abbreviation that is fairly rare (McNamee 1981, p. 118). Only one scribe wrote the text, and it is correctly written.

Line-length and thus the approximate width of the writing space are fairly well secured by a quotation from Thucydides, and this sets the length of lines 2 and 3 at 79 and 76 letters, respectively. Additionally, an extensive quotation from Philochorus occupying lines 4-8 is also very close in wording to a passage in the Aristophanic scholia. The quotation is followed by a gloss preserved in the *sch. vet. in Eur. Tr.* 9. Thus lines 4 through 8 can also be tentatively restored with letter-counts in the same range as lines 2 and 3, at 76, 77, 79, 79, and 77 letters, respectively. Since neither left nor right margin survives, the exact start- and end-points of the original lines are unknown. The text presented here generally follows the ed.pr., with a few entirely adjustments *exempli gratia* at the beginning or end of lines 4 through 8 to make their length more or less uniform.

The first editors believed the text came from a recycled book roll, and that its blank back, with its horizontal fibers, was unwritten papyrus at the end of some literary text. No other book roll is dated anywhere near so late, however, and this theory can be set aside. Nor, evidently, does the text come from a codex. The preserved comment deals with a passage very early in the play, so whatever will have followed it ought to have been written on the back of this fragment, but the back is blank. Nor is it likely the writing comes from a broad upper or lower margin whose opposite side happened to be blank.[1] The variable color of the three remaining strips of papyrus on the back leave the impression, in any event, that that side was not intended for writing.

Undoubtedly the only explanation is that the text was written on a loose sheet of papyrus and never contained more than this excerpt of commentary. Two facts support this. First, the collesis crosses through and above line 6 and runs across the fibers in the same direction as the script. Thus the orientation of the fragment is atypical for either roll or codex, where handwriting typically crosses the collesis at an angle of 90°, no matter the direction of the fibers.[2] Secondly, it had become customary by the fourth century for letters and documents to be written *transversa charta* (according to Fournet 2007, p. 359, 86.5% of petitions of the fifth to seventh centuries are written across rather than along the fibers). It would be normal, then, for someone making a short note on a loose sheet of papyrus to orient it as he would a sheet on which he intended to write a letter or a document.

Why someone would copy such deeply learned material on a loose sheet of paper, however, is hard to guess. The writer may have wanted to record something too extensive to fit into the margins of his copy of *Troades* and got around the problem by slipping this loose piece, like a bookmark, among the pages of his codex. An intriguing possibility, impossible to prove, is that the fragment is a sort of proto-scholion, excerpted from one or more sources, quickly written on a disposable piece of papyrus, and intended to be eventually compiled with many other such slips in proper order. Some such process, used in modern times by compilers of dictionaries, may lie at the genesis of variorum scholia (Murray 2001).

In precision, substance, and learning, the text is remarkable among surviving ancient commentaries on papyrus, whether free-standing or in the form of marginal notes. Of the other three heavily annotated, large-format papyri of late antiquity, only the Callimachus approaches it in these features. The fragment starts in the middle of a comment on *Troades* 9-10 ὁ γὰρ Παρνάσιος / Φωκεὺς Ἐπειός. The writer's focus is historical and Athenian, and deals, in particular, with the "Sacred Wars" between Athens and Sparta of the early 440s B.C.E. (see Costa 2007, p. 250 n. 3 for a summary of recent bibliography and discussion). The long quotations from Thuc. 1.112.5 and Philochorus *Atthis* Book 4 (which the writer mistakenly identifies as Book 5), are offered in

---

[1] Large-format codices from late antiquity with notes of comparable length are TM 59424 (Callimachus, with notes in the bottom margin 75 or more letters long; see McNamee 2007, pp. 202-219), TM 59217 ⇒ Aratus 2 CLGP, McNamee 2007, pp. 178-183, and TM 62559 (Pindar, McNamee 2007, pp. 306-308); notes in the latter two are extensively restored.

[2] Interestingly, the calculated line-length in the papyrus, 28 cm, is well within the normal range for the length of colleseis, as these can range from 19 to 33 cm (Johnson 2009, p. 257).

support; see *BNJ* 328 F 34c (with note). One, or perhaps two glosses on Παρνάςιος occupy the last two surviving lines of the text. The Euripidean scholia, by contrast, are literary and mythological, not historical. They begin and end with glosses, in one case supported by quotations from Homer, which the papyrus does without. Relevant history is briefly summarized: Thucydides is cited but not quoted and Philochorus not mentioned, but the genealogy of Epeios is traced through four generations. There is, however, a close match for the papyrus' Philochorus material in the *sch. in* Aristoph. *Av.* 558 which deal with Pisthetaerus' suggestion that the birds initiate a ἱερὸν πόλεμον.

Recto, transv. charta? (↓)

— — —

π]αλιν Φωκεῦς[ιν

"Λακεδ]αιμόνιοι δὲ μετὰ ταῦτα τὸν ἱερ[ὸν καλούμενον πόλεμον ἐςτράτευςαν, καὶ

κρατήςαντες τοῦ ἐν

Δελφ]οῖς ἱεροῦ παρέδοςαν Δελφοῖς· . [

   Φι]λόχορ(ος) δὲ ἐν τῆι δ̄· "ἐν τούτοις πε[ρὶ

5   π]όλεμον ἐπολέμηςαν Ἀθηναῖοι. [

     ]εν ἔμπροςθεν, ἐπεὶ Φωκεῖς κ[ατειλήφεςαν

    ] . Δελφῶν ἔλαβον. Ἀθηναῖοι δὲ τρ[

    Π]αρνάςιον ἔφη τὸν Ἐπειὸν διὰ̣ [

[. . . . . τ]οῖ̣ς Φωκευ[ςι

— — —

3 ἱ̈εροῦ· pap. The mark above the first letter has the shape of a circumflex accent but is presumably a quickly made trema   .[a straight vertical stroke, suitable for the vertical shaft of κ 4]λ̣.χ̣, with a malformed o written between the upper branches of χ and ρ between the lower; Eitrem-Amundsen read ξ pap.   7]. a stroke descending from upper left to lower right and ending about the midpoint of the writing space: possibly the abbreviation stroke ', although the scribe does not employ brachygraphic abbreviations in what remains. Alternatively, perhaps υ (cf. the curved right branch of the letter in lines 3 ἱεροῦ and 4 τούτοις) (SP); α impossible.

---

3 κ[αὶ?   4 Φι]λόχορ(ος) McNamee: Φι]λόχο(ρος) Eitrem-Amundsen, Costa   δ̄ corr. Eitrem-Amundsen, ξ pap.   7 π](αρὰ)? McNamee:]. ἱερο]ῦ̣, μαντείο]υ̣? SP   8 διὰ̣ McNamee: δ[ιὰ Eitrem-Amundsen

... back to the Phocians, (as Thucydides [1.112.5] says:) "The Spartans after this (conducted the so-called) Sacred (War, and once they had taken control) of the sanctuary at Delphi they handed it over to the Delphians; (?and again later the Athenians....") ...Philochoros in book 4 (*BNJ* 328 F 34c): "...in the meantime, about...the Athenians fought.... war ... previously, after the Phocians (seized...) ...took ...the Delphians. But the Athenians...(fought)...a third.... He called Epeius 'Parnassian' (*Tr.* 9) because... (with) the Phocians....

1-7   The connection between the Sacred Wars and the Euripidean play is the reference in *Tr.* 9 to Epeios as Phocian. The papyrus comment begins with a summary of the so-called Sacred Wars over control of the oracle at Delphi, in which Athens and Sparta engaged in the early 440s B.C.E. on behalf of their proxies the Phocians and Delphians, respectively. The writer substantiates the facts with two fairly long quotations from Thucydides and Philochorus. These wars are also treated, at greater length, in *sch. vet. in* Aristoph. *Av.* 558 = *FGrHist* 328 F 34a, which also draws on Philochorus. The Euripidean scholia on this line cite Thucydides but focus less on history than on grammatical issues (glosses, supportive Homeric quotations, a genealogy).

1   Restore, e.g., ...Φωκέας, Ἀθηναίων δὲ ἔμπ]αλιν Φωκεῦς[ιν αὐτὸ παραδόντων αὖθις, ὡς Θουκιδίδης μέν φησι ἐν τῆι αʹ. Cf. the *sch. vet. in* Eur. *Tr.* 9 (correspondences with the text of the papyrus are in bold): Λακεδαιμονίων μὲν ἀποδόντων Δελφοῖς τὸ ἱερὸν μετὰ τὸ καταπολεμῆσαι Φωκέας, Ἀθηναίων δὲ **ἔμπαλιν Φωκεῦσιν** αὐτὸ παραδόντων αὖθις, ὡς Θουκυδίδης φησί. Noteworthy is that the scholion omits the lengthy Thucydidean quotation.

2-4   The writer quotes Thuc. 1.112.5. Restore, e.g., "Λακεδ]αιμόνιοι δὲ μετὰ ταῦτα τὸν ἱερ[ὸν καλούμενον πόλεμον ἐστράτευσαν, καὶ κρατήσαντες τοῦ ἐν | Δελφ]οῖς ἱεροῦ παρέδοσαν Δελφοῖς· κ[αὶ αὖθις ὕστερον Ἀθηναῖοι κρατήσαντες παρέδοσαν Φωκεῦ|σιν." The Thucydidean text establishes the probable length of line 2 and, presumably, of the rest of the papyrus, although if the measurement is correct, part of the Thucydidean text was omitted in line 3. In the quotation that follows, a possible omission is italicized (cf. Eitrem-Amundsen 1957, p. 148; Stroppa 2009, p. 317 n. 44): **Λακεδαιμόνιοι δὲ μετὰ ταῦτα τὸν ἱερὸν** καλούμενον πόλεμον ἐστράτευσαν, καὶ κρατήσαντες τοῦ ἐν **Δελφοῖς ἱεροῦ παρέδοσαν Δελφοῖς· καὶ** αὖθις ὕστερον Ἀθηναῖοι *ἀποχωρησάντων αὐτῶν στρατεύσαντες καὶ* κρατήσαντες παρέδοσαν **Φωκεῦσιν.**

3-5   Restore, e.g., [Φωκεῦ|σιν, ὡς Φ]ιλόχορ(ος) δὲ ἐν τῆι δʹ· "ἐν τούτοις πε[ρὶ τοῦ ἐν Δελφοῖς ἱεροῦ τὸν ὕστερον ὑπὲρ Φωκέων ἱερὸν καλού|μενον π]όλεμον ἐπολέμησαν Ἀθηναῖοι...." Cf. *sch. vet. in* Aristoph. *Av.* 558: νικήσαντες δὲ **Φωκεῦσι** πάλιν ἀπέδωκαν, **ὡς Φιλόχορος (ἐν τῆι δʹ V)** λέγει... and, later in the scholion, καθάπερ καὶ **Φιλόχορος ἐν τῆι δʹ** λέγει "... ὑπὲρ τοῦ ἐν Δελφοῖς ἱεροῦ."

3   ἱεροῦ· The punctuation may mark a comma-like pause in the text.

4   ἐν τῆι δ: ε̄ written mistakenly instead of δ. Philochorus treated the period of the Sacred Wars in Book 4; cf. Costa 2007, p. 254; Jacoby in *FGrHist* 3B Suppl. vol. 1, Text, pp. 251-252; *sch. vet. in* Aristoph. *Av.* 558 (quoted above, comment on lines 3-5). The feminine article preceding the numeral is anomalous, τῶι (βιβλίωι) being expected; *sc.* cυγγραφῆ, ἱcτορίᾳ?

5-7   Reading ἱερο]ῦ or μαντείο]υ (Perrone) at the beginning of line 7 introduces a syntactical puzzle. I prefer to see the traces as an abbreviation mark and read π(αρά) with the *sch. in* Aristoph. *Av.* 558. This is not a perfect solution either, however, as the no such abbreviations survive in the papyrus. Restore, e.g., [ἄλλος γὰρ πόλεμος Λακεδαιμονίοις πρὸς Φωκέας ὑπὲρ Δελφῶν | γέγον]εν ἔμπροσθεν, ἐπεὶ Φωκεῖς κ̣[ατειλήφεσαν τὸ ἱερόν· καὶ κρατήσαντες Λακεδαιμόνιοι τὸ μαντεῖ]ον ?παρ]ὰ Δελφῶν ἔλαβον. Cf. *sch. vet.* in Aristoph. *Av.* 558: πρότερος μὲν Λακεδαιμονίοις πρὸς Φωκεῖς ὑπὲρ Δελφῶν, καὶ κρατήσαντες τοῦ ἱεροῦ Λακεδαιμόνιοι τὴν προμαντείαν παρὰ **Δελφῶν ἔλαβον**. In lines 6-7 the ed.pr. adopted the scholiast's τὴν προμάντειαν, which may be preferable to μαντεῖ|ον, depending on space available.

7-8   Restore, e.g., Ἀθηναῖοι δὲ τρ[ίτωι ἔτει τοῦ προτέρου πολέμου τὸ ἱερὸν πάλιν ἀπέδωκαν Φω|κεῦσι. Cf. *sch. vet.* in Aristoph. *Av.* 558: "ὕστερον δὲ **τρίτωι †ἔτει** τοῦ πρώτου πολέμου Ἀθηναίοις πρὸς Λακεδαιμονίους ὑπὲρ Φωκέων. καὶ **τὸ ἱερὸν ἀπέδωκαν** Φωκεῦσι." †ἔτει: sc. μηνί? Jacoby, who notes that the absolute chronology of the Sacred Wars is unclear and doubts that any one lasted as long as three years (*FGrHist* 3B Suppl. vol. 1, Text, p. 320); Costa 2007, pp. 251-253 summarizes the problem.

8-9   At the end of the historical comment, the writer appends a gloss that corresponds to portions of the Euripidean scholia. Restore, e.g., Π]αρνάσιον ἔφη τὸν Ἐπειὸν διὰ̣ [τὸ πλησίον τῇ Φωκίδι εἶναι τὸν Παρνασσὸν ἢ ἐπεὶ Δελ|φοὶ ἐτάττοντο σὺν τ]οῖς̣ Φωκεῦ[σι, although the supplement at the end of line 8 is a bit short. Cf. *sch. vet. in* Eur. *Tr.* 9: **Παρνάσσιον** αὐτὸν εἶπε Φωκέα ὄντα **διὰ** ⟨τὸ⟩ τάττεσθαι Δελφοὺς ὑπὸ **Φωκεῦσιν**. ... ἄλλως· ὁ Φωκεὺς Παρνάσιος εἴρηται, ἐπεὶ Δελφοὶ σὺν τοῖς Φωκεῦσιν ἐτάττοντο. ἢ διὰ τὸ πλησίον τῇ Φωκίδι εἶναι τὸν Παρνασσόν.

The text, with the restorations suggested above, might then read:

...Φωκέας, Ἀθηναίων δὲ ἔμπ]αλιν Φωκεῦς̣[ιν αὐτὸ παραδόντων αὖθις, ὡς
    Θουκιδίδης μέν φησι ἐν τῆι α΄·
"Λακεδ]αιμόνιοι δὲ μετὰ ταῦτα τὸν ἱερ[ὸν καλούμενον πόλεμον ἐστράτευσαν, καὶ
    κρατήσαντες τοῦ ἐν
Δελφ]οῖς ἱεροῦ παρέδοσαν Δελφοῖς· κ̣[αὶ αὖθις ὕστερον Ἀθηναῖοι κρατήσαντες
    παρέδοσαν Φωκεῦ-
σιν," ὡς Φ]ι̣λόχορ(ος) δὲ ἐν τῆι δ΄· "ἐν τούτοις πε[ρὶ τοῦ ἐν Δελφοῖς ἱεροῦ τὸν
    ὕστερον ὑπὲρ Φωκέων ἱερὸν καλού-
5 μενον π]όλεμον ἐπολέμησαν Ἀθηναῖοι· [ἄλλος γὰρ πόλεμος Λακεδαιμονίοις πρὸς
    Φωκέας ὑπὲρ Δελφῶν
γέγον]εν ἔμπροσθεν, ἐπεὶ Φωκεῖς κ̣[ατειλήφεσαν τὸ ἱερόν· καὶ κρατήσαντες
    Λακεδαιμόνιοι τὸ μαντεῖ-
ον παρ]ὰ Δελφῶν ἔλαβον· Ἀθηναῖοι δὲ τρ[ίτωι ἔτει τοῦ προτέρου πολέμου τὸ
    ἱερὸν πάλιν ἀπέδωκαν Φω-

κεῦcι· Π]αρνάcιον ἔφη τὸν Ἐπειὸν διὰ̣ [τὸ πληcίον τῇ Φωκίδι εἶναι τὸν Παρναccόν
  ἢ ἐπεὶ Δελ-
φοὶ ἐτάττοντο ὑπὸ (or cὺν?) τ]οῖc Φωκεῦ[cι

(... the Phocians, and the Athenians giving it back) again to the Phocians, (as
Thucydides says in Book 1:) "The Spartans after this (conducted the so-called
Sacred War, and once they had taken control) of the sanctuary at Delphi they
handed it over to the Delphians; and (again later the Athenians, having gained
control of it, handed it back to the Phocians.") As Philochoros (says) in book 4:
"In the meantime, the Athenians fought (the second so-called Sacred War over
the sanctuary at Delphi on behalf of the Phocians. For the Spartans had another war against the Phocians over Delphi) previously, when the Phocians (had
captured the sanctuary. The Spartans, once they got control of the seat of the
oracle,) took it from the Delphians. But the Athenians (in the third year of the
former war gave the sanctuary back again to the Phocians.") He called Epeius
'Parnassian' because of (Parnassus' proximity to Phocis or because Delphi
was aligned with) the Phocians.

Schede

(a)

P.Hib. II 172, coll. IV 9, 16, 19, V 1 [⇒ III: Lexica]

Saec. IIIᵃ. MP³ 2129; LDAB 3535; TM 62370.

Nella lista di composti registrati da P.Hib. II 172, attinti essenzialmente dalla poesia epica, lirica corale, tragica e commentati o chiosati, talora, nei materiali lessicografici, scoliastici, grammaticali più tardi, se ne trovano alcuni per i quali la fonte è con ogni verosimiglianza Euripide; per altri – benché attestati nell'opera del drammaturgo – possono darsi diverse possibilità.

Nella prima categoria rientrano ἀγχίπλους di col. IV 9 (= *SH* 991, 85) 'breve', 'vicino' (in riferimento a navigazione), presente soltanto in Eur. *IT* 1325[1], e δοριάλωτος 'catturato con la lancia' di col. IV 16 (= *SH* 991, 92), tratto probabilmente da Eur. *Tr.* 518[2], considerato che le restanti attestazioni sono in prosa (Erodoto, Isocrate, Senofonte, Demostene, Eschine etc.). Analogamente δοριπετής 'causato da colpo di lancia' (col. IV 19 = *SH* 991, 95) occorre nel solo Euripide (*Andr.* 653, *Tr.* 1003, *Cycl.* 305)[3], così come anche καλλιβλέφαρο[c] 'dalle belle palpebre' (col. V 1 = *SH* 991, 104) è documentato, fino al III sec. a.C., esclusivamente nel dramma euripideo *Ione* (v. 189: si tratta, in realtà, di restituzione degli editori moderni [καλλίφαρον **L**], ritenuta però, sicura)[4].

Un caso particolare è rappresentato da λιθόδμητον (col. IV 14 = *SH* 991,

---

[1] Cfr. Hsch. α 901 Latte-Cunningham ἀγχίπλους· εὐδιακόμιστος. καὶ ὁ παρεστώς. καὶ σύνεγγυς. Εὐριπίδης Ἰφιγενείᾳ τῇ ἐν Ταύροις. Si noti che nel codice Marciano di Esichio si legge ἀγχίπους, elemento che potrebbe indurre a correggere il testo di Euripide, oppure, viceversa, come è stato fatto, a intervenire in Esichio. "En effet εὐδιακόμιστος semble se rapporter à ἀγχίπλους" – osservava Weil 1907, p. 549 – "mais l'autre sens, ὁ παρεστὼς καὶ σύνεγγυς, convient parfaitement à ἀγχίπους. Je suis donc disposé à croire que dans cet article d'Hésychios, comme dans plus d'un autre, deux gloses différentes ont été confondues".

[2] Cfr. Hsch. δ 2209 Latte-Cunningham *δοριάλωτος· αἰχμάλωτος, ὑπὸ δόρατος ληφθείς, *Sud.* δ 1380 Adler δοριάλωτος· αἰχμάλωτος, *EM.* p. 60, 19s. αἰχμάλωτος· ὁ τῇ αἰχμῇ ἁλωτός, ὅ ἐστι δορί· ἔνθεν αἰχμάλωτον λέγομεν, καὶ δοριάλωτον κα[λοῦμεν τὸν ἐν] πολέμῳ ληφθέντα διὰ δόρατος, ἤγουν αἰχμῆς ἀμφήκους καὶ σπάθης καὶ τὰ λοιπά, p. 283, 36 δορυκτήτην· δοριάλωτος, αἰχμάλωτος, *sch. vet.* Eur. *Hec.* 478, 2 Schwartz δοριάλωτος, ὑπὸ τὴν κτῆσιν καὶ δεσποτείαν γινομένη τῶν Ἑλλήνων. Cfr. pure *sch. vet. rec.* Th.M., Tricl., Mosch. et anon. Eur. *Hec.* 100-154, 4 Dindorf δοριάλωτος γενομένη (*sc.* Ἑκάβη) παρὰ τῶν Ἀχαιῶν, 105 ἀνέστηκεν· ... δοριθήρατος· αἰχμάλωτος. ἤγουν δοριάλωτος. αἰχμάλωτος γενομένη δηλονότι, 494, 4 Dindorf ἀνετράπη, ἠφανίσθη. καὶ νῦν ἡ αὐτῆς πόλις πᾶσα ἠφάνισται δοριάλωτος.

[3] Il termine viene commentato in *sch.* Eur. *Andr.* 653 Dindorf δοριπετῇ· δορίπληκτα, δόρατι ἀνῃρημένα.

[4] Cfr. Martin 2018, p. 184. Cfr. pure Ap. Dysc. *Adv.* (*GG* II 1/1) p. 196, 26, Theognost. *Can.* 522 βλέφαρον παρὰ τὸ βλέπω καὶ αἴρω, βλεπέαρόν τι ὄν· τὰ γοῦν παρ' αὐτὸ τὴν αὐτὴν ἀποίσει γραφήν· καλλιβλέφαρος· κυανοβλέφαρος· εὐβλέφαρος, *EGen.* β 138 Lasserre-Livadaras τοῦ βλέποντος φάρος· ἢ παρὰ τὸ ἐν τῷ βλέπειν αἴρεσθαι. τὰ γοῦν παρ' αὐτῷ συγκείμενα τὴν αὐτὴν φυλάττει γραφήν, οἷον καλλιβλέφαρος κυανοβλέφαρος.

89), che nell'elenco di P.Hib. compare subito dopo i composti θεόκτιτ[ο]ν e θεόγνη[τ]ον, a cui è evidentemente associato: sotto di esso, infatti, nel papiro è posta una *paragraphos*, a separare il blocco di termini contenente, tra gli altri, i suddetti vocaboli, da quello successivo. La ragione della presenza di λιθόδμητον nella serie potrebbe risiedere nel significato affine della seconda parte del composto[5] -δμητον e -κτιτον[6], ma non è escluso – come ha osservato Rossini 2019, pp. 77-78 – che essa sia dovuta anche al fatto che nella tradizione del Marc. gr. 471 (**M**, XI sec.) λιθόδμητον rappresenta una *varia lectio* di Eur. *Hec.* 23 θεόδμητον, nata forse, secondo la studiosa, "da una *epanorthosis* relativa ai presupposti mitologici del testo" (p. 78). Del resto l'aggettivo θεόδμητος indica 'costruito dagli dèi', ma l'altare di Atena a Troia, a cui l'attributo è riferito nel testo euripideo, non era, secondo la tradizione, una creazione divina. Ciò, secondo Rossini, potrebbe aver indotto un copista/esegeta antico, attento alla correttezza 'teologico-mitologica' del testo, a sostituire θεόδμητον con λιθόδμητον, secondo un uso che si riscontra tipicamente negli interventi alessandrini e in particolare zenotodei volti, ad esempio, a ripristinare la coerenza contenutistica dei testi e ad eliminare quanto si riteneva ἀπρεπές. Si dovrà, tuttavia, ricordare che θεόδμητος può essere inteso anche come 'costruito per gli dèi'[7] e non scarterei la possibilità che λιθόδμητος sia da intendersi quale interpolazione d'attore o banalizzazione di un copista[8]. Il fatto che in un'annotazione marginale presente in **M** in corrispondenza del verso di *Hec.* 23, recante λιθόδμητον, il medesimo copista che ha vergato il testo annoti: γράφεται πρὸς θεοδμήτῳ fa ipotizzare, in ogni caso, a Rossini 2019, pp. 78-79 che "a partire da materiali di chiosa e/o commento all'*Ecuba* in cui i due termini θεόδμητον e λιθόδμητον – lemmatizzati al neutro o all'accusativo – si trovavano accostati, sia giunto in P.Hib. II 172 solo il secondo: θεόδμητος è infatti coerente sia per composizione, sia per significato con i due precedenti, mentre λιθόδμητος sarebbe stato inserito perché correlato al primo per via filologico-erudita come in numerosi altri casi

---

[5] Cfr. Turner 1955, p. 1: "the arrangement is not alphabetical, but by rough groupings based on one or other elements of their formation or of meaning".

[6] Cfr. pure Hsch. θ 264 Latte-Cunningham θεοδμήτων· ὑπὸ θεοῦ ᾠκοδομημένων δεδομημένων, θεοκτίστων, *EGud.* p. 258, 24-26 Sturz θεόδμητον, παρὰ τὸ θεὸς καὶ τὸ δομῶ, ὃ σημαίνει τὸ κτίζω, θεοδόμητον, καὶ κατὰ συγκοπὴν θεόδμητον, καὶ κατ' ἀναβίβασιν τοῦ τόνου. σημαίνει τὸ θεόκτιστον, *sch. rec.* Pind. *O.* 3, 12 Abel θεόδματον· τουτέστι τὸ θεόκτιστον.

[7] Cfr. *sch. vet. rec.* Thom. M., Tricl., Mosch. *et anon.* Eur. *Hec.* 23, 5 Dindorf θεοδμήτῳ· οὐχ ὅτι θεόδμητος ἦν ὁ βωμὸς τῆς Ἀθηνᾶς, διὰ τοῦτο θεοδμήτῳ λέγει, ἀλλὰ τῷ τῇ θεᾷ παρὰ τῶν Τρώων δομηθέντι· ἢ τῷ θείως καὶ θαυμαστῶς κτισθέντι. θεοκατασκευάστῳ. τῷ δομηθέντι διὰ τοὺς θεούς. Per altre spiegazioni, cfr. *e.g. sch. vet. rec.* Thom. M., Tricl., Mosch. *et anon.* Eur. *Hec.* 906, 2-4 Dindorf ἔλεγον πρὸ τῆς πορθήσεως τῆς Ἰλίου εἶναι ταύτην ἀπορθήτως ὡς θεόδμητος· ὁ γὰρ Ποσειδῶν καὶ ἕτεροι θεοὶ ἔκτισαν ταύτην, καὶ ἕνεκα τούτου ἐκάλουν αὐτὴν ἀπόρθητον, cfr. pure *sch.* Eur. *Hip.* 974 Dindorf.

[8] Cfr. Matthiessen 2010, p. 260 che si richiama a Page 1934, pp. 100-101, dove tale esempio è inserito tra "accidental interpolations".

nel papiro". Il che dimostrerebbe inoltre, in ultima analisi, che la variante di **M** avrebbe origine almeno nel III sec. a.C.

Si tratta di ipotesi che, pur con la debita cautela, meritano di essere riferite.

Attestati in Euripide, ma non esclusivamente, sono i composti di P.Hib. II 172 δηιάλωτος 'preso dal nemico', 'prigioniero' (col. IV 15 = *SH* 991, 91), presente in *Andr.* 105 e in Aeschl. *Sept.* 72 (cfr. al riguardo *sch. rec.* Aeschl. *Sept.* 69, 4 Dindorf); ἰςόθεος 'uguale agli dèi' (col. II 16 = *SH* 991, 40), usato dal tragediografo in *Tr.* 1169, *IA* 626, altresì molto diffuso in poesia a partire dall'epica omerica (vd. i numerosi scolii omerici su tale aggettivo) e utilizzato da Esiodo, Pindaro, Eschilo, Sofocle, Bacchilide; analogamente εὐρύχορος (col. II 20 = *SH* 991, 44), 'vasto', 'spazioso' si trova in Eur. *Bac.* 86; in precedenza, nondimeno, si era già riscontrato nei poemi omerici (diversi sono gli scolii relativi, che lo chiosano), nella poesia greca arcaica e in Bacchilide. Infine ποντομέδων 'signore del mare' (col. III 11 = *SH* 991, 59), epiteto di Poseidone, compare nell'*Ippolito* (v. 744), oltre che in Pindaro, Simonide, Eschilo (vd. gli scolii ai passi di tali autori), per limitarsi all'àmbito della produzione lirica e drammatica; così δορυςςοῦς 'che brandisce la lancia' (col. V 8 = *SH* 991, 111) è presente in Eur. *Her.* 8 riferito all'esercito (δορυςςοῦν ςτρατόν), ma anche in Soph. *OC* 1313 οἷος δορυςςοῦς Ἀμφιάρεως e, quanto a χάλκαςπ[ις 'dallo scudo di bronzo' (col. V 26 = *SH* 991, 102), esso è attestato sì, in *HF* 795 e *IA* 764, ma anche in Pindaro, Bacchilide, Sofocle (e gli scolii a Pindaro e Sofocle si soffermano sul composto).

Infine, in col. IV 18 (= *SH* 991, 94) sarei propensa a leggere δορικτήτη in luogo di δορίκτητος di Turner 'conquistato con la lancia', composto attestato in Euripide (*Andr.* 155, *Hec.* 478) e Licofrone (933, 116) nonché oggetto di considerazione da parte di scoliasti e lessicografi[9]. Se il lemma è al femminile, come altre volte nel papiro, ne indicherei la fonte non in Euripide, bensì in Omero (*Il.* IX 393)[10].

ELENA ESPOSITO

***

---

[9] Cfr. Hsch. δ 2212 Latte-Cunningham, *sch.* Eur. *Andr.* 155 Dindorf, *sch. vet. rec.* Thom. M., Tricl., Mosch. et anon. Eur. *Hec.* 478, 3 Dindorf, *sch. vet.* Eur. *Hec.* 444, 40 Schwartz; *sch. vet.* Lycophr. 1359b Leone.

[10] Ap. Soph. 59, 31 Bekker, Hsch. δ 2272 Latte-Cunningham, *sch.* D Hom. *Il.* IX 393/Z^s van Thiel, *sch. vet.* Hom. *Il.* IX 393a1 Erbse.

(b)

P.Hib. II 179 verso

Saec. IIIᵃ: 280-240ᵃ Turner. MP³ 391.100; LDAB 130715; TM 130715 (recto: LDAB 1036; TM 59926)

Seven fragmentary pieces of a papyrus roll from a mummy. The recto writing is tiny capitals with some cursive features, difficult to decipher. The diminutive height of the original roll, 15.5 cm, is indicated in fr. 1, whose top and bottom margins survive along with thirty lines of fragmentary text. It was first published as poetical fragments whose vocabulary and style Turner thought suited a satyr play (Turner 1955, p. 17), but Kannicht 1976 identified in it early passages from the play *Heracles*. Luppe (ap. Kannicht 1976), Cropp 1982, Musso 1983, Luppe 1993, and Janko 2001 made further advances in deciphering and ordering the fragments as four consecutive columns. For the most recent arrangement of the fragments see Janko 2001, p. 5.

There is little consensus about the exact nature of the text on the recto, which shows large and small discrepancies with the received text of Euripides' *Heracles*. Recto col. i (fr.1) consists of a few trimeters from a prologue that was different from that of the traditional play, followed by a parodos sung by a chorus of elders, as in the received *Heracles*—except in the papyrus the chorus' lines are anapaests, not lyric as in manuscripts LP. At the bottom of the column are four unknown iambic lines, possibly lyric. On the basis of the content, the fragment evidently comes from near the beginning of the play. Recto col. ii (frr. 4, 3, 7) evidently followed recto col. i (fr. 1) immediately and contains parts of the first episode as known from the tradition, namely, the announcement of Lycus' approach and parts of the speech in which he berates the absent Heracles (*HF* 136-143, 146-160, and 160-65). The text varies significantly, however, from the familiar version. Recto col. iii (frr. 2 col. i, 6, 5) contains the end of Lycus' speech and part of Amphitryon's response (*HF* 167-70, 183-184, 186), again with many divergences from the received text. Recto col. iv (fr. 2 col. ii) contains the beginning of Lycus' retort at *HF* 238 but omits a great deal of the preceding speech by Amphitryon. This is traditionally 66 lines long, but the papyrus has room for only 32 lines. Especially interesting (see below) is the evident omission of Amphitryo's arguments for the superiority of the bow over the spear (*HF* 188-205).

The extreme divergence from tradition has produced multiple conjectures about the nature of the original text. Luppe, Janko, and Kannicht regard it as an alternate version of the known *Heracles* (Luppe 1977, 1993; Janko 2001; Kannicht 2004, pp. 943-946). Kannicht 1976 thought it fragments of Euripides *Heracles* combined with some other play about Heracles. Bond 1981 and

Cropp 1982 regard it as excerpts from the known *Heracles* mixed with other works. Musso 1983 suggests the papyrus is a copy of the play with commentary interspersed with text, in the manner of the Lille Callimachus (first half of saec. II[a]). Carrara usefully summarizes the theories offered through 2009 and sees two practicable alternatives: either the text is a collection of extracts, as Bond and Cropp think, or it is a "rielaborazione" of the Euripidean play (Carrara 2009, pp. 84-90). More recently Meccariello 2019 regards the text as a modification, rather than a complete second version, of the known *Heracles*.

On the verso a second scribe wrote in "a rough semi-cursive" (Turner 1955, p. 17) that is an "upright, bilinear hand, much larger than on the recto" (Janko 2001, p. 5). What survives consists of (1) eight damaged lines written at the top of the back of recto col. i (fr. 1). This portion is broken at the top, left, and right sides, except for the right ends of lines 4 and 5, which are complete (Janko 2001, p. 6). The papyrus surviving below line 8 is blank. (2) Four fragmentary lines, the first three of which show a clear left margin, written on the back of recto col. ii (fr. 4, which comes from the top of the column). Fibers on the backs of frr. 3 and 7, which fall lower in the same column (recto col. ii), are stripped. (3) Five lines, damaged by plaster at the top, broken at the sides, and with blank papyrus below, written on the back of recto col. iii, about mid-column (fr. 6; the back of fr. 5, which is placed lower in recto col. iii, is blank). There is no writing on the back of recto col. 4 (fr. 2 col. ii). The verso texts seem to constitute, then, two or possibly three separate passages of writing, i.e., one on the back of recto col. i (fr. 1) and one or two on the back of recto cols. ii and iii, all written at the top of the roll (see Janko 2001, pp. 5-6).

A not unreasonable hypothesis would be to understand the verso text as a commentary on some text. If so, the unconventional *Heracles* of the recto is obviously the closest available candidate, and there are suggestions it could be the subject. (A transcription of the verso text is appended below.) The strongest evidence that it is exegetic is two grammatical terms that would be at home in a commentary. Kannicht recognized ἐπανορ[θ- on the back of recto col. 1 (fr. 1 = verso col. i.8 in the transcription below), a word referring to revision or correction and employed with some frequency by Plato (Kannicht 1976, p. 131). Janko spotted]ϲυνειρον[τ- on the back of recto col. 2 (fr. 4 = verso col. ii.3 in the transcription below), which Philodemus uses of the flow of sounds, but which can also apply to continuity in discourse or reasoning (cf. Janko 2001, p. 5, n. 12). Other, less conclusive evidence for a commentary specifically on *Heracles* emerges in certain words and phrases: (1) δοῦλος on the back of recto col. 1 (fr. 1 = verso col. i.5 in the transcription) appears in the traditional version of Amphitryon's long rhetorical defense of his son's skill at archery. The papyrus omits the entire passage (*HF* 170-209). (2) ἀ]ρετή[on the back of recto col. 3 (fr. 6 = verso col. iii.1), the essential subject of that speech, does not actually figure in it.

A commentator endeavoring to explain the omission of Amphitryon's long speech from the play, however, might conceivably employ both this word and δοῦλος. (3) νέ]|κυι cωρόν[on the back of recto col. 2 (fr. 4 = verso col. ii.2), if correctly read by Janko, might contain a form of νέκυc, a word with obvious relevance in the play; cωρόν could be applied to the heap of corpses left by Heracles' rampage. But the syntax of the phrase is problematic and other readings possible. (Kannicht's]κυι ὡρονο[is also hard to interpret in relation to the play.) (4) θορυβ[- on the back of recto col. 3 (fr. 6 = verso col. iii.2) suitably describes the mayhem of the murders as well as Heracles' mental turmoil. It does not occur in the play. (5)]μαχαρμα[on the back of recto col. 3 (fr. 6 = verso col. iii.3) might derive from Hom. *Od.* 19.471 (τὴν δ' ἅμα χάρμα καὶ ἄλγοc ἕλε φρένα), as the ed.pr. tentatively suggests. That Homeric line describes Eurykleia's simultaneous joy and pain upon recognizing Odysseus and, in commentary on Euripides' play, might be relevant to Heracles' clash of emotions on his return from Hades (*HF* 523-530), or to the chorus' χαρμοναὶ δακρύων ἔδοcαν ἐκβολάc at *HF* 745. But both these passages come much later in the play than the text preserved on the recto of the papyrus. Nor is the Homeric identification certain.[11] The collected evidence, then, suggests but does not demonstrate that the text on the verso of P. Hib. is commentary on Euripides *Heracles*.

If the verso text is in fact commentary, it is remarkable for at least two reasons. First, commentary was not conventionally written on the back of literary texts, although of course practices familiar to us from later periods may not have been customary in the first half of saec. III[a], for which evidence is virtually non-existent. In later papyri there is only one concrete example of exegesis written on the back of the text it explains, plus one other papyrus that may have carried such commentary. The former example is ⇒ Apollonius Rhodius 4, saec. I/II[p] (MP[3] 103; LDAB 258; TM 59163), with short notes accompanied by ἔcω ("see inside") on the back of the poetic text. The latter is a copy of Stesichorus (MP[3] 1485.1; LDAB 3969; TM 62781; saec. I[a]-I[p]) where ἔξω ("see the outside of the roll") may be read in a broken marginal note and could refer to commentary on the back; no writing is reported on reverse of this papyrus. On words such as ἔcω used to send a reader to the other side of a roll, see the references at Turner 1987, p. 14, n. 71.[12]

Secondly, even the existence of commentary in a papyrus of this early date would be extraordinary. The earliest known surviving commentary is that on

---

[11] In an interesting coincidence, the same passage from the *Odyssey* is quoted in the scholia to Pind. *N.* 1.85a to illustrate the mixed emotions Amphitryon feels on discovering the infant Heracles strangling the snakes sent to kill him.

[12] An entirely different sort of case is Philodemus' opisthographic draft of *Academicorum Historia*, in which ὀπίcω on the front refers to the author's notes on the back (P.Herc. 1021; LDAB 3614; TM 26441).

Orphic hymns preserved in the Derveni papyrus of saec. IVᵃ (MP³ 2645.2; LDAB 7049; TM 65795; 325-275ᵃ Turner GMAW, 350ᵃ Janko 2002). The earliest known exegetic writings on classical Greek literature are by Euphronius, who is frequently cited in Aristophanic scholia and credited with ὑπόμνημα on Aristophanes' *Plutus* (Orus *Orthographia* 283r ἐκτείνουϲι τὸ α, ὡϲ Εὐφρόνιοϲ ὁ γραμματικὸϲ ἐν ὑπομνήματι Πλούτου Ἀριϲτοφάνουϲ, cited by Pfeiffer 1968, pp. 160-161 with note). His date is uncertain, but his knowledge of critical *semeia* in manuscripts of the comedian suggests he was a younger contemporary of Aristophanes of Byzantium (265-190 BCE); on his disputed dates, see Novembri 2020 and Montana 2020, pp. 200-203. His period of activity, given this fact, would postdate the writing of P.Hib., or overlap it by a few years. The papyrus, that is, possibly predates Euphronius, the earliest known author of hypomnemata on Greek literature. Thus the text on its verso, if it is a commentary on *Heracles* or any other literary work, is probably the earliest surviving primary evidence for scholarly exegesis of classical literature.

The transcription below is that of Kannicht 1976, p. 130, with modifications by Janko 2001, p. 6. The apparatus is the work of W.E.H. Cockle and E.G. Turner, supplemented by Janko.

P.Hib. 2.179 verso

col. i (Fr. 1)

```
        —   —   —
1        ]...[
    ].α..αρϲι.[
    ].ο.παχογ[
   ]γμα[.].υϲ..
5  ]οϲ δουλοϲ
      ` ..ο.´
    ]...μαιτευ.[
   ]ημι.α[.]τειον[
   ].ο[.].τ.επανο.[
```

vacat

col. ii (Fr. 4)

— — —

1 . . . ε̣α̣τ̣[
   κυιϲωρονο̣[
   ϲυνειρο̣ν̣[
   ]κ̣ο̣τ̣ω̣ν̣

— — —

col. iii (Fr. 6)

— — —

1   ]ρ̣ετη[
   ] . . . [ ] . θορυ . [
      ]μαχαρμα[
      ]πηϲαν[
5   ]ταλ[

— — —

Col. i (fr. 1)   1   ϲ[, ο[, or the right hand of κ[2   perhaps α̣ . . ι̣; for ρ perhaps read ι̣; at end a horizontal at mid-height   4   perhaps]φυϲ or ψυϲ? A horizontal joins the right hand of ϲ at mid-height   6   possibly]α̣πω; suprascript illegible   7   ]ημ̣ . α̣[: "μ is like a capital λ overwritten with blacker ink to the right; and the two following letters are in the blacker ink; after ι are traces like the left side of χ fusing to the right in a small circle"   8   perhaps]υ̣ϲ[; after] . τ̣, a high curve like the top right hand of ο; at the end stray ink

col. ii (fr. 4)   1-3: the clear left margin was noticed by Janko 2001, p. 6   1   ] . . ., first trace of a possible]κ, then traces of the feet of two letters which E.G.T. took as πα; ε̣α̣τ̣[: E.G.T. reads ε̣ as ρ (] . . πα̣ρα), but the foot of ρ does not seem to curl so much to the right   2   ο[, ϲ[, ω[are possible   3   ]κ or perhaps]π seem possible   4   some ink-traces might allow]κε̣

col. iii (fr. 6) 1-2: the ed.pr. and Kannicht give line 2 as]μοι[, but this is a mistranscription of θορ in the actual line 2 (Janko)   2   before θ, the right hand of a vertical, perhaps with a descending stroke to the left at the top; . [, trace of a high horizontal and a foot: β[ed.pr.   5   ]ταλ[ed.pr., obscured by plaster.

Index papyrorum

Indice I.2.5.1